THE[OLOGY WITHOUT W]ORDS

This book is a study of a Christian theology without words, focussing on theology in the Deaf Community. Deaf people's first and preferred method of communication is not English or any other spoken language, but British Sign Language – a language that cannot be written down. Deaf people of faith attend church on a regular basis, profess faith in God and have developed unique approaches to doing theology. While most Western theology is word-centred and is either expressed through or dependent on written texts, theology in the Deaf Community is largely non-written. This book presents and examines some of that theology from the Deaf Community and argues that written texts are not necessary for creative theological debate, a deep spirituality or for ideas about God to develop.

D0303909

Explorations in Practical, Pastoral and Empirical Theology

Series Editors: Leslie J. Francis, University of Warwick, UK
and Jeff Astley, Director of the North of England
Institute for Christian Education, UK

Theological reflection on the church's practice is now recognised as a significant element in theological studies in the academy and seminary. Ashgate's new series in practical, pastoral and empirical theology seeks to foster this resurgence of interest and encourage new developments in practical and applied aspects of theology worldwide. This timely series draws together a wide range of disciplinary approaches and empirical studies to embrace contemporary developments including: the expansion of research in empirical theology, psychological theology, ministry studies, public theology, Christian education and faith development; key issues of contemporary society such as health, ethics and the environment; and more traditional areas of concern such as pastoral care and counselling.

Other titles in the series include:

Reconstructing Practical Theology
The Impact of Globalization
John Reader
978-0-7546-6224-2

The Bible and Lay People
An Empirical Approach to Ordinary Hermeneutics
Andrew Village
978-0-7546-5801-6

Inspiring Faith in Schools
Studies in Religious Education
Edited by Marius Felderhof, Penny Thompson and David Torevell
978-0-7546-6031-6

Deaf Liberation Theology
Hannah Lewis
978-0-7546-5524-4

Theological Reflection and Education for Ministry
The Search for Integration in Theology
John E. Paver
978-0-7546-5754-5

Theology without Words
Theology in the Deaf Community

WAYNE MORRIS
University of Chester, UK

ASHGATE

Published by
Ashgate Publishing Limited
Gower House
Croft Road
Aldershot
Hampshire GU11 3HR
England

Ashgate Publishing Company
Suite 420
101 Cherry Street
Burlington, VT 05401-4405
USA

Ashgate website: http://www.ashgate.com

British Library Cataloguing in Publication Data
Morris, Wayne, 1977–
    Theology without words: theology in the deaf community. – (Explorations in practical, pastoral and empirical theology)
    1. Church work with the deaf 2. Deaf – Religious life 3. Theology 4. Nonverbal communication
    I. Title
    259.4'42

Library of Congress Cataloging-in-Publication Data
Morris, Wayne, 1977–
    Theology without words : theology in the deaf community / Wayne Morris
        p. cm. – (Explorations in practical, pastoral, and empirical theology.)
    Includes bibliographical references
    ISBN 978-0-7546-6222-8 (hardcover : alk. paper)
    ISBN 978-0-7546-6227-3 (pbk. : alk. paper)
  1. Church work with the deaf. 2. Deaf – Religious life. 3. Theology. 4. Nonverbal communication.
    I. Title. .

    BV4463.M67 2008
    230.087'—dc22

                                                                    2007052597

ISBN 978 0 7546 6222 8 (Hbk)
ISBN 978 0 7546 6227 3 (Pbk)

Printed and bound in Great Britain by MPG Books Ltd. Bodmin, Cornwall.

To all the members of the Deaf Church of Christ the King, Birmingham, for their love, support and friendship and their willingness to participate in this book.

Contents

Acknowledgements

This book began as a PhD thesis with the University of Birmingham and so I would like to begin by thanking my supervisor, Professor John Parratt, for encouraging me to pursue this research from the beginning, for guiding me throughout, and for the meticulous criticism and advice he has offered so wisely. Thank you also to Professor John Hull for his encouragement to rework and publish my original thesis.

Past and present members of the Deaf Church of Christ the King in Birmingham must be thanked not only for welcoming me among them, but for allowing me to conduct this research. Other Deaf churches, along with their chaplains, have welcomed and helped me with this research – too many to thank all of them individually – but I am grateful to them all. I must also mention colleagues and friends from Archbishops' Council, Committee for Ministry of and among Deaf and Disabled People, and members of Deaf Anglicans Together (formerly National Deaf Church Conference). In conversations I have often been challenged to rethink my assumptions and theologies and I thank all those Deaf people who have been patient in accompanying me through this research. Thank you also, to Julie White who made my visit to Zimbabwe in 1999 possible and for putting me in touch with the Deaf community in Harare.

Thank you to colleagues at Church Action on Disability who have offered wise counsel throughout my time there and also to colleagues at the University of Chester.

I am extremely grateful to those who have offered comment on the text of this book including Ruth Ackroyd and Ros Hunt.

Thanks must go to the St Luke's College Foundation for a grant to conduct the initial research as well as to the University of Birmingham.

Finally, I am grateful to so many people whose support has been so crucial to completing this project. Among them are friends at All Saints' Church, Gobowen, my Grandmother, Mavis Berridge, Christine and David Latham, and my friend Kevin Jones without whose support this work would not have been finished.

List of Abbreviations

ASL   American Sign Language

BDA   British Deaf Association

BID   Birmingham Institute for Deaf People

BSL   British Sign Language

FDP   Federation of Deaf People

NHS   National Health Service

RNID   Royal National Institute for Deaf People

SSE   Sign Supported English

Introduction

'In the Beginning was the Word'

'In the beginning was the Word, and the Word was with God, and the Word was God' (John 1.1). This opening verse from John's Gospel is perhaps one of the most well known and used Christological statements from the Bible and Church tradition. The theology of Christ as 'the Word', due to its Hellenistic philosophical origins, has tended to associate the nature of God, revealed in Christ Jesus, with Western concepts of reason and intellectual capacity (logos referring to reasoned debate) which, Frances Young argues, theology traditionally suggests, are those human qualities that most closely reflect the image of God[1]. In other words, God in his essence is a reasoning intellectual being and those same qualities in us are the *Imago Dei*. In some traditions, 'the word of the Lord' is a phrase used to describe the Bible. In the Church of England's service book, *Common Worship*, each passage read from the Bible, excluding the Gospel, concludes with the reader saying, 'This is the *word* of the Lord' [my italics][2]. This second use of 'the word' (note the use of the definite article) further reinforces the idea that God is a being whose relationship with humanity is intellectual in nature and that he has chosen to communicate with humanity through what is essentially a product of intellectual development: the written text[3]. Jesus, the Bible and, finally, preaching is what Barth has identified as the three dimensions of the Word of God[4]. Preaching is essentially an oral, word-centred approach to theology, usually involving only the one person presenting a monologue[5] and the rest of the people listening to what is said.

The implications of describing Jesus Christ or the Bible or preaching as 'the Word' and therefore the source of theology is brought into sharp focus when one encounters members of the Deaf community because for Deaf people, words – spoken or written – are thought to be a peculiarly hearing phenomenon. By 'Deaf People' I am referring to those profoundly Deaf people who use British Sign Language (BSL) as a first or preferred language and not those who develop an acquired hearing loss

---

[1]   Young, F., 'Imago Dei', *Ecumenical Disability Advocates Network* (Nairobi, 2002), pp.3–4.

[2]   Church of England, *Common Worship: Services and Prayers of the Church of England* (London, 2000), p.172.

[3]   Pinker, S., *The Language Instinct* (London, 1994), p.189.

[4]   Hart, T., *Regarding Karl Barth* (Carlisle, 1999), p.28. See the full discussion in: Barth, K., *Church Dogmatics: The Doctrine of the Word of God* (Edinburgh, 1956), Vol I.ii.

[5]   Some models of preaching, including in Deaf worship, involve a more interactive approach. A discussion of Interactive Preaching and its value in hearing contexts can be found in, Pearson, B. 'Interactive Methods of Preaching', in Hunter, G. et al., *A Preachers Companion: Essays from the College of Preachers* (Oxford, 2004), pp.107–10.

later in life after learning a spoken language[6]. When discussing sign language, Deaf people consciously use 'signs' to refer to the individual parts of communication, instead of 'words', which are reserved for parts of speech or the text only. So the argument that follows here begins with the situation that one of the most important Christological and theological statements of Christian faith, along with the other dimensions of the 'Word' as revelation and thus the source of theology, is, in the language that is used, potentially deeply problematic to many Deaf people.

Writing a book on the theology of the Deaf community itself creates a dilemma concerning the way the arguments that follow will be presented. The dilemma is that, unlike most other languages that are spoken, BSL is communicated not by sound or by text, but by using visual and spatial means. There are no fixed set of symbols such as the English alphabet that can be used to express BSL in an intelligible written format[7]. While BSL is a full and complete language capable of communicating complex ideas, it is a language used by a community for whom the written text is inaccessible other than through a second language and culture used by hearing people[8]. While some Deaf people use English well, many find difficulties in learning spoken languages because one's ability to articulate individual words is largely dependent on being able to know what a word should sound like. Whilst Deaf people often do learn English to varying degrees, they do not communicate easily in either spoken or written English but do communicate easily in their first or preferred language, BSL. At once a problem is encountered, therefore, in terms of *writing* a book on the theology of Deaf people. Not only is this book itself largely inaccessible to Deaf people, if Deaf people express themselves most readily in BSL, then inevitably, they will also express their theology in their preferred mode of communication as well. Thus anything I have included about Deaf people's theology has relied on my ability to interpret and translate from BSL and Deaf culture into English, hearing cultural terms. While many modern Western theological traditions such as feminist and black theologies would put experience[9] as the primary source for theology rather than the written word or 'Word' as revelation, they are still mostly word-centred in their articulation of that experience and theological reflection on it because it is done almost entirely by hearing people.

Reflecting on these dilemmas has been important from the outset in terms of how this book may have something to contribute to theological study. Firstly, it has been necessary to think about who the prospective audience might be. Inevitably, in preparing a book for publication, it is directed at a hearing audience for whom the English text is easily accessible. Secondly, I think that Deaf people's theology has much to contribute to the field of theological enquiry both in terms of the content

---

[6]   The definition of 'Deaf People' and the 'Deaf Community' is explored more fully in chapter 1.

[7]   Brien makes use of a series of written symbols representing such aspects of BSL as hand shape, movement, etc. However, this system is fairly esoteric and unintelligible as a written format of BSL used by few, if any, Deaf people. See Brien, D. (ed.), *Dictionary of British Sign Language/English* (London, 1992).

[8]   Sutton-Spence, R. and Woll, B., *The Linguistics of British Sign Language: An Introduction* (Cambridge, 1999), p.2.

[9]   See the discussion of this in chapter 4.

of Deaf theology and because of the non-literary methodologies employed by Deaf people. Because Deaf culture is a non-literary culture (only by using English or some other written language is literacy accessed) they are excluded from many of the sources of Christian theology such as the Bible, Church tradition, and modern theological research. But Deaf people do do theology, yet their theology, for want of a better term, is 'oral'. 'Oral' is not the right word for reasons that are both obvious now and will become obvious later. To put it another way, therefore, Deaf theology is lived, it is temporary and not fixed for 'eternity' in written creeds or in texts such as this, but is based on reflective experience expressed through BSL, relevant to a particular moment in history. In our highly literate culture in Britain, in our 'wordy' theologies and liturgies, even in describing God as the 'Word' it is hard to think of doing theology without the words of texts and speech. Deaf people, however, challenge theological enquiry with an alternative way of doing and articulating theology through spatial and visual media and for these reasons this book will hopefully be of interest to hearing people and a challenge to them. At the same time, however, I hope that some Deaf people will also be able to make use of what follows here, even if it is written in, what is for many, their second language.

In light of the above the argument that follows is divided into three parts. The first part is necessarily didactic in nature. Little work at all has been done on theology and Deaf people, and this is the first to study in depth the theology of the Deaf community itself[10]. Little is known about the Deaf community among theologians or more generally in society in terms of who they are and what the issues are that are important to them, although through the work of Deaf people, this is slowly changing. Thus in the first part I aim to provide a discussion of the Deaf community in Britain with some references to other contexts to reflect part of the international dimension of what it means to be a member of the Deaf community (chapter 1). Chapter 2 then will look at some of the arguments concerning whether BSL is a full language and explains some of the ways in which BSL works as a language. In this chapter I aim only to discuss the grammar of BSL inasmuch as it is necessary to understand the grammar for our purposes here. I then examine the use of BSL in education. An insight into both of these issues (language and education) are crucial for understanding the theology of Deaf people as a whole because theology can only be expressed through some mode of communication – usually, though not exclusively, language[11].

The second part of this book focuses on method. This part is divided into three chapters. Firstly, I outline the methodology used to obtain the data I acquired

---

[10] A number of PhD theses have been produced on aspects of theology and Deafness including one at Birmingham University looking at the Deaf Community and Liberation Theology: Lewis, H. (2002). Hitching, R., *The Church and Deaf People: A Study of Identity, Communication and Relationships with Special Reference to the Ecclesiology of Jörgen Moltmann* (Carlisle, 2003), is the resulting publication of Hitching's PhD with London Bible College. However, there is no academic research, published or otherwise, that has investigated the theology that emerges from and exists among the Deaf community.

[11] Begbie, J. (ed.), *Beholding the Glory: Incarnation Through the Arts* (London, 2000) brings attention to the way theology can be expressed through means other than language, namely disciplines within the arts.

(chapter 3) mainly through fieldwork. Secondly, I aim to outline some of the methods employed by Deaf people in their theology, as I have discovered them through my research (chapter 4), and these methods are particularly challenging to Western styles of theology. The third chapter in this part (chapter 5) provides a short study and critique of the images of God in the Bible as Deaf people have learned, understand and interpret them, from my perception of Deaf theology. I have included this as a separate study because, for many, at least in Protestant traditions, the Bible is the most important, and sometimes only authoritative source and reference point for theological study[12] while also being important in Catholic and Orthodox traditions for theology. I discovered that the Bible is problematic as a source for Deaf theology not only because it is written text, but also because of the language and images it uses about God.

The third part of the book contains two chapters that focus specifically on the content of Deaf theology. I immediately acknowledge here that theological method and content are not mutually exclusive from each other and discussion of both method and content is present in both parts, it is simply that Deaf people's methods for doing theology and what they actually express as their theology are brought into focus at different times. Chapter 6, therefore, explores issues surrounding ecclesiology and liturgy as the primary contexts in which theology is explored and lived. Finally, chapter 7 will focus on Deaf perspectives on the nature of God. This final chapter aims to bring together the themes highlighted in the thesis and apply them practically to the way that Deaf people understand and express their perspectives on the nature of God.

The purpose of this book is to investigate the nature of Deaf theology. As I am a hearing person conducting this research, this presents certain limitations. I am an outsider to the Deaf community and my culture and background are hearing. BSL is also my second language and so much of my thinking and reflecting takes place using English which must influence my own intellectual framework for reflection[13]. Despite this, I am convinced that Deaf people have important contributions to make to theology, which makes this exercise worthwhile. Further, with my knowledge of BSL and the Deaf community learned through getting to know and be alongside Deaf people, I dare to think I may be able to challenge hearing people's perspectives of Deaf people, hearing methods for doing theology and hearing theologies about the nature of God. Thus I admit that the audience for this thesis is primarily a hearing audience and it is they whom I seek to inform and challenge. I accept my own limitations as a hearing person and as an individual in doing this and can only encourage hearing people to seek ways of engaging with many members of the Deaf community to develop a better understanding of Deafness. I am committed to encouraging a better understanding of the Deaf community in society and to pursuing greater justice and equality for Deaf people. In some way, it is my hope that this book will contribute to that process.

---

[12] See the discussion above and White, J.F., *Introduction to Christian Worship*, Revised Edition, (Nashville, 2000), also identifies this threefold understanding of the Word as an important part of Protestant Theology, pp.131–2.

[13] See the discussion of Derrida, postmodernism and poststructuralism in chapter 4.

PART I
The Deaf Community and their Language

Chapter 1

A Sense of Deaf Identity

Introducing the Deaf Community

Estimates suggest that between 50,000 and 100,000 Deaf people live all over the United Kingdom[1]. The Deaf community includes men, women and children, people from across the variety of ethnic groups present in the UK, with different expressions of sexual orientation. They can be found in rural and urban environments and across all levels of the class system. Some Deaf people live with other impairments such as autism, blindness, or physical impairments while others do not[2]. A few Deaf children are born to Deaf parents while the majority are not[3]. Deaf experiences of education are also diverse, some are taught primarily through oral means[4], some by a bilingual approach[5] and others somewhere in between using a method of total communication[6].

The Deaf community does not include everyone in society who has a hearing loss. Indeed, the Royal National Institute for Deaf People (RNID) suggests that one in every seven people in society lives with some level of hearing impairment, which amounts to somewhere in the region of nine million people[7]. This group should be distinguished from the 50,000 to 100,000 members of the culturally Deaf

---

[1]   Alker, D., *Really Not Interested in the Deaf* (Darwen, 2000), p.27 estimates that there are about 100,000 Deaf people in the UK. Other statistics provided by the Royal National Institute for Deaf People (RNID), *Facts and Figures on Deafness and Tinnitus* (London, 2003) estimate 50,000; British Deaf Association (BDA), *What is BSL?* (London, 2004) estimate 70,000. This reflects the lack of research into the Deaf community as a distinct group.

[2]   Ladd, P., *Understanding Deaf Culture: In Search of Deafhood* (Clevedon, 2003), p.63.

[3]   *Ibid.*, p.42.

[4]   The Oral Approach to Deaf Education involves the Deaf child being taught primarily through English with no sign language use. See Watson, L., 'Oralism – current policy and practice', in Gregory, S. et al. (eds), *Issues in Deaf Education* (London, 1998), p.69.

[5]   The bilingual approach to Deaf education involves the Deaf child learning BSL as their first language and then beginning to learn English through BSL in the same way that anyone would learn English as a second language. See Pickersgill, M., 'Bilingualism – current policy and practice', in Gregory, S. et al. (eds), *Issues in Deaf Education* (London, 1998), pp.88–97

[6]   Total Communication involves using a combination of English and Signs together in teaching along with mime, gesture and drawing – any means to get the message across. See Watson, L. et al., *Deaf and Hearing Impaired Pupils in Mainstream Schools* (London, 1999), p.36.

[7]   Royal National Institute for Deaf People, *Facts and Figures on Deafness*, estimate that there are 9 million deaf and hard of hearing people in the UK.

community. The Deaf community or Deaf people, who are the focus of this book, includes people who are profoundly Deaf – usually being Deaf at birth or before spoken language is acquired – they use BSL as their first or preferred language, identify with the culture of Deaf people and meet regularly together for corporate social, religious and political activities[8]. The traditional focus of Deaf communities were Deaf clubs, now declining in significance as Deaf people meet together in similar contexts to and alongside hearing people[9]. In this book, in line with current convention in the Deaf community, the use of the upper case 'D' refers to culturally Deaf people who use sign language, while the lower case 'd' refers to people with a profound hearing loss who use English to communicate[10].

No chapter of a book or a book on its own could do justice to the Deaf community by trying to sum up their rich and varied experiences in a few thousand words. Paddy Ladd's seminal work, *Understanding Deaf Culture: In Search of Deafhood* (2003) provides many helpful insights for anyone who would want to read about the Deaf community in more detail. For our purposes here, I aim only to provide an introduction to the Deaf community, based on the available (though limited) literature on the subject and my own experiences with the Deaf community in Birmingham. In this introduction to the Deaf community, therefore, I will firstly outline the medical and social models of disability, and the impact these models have had on the Deaf community and the articulation of Deaf identity. Secondly, I will focus more specifically on the Deaf community and their continually developing sense of identity rooted in what has become known as 'Deaf culture'.

Disability and the Deaf Community: In Search of an Understanding

Traditionally, both disability and Deafness have been understood among many people in the UK as primarily medical conditions or illnesses. Over the past thirty years or so, disabled people and Deaf people have made considerable efforts to distance themselves from such a perspective and have made reference to themselves using a 'social' rather than a 'medical' perceptual framework[11]. In more recent times, the Deaf community has further developed thinking surrounding Deaf identity and now argues that Deaf people should not be perceived primarily as disabled, but as a cultural and linguistic minority group[12]. These models and their development are outlined below. Some Deaf people may feel angry that I have decided to begin discussing an understanding of the Deaf community by beginning with 'disability'. I have done so because many hearing non-disabled people still see being Deaf as a

---

[8]   Alker, D., 'The Changing Deaf Communities', in International Ecumenical Working Group, *The Place of Deaf People in the Church* (Northampton, 1996), pp.178–9.

[9]   Ladd, P., *Understanding Deaf Culture*, p.47.

[10]   See Ladd, P., *Understanding Deaf Culture*, p.33. If a quotation is used by an author who does not follow this convention, I have not changed their particular way of referring to Deaf people.

[11]   Swain, J. et al., *Controversial Issues in a Disabling Society* (Buckingham, 2003), pp.22–5.

[12]   Ladd, P., *Understanding Deaf Culture*, p.35.

disability or even an illness even if that is not how Deaf people today understand themselves. By beginning at where most people are at the present moment and recalling that the main audience for this book will be hearing people, I hope that the arguments that follow will help to transform the more general social understanding of the Deaf community, so that it will be recognized that Deaf people are a unique group of people who should be viewed as a community in their own right, without needing to make reference to anyone else.

The Medical Model

Pamela Knight describes the 'medical model' as a response to disability that, in effect, understands impairment as an illness and places the responsibility for the condition and its consequences, personal and social, with disabled people themselves. She explains: 'It is *their* functional limitation which is the root cause of the disadvantages experienced, and these disadvantages can only be rectified by treatment or cure'[13]. Based on guidelines from the World Health Organization[14], McCloughry and Morris label and then define three dimensions to the way disability is understood in the medical model[15]:

- *Impairment*: Any loss or abnormality of psychological or anatomical structure or function.
- *Disability*: Any restriction or lack (resulting from an impairment) of ability to perform an activity in the manner or within the range considered normal for a human being.
- *Handicap*: A disadvantage for a given individual resulting from an impairment or disability, that limits or prevents the fulfilment of a role (dependent on age, sex, social and cultural factors) for that individual.

Both disabled people and the World Health Organization no longer work with these definitions, though they continue to reflect the attitudes of many towards disabled people in society – that impairment and its consequences are the problem of disabled people and that any difficulties they experience are their own responsibilities.

The term 'handicap' demonstrates another attitude towards disabled people as it derives from 'cap-in-hand' implying that disabled people are the objects of charitable benevolence rather than empowered individuals with a contribution to make to society. This benevolence that arises from the sense of pity of non-disabled people towards the 'tragedy' of disabled people should be seen as a consequence of the medical model. Many in the medical profession and many in society at large still

---

[13] Knight, P., 'Deafness and Disability', in Gregory, S. et al. (eds), *Issues in Deaf Education* (London, 1998), p.215.

[14] This language is no longer used by the World Health Organization. New Guidelines were published in 2001 under the title of 'International Classification on Functioning and Disability'. See: World Health Organization, *Towards a Common Language for Functioning, Disability and Health* (Geneva, 2002).

[15] McCloughry, R. and Morris, W., *Making a World of Difference: Christian Perspectives on Disability* (London, 2002), p.9.

live with the perception that disability is an illness that needs to be cured and if this is not possible, the individual disabled person is to be pitied[16]. This model ignores the experiences of many disabled people who live relatively happy lives as disabled people and do not necessarily seek or hope for medical intervention to change their condition. Most impairments cannot be cured medically, and so disabled people are perceived as an 'abnormal' and an undesirable presence in society with little to offer.

The Social Model

The social model of disability, while recognizing that impairment exists at the level of the individual person, though is not the fault of a disabled person, argues that many problems that disabled people experience in terms of leading a full life in society are due to social inequalities[17]. The language of 'Impairment' and 'Disability' has been redefined by disabled people, and the term handicap, at least in official documents in Britain[18], has largely been dropped. McCloughry and Morris again outline the language used in the social model of disability as follows:

- *Impairment*: Lacking part or all of a limb or having a defective limb, organ or mechanism of the body.
- *Disability*: The disadvantage or restriction of activity caused by a contemporary social organization which takes no or little account of people who have physical impairments and thus excludes them from participation in the mainstream of social activities[19].

I would add to the definition of disability that individuals as well as organizations can disable people with impairments. By challenging the medical model, the social model advocates a perspective on disability that does not place the blame on to the disabled person for her inability to participate in society. It recognizes that disabled people are an oppressed social group who, if social and environmental barriers are removed, can participate in the mainstream of society[20].

Assessing the Medical and Social Models

The medical model has obvious limitations in terms of its ability to provide a framework in which to discuss disabled people's experiences and identities because it defines them almost entirely in terms of them having a medical *problem*. It would be inappropriate, however, for disabled people and society to discount medicine from having a contribution to make towards the greater welfare of disabled people generally. Many disabled people, for example, live with chronic pain, label

---

16   Swain, J. et al., *Controversial Issues*, p.23.

17   *Ibid.*, p.24

18   See for example, Disability Rights Commission, *Code of Practice: Rights of Access Goods, Facilities, Services and Premises* (London, 2002).

19   UPIAS, *Fundamental Principles of Disability* (London, 1976), pp.3–4.

20   Swain, J. et al., *Controversial Issues*, p.24.

themselves as disabled, and use medical help to alleviate the pain. In such instances, medicine has an important role to play. Assessments made by medics of a particular condition are important in terms of defining an impairment as well as working to enable that person to live their life to the full. However, difficulties develop when it is perceived that living life to the full can only be achieved by medical intervention, with the purpose of cure, or as near to it as possible. Sometimes medicine can help, at other times it will do more harm than good. As will be discussed later, this has been particularly true for Deaf people.

The social model also presents limitations. Commenting on the social model, French argues:

> Viewing a mobility problem as caused by the presence of steps rather than by the inability to walk, or regarding the inability to access information as due to the lack of sign language rather than to a hearing impairment is easy to comprehend ... However, various profound social problems that I encounter as a visually impaired person, which impinge upon my life far more than indecipherable notices or the lack of bleeper crossings, are more difficult to regard as entirely socially produced or amenable to social action. Such problems include my inability to recognize people, being nearly blinded when the sun comes out, and not being able to read non-verbal cues or emit them correctly[21].

The definition of 'disability' in the social model, while purposeful for many living with a physical, and indeed sensory impairment, does not necessarily describe the reality of life for all disabled people such as French. A person with, for example, a learning difficulty will never be able to achieve so much academically as a child without a learning difficulty, regardless of society. Society cannot resolve this matter, and so the impairment as well as the social disability will contribute to the limitation a disabled person lives with. Knight further explains: '... the social model itself is also criticized for having the goal of 'normality' for disabled people ... Each society has expectations, beliefs and values of its own which constitute a concept of normality for that particular society. The social model incorporates the assumption that all members of that society must aspire to the same norms'[22]. A child with a learning difficulty will feel more oppressed by pressure to succeed academically than by the recognition that this child's abilities and gifts will lead them in different directions to the so-called 'norm'. Contrary to popular opinion, disabled people and non-disabled people cannot do everything they set their minds to; all must live with and accept that certain limitations, other than social ones, are placed on their lives and that limitation itself can be a source of creativity[23]. The social model aims to achieve greater equality in society by recognizing the social barriers that limit disabled people from participating in society equally.

---

[21]   French, S., 'Disability, impairment or something in between?' in Swain, J. et al., *Disabling Barriers – Enabling Environments* (London, 1993), p.17.

[22]   Knight, P., 'Deafness and Disability', p.216.

[23]   Frances Young argues that limitation itself can be creative in Young, F. (ed.), *Encounter with Mystery: Reflections on L'Arche and Living with Disability* (London, 1997), p.165.

Based on the work done by disabled people[24] and the World Health Organization[25], a new approach is needed which brings together these two perspectives of the medical and social models. This approach would involve respecting disabled people as unique human beings with gifts and abilities. It would accept that social barriers suppress the ability of many disabled people to participate fully in society. It would recognize that medical intervention can be useful for many disabled people, provided it is not imposed on disabled people. Choice and freedom are paramount. This new approach would also recognize that disabled people are a diverse group of people and no single model is realistically applicable to all. Sally French (above) shows that the social model, like the medical model, cannot be applied universally to all disabled people. To understand the nature of the Deaf community, therefore, a particular approach is needed that recognizes that Deaf people are a unique group of people and should not be lumped together with all other disabled people, thus homogenizing and consequently trivializing their experiences.

The Deaf Community and Models of Disability

Deafness and the Medical Model

Knight argues that the 'medical scenario is the first experience of deafness for most parents'[26]. With 90 per cent of Deaf children born to hearing parents[27], who are likely not to be informed or prepared for the birth of a Deaf child, it is inevitable that they will look to the medical experts who are immediately around them for help and advice. Like the medical model of disability, Knight sums up the medical response to Deafness as follows: 'The diagnosis and degree of deafness in a child is a medical issue. Efforts are made by the medical profession to find the cause of deafness and if possible a cure. If no cure is possible then provision of appropriate amplification devices is made to compensate for the degree of deafness'[28]. Diagnosis of hearing loss is crucial in order for an assessment of a child's needs to be made. Unless it can be confirmed that a child is unable to hear, and to what degree, no adequate response can be made. As will be seen later, an early diagnosis of Deafness can be crucial in terms of language acquisition. As Knight indicates, once diagnosis is made, in the medical model, a cure is usually sought. If a cure fails, then technology is introduced and many Deaf people do make use of hearing aid technology. The medical model's goal is one in which it is assumed to be ethically right that the Deaf child is enabled to be as much like a hearing child as possible. Ladd comments, 'Playing on those parents fears of "abnormality" and their desire to achieve "normality", they (proponents of the medical approach) then present their medical model which claims that normality

---

24   Significant discussions of the Social Model of Disability include, Oliver, M., *Disabled People and Social Policy: from exclusion to inclusion* (London,1998), and many of the papers in Shakespeare, T. (ed.), *The Disability Reader: Social Science Perspectives* (London, 1998).

25   World Health Organization.

26   Knight, P., 'Deafness and Disability', p.217.

27   Ladd, P., *Understanding Deaf Culture*, p.42.

28   Knight, P., 'Deafness and Disability', p.217.

can only be achieved by denying the realities of deafness and keeping their children away from Deaf communities lest they be "contaminated" by them'[29]. The quest for a cure for Deafness has both historically and in contemporary society had negative consequences for Deaf children.

Harlan Lane describes some of the methods of one French 'doctor', Jean-Marc Itard, who tried to 'cure' Deafness in some children in the nineteenth century:

> He started by applying electricity to the ears of some pupils, since an Italian surgeon had recently found that a frog's leg would contract if touched by charged metal … He also placed leeches on the necks of some of the pupils in the hope that local bleeding would help somehow. Six students had their eardrums pierced, but the operation was painful and fruitless, and he desisted. Not soon enough for Christian Dietz who died following his treatment.[30]

The desire for a cure for Deaf people has had devastating, at times, fatal consequences for Deaf people throughout history. In the contemporary situation, the desire for cure of Deaf people by hearing people continues.

Cochlear implantation is a surgical procedure which inserts a wire through the inner ear to the auditory nerve. The wire is then connected to an attachment, which is placed in the skull behind the ear. By bypassing the outer, middle and inner ear, the wire picks up sound, directs it from the outside and transmits it directly to the auditory nerve[31]. Despite the claims in the early years of this procedure that it could enable a Deaf person to hear, the evidence concerning the success rate of this procedure is ambiguous. Robinson, for example, suggests the younger a child is when the procedure is carried out, preferably under five years of age, the better the response will be in terms of the child's ability to hear and then speak using English[32]. Conversely, Lane argues, and this view is widely held in the Deaf community, the cochlear implant does little to improve hearing and speech and the ability to learn English when implanted in profoundly Deaf children[33]. In the USA, this procedure was only licensed in 1990 and was expected to be popular among Deaf people. However, it has been met with strong resistance by the Deaf community in America, Britain and across the world who argue that this is yet another attempt to turn Deaf people into sorry imitations of hearing people[34]. One of the main objections of the Deaf community to using the cochlear implant in young infants is that they do not

---

[29]   Ladd, P., *Understanding Deaf Culture*, p.35.

[30]   Lane, H., *When the Mind Hears: A History of the Deaf* (Cambridge, 1989), p.132. See also Dimmock, A., *Cruel Legacy: An Introduction to the Record of Deaf People in History* (Edinburgh, 1993), pp.41–3.

[31]   A description of the procedure can be found in Lane, H., 'The Medicalization of Cultural Deafness in Historical Perspective', in Fischer, R. and Lane, H. (eds), *Looking Back: A Reader on the History of Deaf Communities and their Sign Languages* (Hamburg, 1993), p.480.

[32]   Robinson, K., 'Cochlear Implants: Some Challenges', in Gregory, S. et al. (eds), *Issues in Deaf Education* (London, 1998), p.198.

[33]   Lane, H., 'The Medicalization of Cultural Deafness in Historical Perspective', pp.480–1.

[34]   Ladd, P., *Understanding Deaf Culture*, pp.30–1.

have any choice about whether to make use of the procedure[35]. If it proves not to have any significant effect among Deaf infants, the risk of undertaking serious surgery on small babies, with no clear evidence to prove that it works, cannot be justified.

Lane argues,

> We have come to look at Deaf people in a certain way, to use a certain vocabulary of infirmity, and this practice is so widespread among hearing people, and has gone on for so long, and is so legitimized by the medical and paramedical professions, that we imagine we are accurately describing attributes of Deaf people rather than choosing to talk about them in a certain way[36].

Deaf people do not perceive the condition of Deafness purely in terms of being like a hearing person who is unable to hear. Rather than determining their identity in these negative terms, a more positive framework is used as will be outlined shortly.

One point that is important to note, however, is that medical diagnosis should remain as a factor in the lives of Deaf and disabled people. A quick diagnosis that a child is profoundly Deaf, for example, can lead to action being taken quickly by parents to ensure that their child is exposed to BSL as their first language[37]. Without this, parents may be in ignorance about their child's Deafness and not be able to do anything positive or negative for the first few crucial years of life when language is most readily learned[38]. As explained in chapter 2, Deaf infants acquire BSL at a much faster rate than English. Medical diagnosis should continue to be important for Deaf children and this is happening with the introduction of the 'Newborn Hearing Screening Programme' where all babies will have a hearing test within the first few weeks of life[39]. However, what will need to change is what happens after the diagnosis has taken place, for Deaf people to be able to develop in terms of Deaf culture using British Sign Language, rather than being forced to become more like hearing people.

Deafness and the Social Model

Many Deaf people acknowledge that the social model of disability has had many positive consequences for the Deaf community. It recognizes that being unable to hear, like being unable to see or walk, should not be perceived as a reason for exclusion from society. An example of one Deaf man's experience of going into hospital demonstrates the way that Deaf people can experience social exclusion:

> I didn't understand the nurses, they talked to me, but I couldn't lip-read them. I asked for a bottle, but nothing happened. It was painful … they wrote things down for me, but I

---

[35]   *Ibid.*, p.31.

[36]   Lane, H., 'The medicalization of cultural Deafness in historical perspective', p.482.

[37]   The benefits of introducing BSL early in a Deaf child's life are demonstrated in Watson, L. et al., *Deaf and Hearing Impaired Pupils*, pp.33–4.

[38]   See the discussion in chapter 2.

[39]   National Health Service, *Newborn Hearing Screening Programme: Information for parents to be and parents of new born babies* (London, 2002).

couldn't read because I only have one eye ... I couldn't see anything they wrote – I left my glasses at home[40].

The social model has acknowledged that the primary reason that Deaf and disabled people have been excluded from participating in society has been to do with society itself, like the lack of awareness shown towards the man's needs when he was in hospital and the lack of resources to respond to those needs. Ladd explains, however, that, 'Deaf communities have been swept along with the social model movement largely because they lacked the power to make their own views known.[41]' He criticizes the social model for including Deaf people only because they live with discrimination as a result of physically being unable to hear. If inclusion with and identification with disabled people in the social model ultimately comes down to what appears to be medical diagnosis alone, then Deaf people are not interested, Ladd argues. However, disabled people do not use the social model in this way either. Like Deaf people, disabled people are searching for and beginning to define their own identity in terms of what is positive about their lives as much as by the limitations their impairment presents them with. Full inclusion of Deaf people in society will not be achieved by flashing doorbells, textphones and such like, or even by the provision of BSL interpreters for Deaf people in every context in society. Likewise, a person using a wheelchair will never feel included in a context where other people, regardless of how accessible the building is, do not receive him/her in a positive way.

Inclusion and equality in society for Deaf people and disabled people cannot be brought about simply by introducing acts of parliament that legislate for the provision of what the Disability Rights Commission calls, 'Auxiliary Aids'[42], but by a more fundamental transformation in the perception of Deafness in society and the response that emerges from that. There have been small but important examples of Deaf people being full members of a community alongside hearing people. In the last century, in a place called Martha's Vineyard in the USA, there was a high proportion of people living there who were profoundly Deaf. In that community everyone could sign. It is reported that if a couple of hearing people were speaking and a third Deaf person joined them, they would usually slip into using sign language so that the Deaf person did not feel marginalized. Everyone signed there and Deaf people were included at every level of society[43]. To try to replicate this model throughout Britain would be a mammoth task, and some may think it is not worth it for the relatively small number of Deaf people who live in the UK. To teach even basic sign language in schools, however, would mean that should a hearing and a Deaf person meet, they would be able to communicate. Generations of teaching Deaf children for most of

---

[40]   Taken from an exchange on the video: Visible Communications, *The Invisible Church* (Northampton, 1996).

[41]   Ladd, P., *Understanding Deaf Culture*, p.15.

[42]   Disability Rights Commission, *Code of Practice*, p.61. An auxiliary aid may include BSL Interpreters, loop systems and other assistive technology.

[43]   See the account of this community in Groce, N.E., *Everyone Here Spoke Sign Language: Hereditary Deafness on Martha's Vineyard* (Cambridge, Massachusetts, 1988).

their school life how to speak, has not realized that possibility, but teaching hearing children some signing may begin to break down the communication barriers.

Deafness and Deafhood: Towards a Model of Deaf Culture and Community

Ladd argues for a new perspective on Deafness that he defines as the culturo-linguistic model of Deafness. He explains that this model 'requires that Deaf communities are seen as intrinsic "dual-category members" – that is, that some of their issues might relate to issues of non-hearing [impairment and disability] whilst others relate to language and culture'[44]. Rather than seeing the Deaf community as a disabled group, or as a language minority, Ladd argues that Deaf people are a distinct group which cannot be categorized alongside disabled people or linguistic minorities, but only in their own terms as Deaf people[45]. What distinguishes the Deaf community as a distinct group is what Ladd terms as 'Deafhood'. Ladd explains this concept as follows:

> Deafhood … represents a process – the struggle by each Deaf child, Deaf family and Deaf adult to explain to themselves and each other their own existence in the world. In sharing their lives with each other as a community, and enacting those explanations rather than writing books about them, Deaf people are engaged in a daily praxis, a continuing internal and external dialogue. This dialogue not only acknowledges that existence as a Deaf person is actually a process of *becoming* and maintaining 'Deaf', but also reflects different interpretations of Deafhood, of what being a Deaf person in a Deaf community might mean[46].

What Ladd terms as 'Deafhood' and defines so succinctly here, is the reality of the struggle I have found present in the Deaf communities I have been part of. This struggle to find and articulate what it means to be Deaf will be discussed in more detail below.

Deaf Culture and Disability

Both Ladd and Alker criticize heavily the way that many people in British society 'lump together' the Deaf community, deafened people, and people who are hard of hearing as all 'Deaf', under the more general category of 'the disabled'. This homogenization assumes that all Deaf and hearing-impaired people along with all disabled people pretty much share the same experiences, but there are important marked differences.

Any human being can become a disabled person at any stage of their life, and as people get older, many people do become disabled. The disability movement have coined and use the phrase 'non-disabled'[47] and I have heard some talk about

---

[44] Ladd, P., *Understanding Deaf Culture*, p.16.
[45] *Ibid.*, pp.15–17.
[46] *Ibid.*, p.3.
[47] This phrase is used by government departments and disabled people. See, for example, Grewal, I. et al. *'Disabled for Life?' Attitudes Towards and Experiences of Disability in Britain.*

'temporarily non-disabled people' to point to the reality that no non-disabled human being is exempt from the possibility of becoming disabled because of age, illness, accident, etc. The Deaf community has and uses no such equivalent phrase. Unless people are born Deaf or become Deaf at an early age, there is generally no possibility that a person can become Deaf at any other time in their life because they will have acquired English as their first language. On the whole, disabled people, while living a different life experience to non-disabled people, usually find few problems in communicating orally with one another, though some disabled people do have speech difficulties. The fact that Deaf people use a different language distinguishes them considerably from disabled people in terms of their cultural framework for life as well as the way they interpret the world. Many of the campaigns that Deaf people are engaged in to try to gain equality in society[48] are connected with the issue of language and so this shapes their identity differently.

For the Deaf community, being 'Deaf' will usually not involve coming to terms with a loss as it usually does for deafened people[49] because, as I explained earlier, Deaf people become Deaf at birth or in infancy. Similarly, however, many disabled people do not live with a sense of loss either. Many disabled people, like Deaf people, do not want to be 'non-disabled' and grieve because they have a disabled body. Rather, some often prefer to positively define their identity in terms of their existences as disabled people. Indeed, John Naudé, an Anglican priest who is a wheelchair user, affirms disabled people's humanity as good, arguing that 'every person on God's earth is "wonderfully made", no matter how severe a person's impairment'[50]. Deaf and disabled people find common ground in the fact that they experience discrimination because of social attitudes to impairment and are searching for something positive about their identity in a world that often does the opposite. However, differences must be recognized between Deaf and some other disabled people such as, for example, the way that Deaf people will not generally experience pain as a result of their Deafness, unlike a person with another impairment – such as multiple sclerosis – who might.

Deaf Culture and Loss of Hearing

Doug Alker, the first Deaf chief executive of the Royal National Institute for Deaf People (RNID) begins by defining the Deaf community in terms of individual level of hearing loss. He explains, 'I use the term Deaf (with an upper case D) to refer to people like myself, people who usually have a profound hearing loss. We cannot

---

Research Report No.173 (London, 2002), and Disabled People's Direct Action Network, *Who Represents Disabled People?* (URL: www.johnnypops.demon.co.uk/poetry/articles/dan/pr-oct-2003.htm, 2003).

[48]   For example, one major campaign of many Deaf organizations including the Federation of Deaf People (FDP) and the British Deaf Association (BDA) was to gain recognition of BSL as a language of the UK. See British Deaf Association. *BSL Recognition* (London, 2003).

[49]   Deafened people are those people who experience a severe hearing loss after acquiring spoken language. See RNID, *Facts and Figures on Deafness and Tinnitus*.

[50]   Naudé, J., 'Wonderfully Made', *All People*, 90 (2002): 10.

hear conversations or use the telephone'[51]. He also explains that members of the Deaf community are usually profoundly Deaf from birth or become Deaf at a pre-linguistic age. In making this distinction, Alker refers to two other groups of people with hearing loss. Firstly, in discussing those who are hard of hearing, whom he refers to using the lower case 'd', Alker argues, 'For deaf people, some adjustment on the person (i.e. hearing aid) is sufficient to enable participation in society'[52]. He suggests that to call such people 'deaf' is as erroneous as to call someone who wears spectacles, 'blind', rather, they are 'hard of hearing' or 'hearing impaired'. The second group he refers to are those who are profoundly deaf and have acquired English prior to losing their hearing[53]. They cannot hear with the help of technology though they can speak and think using what Alker refers to as a hearing 'geography'[54]. He argues concerning this group, 'Those who are deaf want to hear again. They want to be "normal" and return to a life experience, which they have enjoyed to a greater degree in the past'[55].

The three categories Alker highlights of 'hard of hearing', '*d*eaf(ened)' and '*Deaf*' are helpful and used by many people with hearing loss to label three sets of experiences, although as Alker rightly points out, many in society do not make these distinctions. However, in my view, Alker is misinformed in his assessment of both hard of hearing and deaf/deafened people. It is rarely the case that technology, such as a hearing aid, will help a person to function normally in society in the same way that spectacles help a person with a sight problem. In the context of meetings, or when there is a background noise, a person who is hard of hearing will still have great difficulty participating in such contexts. A loop system can alleviate but not eradicate this difficulty but some public venues do not have that facility. In this case, there is no difference between a hard of hearing person and a Deaf person to the point that they experience discrimination and exclusion in society, although it is true that the social and political discrimination Deaf people experience is much more serious. Further, it is not true that deaf/deafened people all 'crave' to become hearing again any more than it is true that a person who becomes blind will crave to become sighted again. Some deaf/deafened people will want to change their situation, others will adapt and learn to live and function perfectly well in the world as a deafened person and while they may regret having lost their hearing, they will not crave to have it back. Alker demonstrates clearly here the fact that as these three groups exist, there is a considerable lack of understanding between the three groups.

Some people who were born profoundly Deaf or became Deaf at a pre-linguistic age do not use and have resisted using BSL as their preferred language. Mairian Corker points out that such a position is often not tolerated by the Deaf community[56]. Similarly, however, there is usually a level of suspicion coming from non-sign

---

[51]   Alker, D., *Really Not Interested in the Deaf*, p.24.

[52]   *Ibid.*, p.26.

[53]   *Ibid.*, p.27.

[54]   *Ibid.*, pp.27–9.

[55]   *Ibid.*, p.29.

[56]   Corker, M., *Deaf Transitions: Images and Origins of Deaf Families, Deaf Communities and Deaf Identities* (London, 1996), pp.200–1.

language using pre-lingually deaf people towards members of the Deaf community – in other words the suspicion of each other among people with a hearing loss is present in all groups. Corker argues that the Deaf community's 'boundary with other communities is rigid and does not easily tolerate coexistence of diverse elements in the wider deaf community, as evidenced by the difficulty of gaining access to the Deaf community when in a state of transition or ambivalence about Deafness'[57]. As many people with a profound hearing loss from birth still leave school having been taught orally, many of them only begin to be a part of the wider Deaf community and find a home among Deaf people later in life[58] though many already know sign language and have been part of a smaller Deaf community at school[59].

Firstly, therefore, Deaf people are identified by Alker by their level of hearing loss and the time in their life at which they become Deaf. The second characteristic that identifies a person as Deaf, for Alker, has to do with socio-political concerns: 'Their [Deaf people's] access is possible only if the environment is adjusted to include them as equal members of society. That makes Deafness a social and political issue. It is a struggle for the recognition of and the necessity of that adjustment'[60]. As in the social model of disability, inclusion in society can usually be achieved by changes to society and not the Deaf person. Thirdly, Alker refers to the use of BSL as a defining feature of the Deaf community. There is no technology that can enable a Deaf person to function fully in society. It is only with BSL, Alker argues, that Deaf people can enjoy full participation.

Having been alongside members of the Deaf community for seven years in Birmingham, much of what Alker highlights as features of the Deaf community are easily recognizable. Nevertheless, I would suggest that while a Deaf person's level of hearing loss and political awareness help to define who the members of the Deaf community might be, the over-riding features, and what ought to come first in any attempt to define the Deaf community, is the Deaf person's use of British Sign Language as their first or preferred language, and their identification of themselves as Deaf People. By starting with the level of hearing loss, Alker implies that membership of the Deaf community is determined firstly by medical diagnosis. One's level of hearing loss is important and in fact will determine whether a young child is going to function better as an English or a BSL user and therefore have membership of the Deaf community. However, sign language and culture should be understood as the defining features of the Deaf community because some people who are born with a profound hearing loss do not identify with the Deaf community. In addition, a small number of children who are born with a profound hearing loss and who are brought up with an oral education, do not identify themselves as members of the Deaf community either as children or adults[61].

---

[57]   *Ibid.*, p.200.

[58]   *Ibid.*, pp.200–1.

[59]   Taylor, G. and Darby, A., *Deaf Identities* (Coleford, 2003). p.41.

[60]   Alker, D., *Really Not Interested in the Deaf*, p.26.

[61]   See Corker, M., *Deaf Transitions*, pp.200–1.

The Deaf Community and Hearing People

As explained earlier, the Deaf community in Britain consists of between 50,000 and 100,000 Deaf BSL users. On the periphery of this community are approximately 250,000 hearing people who use BSL[62]. It may be argued that certain hearing people could be included in a definition of the Deaf community such as, for example, hearing children of Deaf parents. I suggest, however, that the Deaf community can be envisaged as a series of concentric circles. At the centre are profoundly Deaf sign language users, then moving outwards, would be hearing children of Deaf parents, hearing parents of Deaf children, other hearing family members, hearing friends of Deaf people, BSL interpreters, hearing employees who work with Deaf people. Together, all of these people influence the lives of Deaf sign language users, though not always necessarily in a positive way. And so, for a study of the Deaf community, it may be helpful to distinguish between profoundly Deaf sign language users and other more peripheral members of the Deaf community because Deaf sign language users do not live in isolation from the rest of society.

While the Deaf community may include hearing people at its edges, for our purposes here, I will focus only on those Deaf people whose first or preferred language is BSL. Those members of the Deaf community who are on the periphery, because they are hearing and use a hearing mental geography determined by a world of sound, will not share the same cultural worldview and theological insights that profoundly Deaf Sign Language users will have. As the son of a mother who became blind, despite all the insights that has given me in to the world of blindness, I can still never know the reality of what it means to live as a blind person in the world, because I am sighted. The same will be true for hearing people, however close they may be to Deaf people, they will not have a full understanding of Deaf experience and subsequently Deaf theology(-ies). As a hearing person, that puts me at a disadvantage also as I write here. However, I simply aim to share and reflect on those insights that Deaf people have shared with me, not claiming that I know what it is like to be Deaf, recognizing that I will only ever understand in part.

The Deaf Community and Cultural-Linguistic Minority Groups

It has already been argued and it will be demonstrated further in chapter 2, that BSL is a full language with its own grammar and that it has the ability to communicate complex and detailed ideas. For Deaf people it is their first or preferred language for communication. BSL is not the majority language in this country and so at first glance, it would appear that there would be no problems in defining Deaf people as a linguistic minority. However, the main difference between BSL users in Britain and say, Urdu, Hindi, Arabic, Polish or Welsh speakers, is that not everyone is convinced that BSL is a language, least of all, those who advise parents of Deaf children, many Deaf educationalists and many politicians.

Ladd asks 'Why is it we [Deaf people] who must strive to raise funds in order to accumulate evidence which "proves" that our sign languages are *bona fide*

---

[62]   Alker, D., *Really Not Interested in the Deaf*, p.27.

languages, and that the collective lives of Deaf people are *bona fide* cultures?'[63] After years of campaigning by the Deaf community, in March 2003, the British government officially recognized BSL as a minority language in the UK[64]. One million pounds (an extraordinarily small amount) was consequently set aside to fund work to improve access for Deaf people to society through BSL and much of the money has been allocated to training interpreters and BSL tutors[65]. In practice, this recognition has yet to make any impact on British society in the short term, but its long-term ramifications will be especially interesting in education, employment legislation and access to work, medical care, the legal system, social services and all sectors of society where Deaf people use a service or are employed as part of the provision of those services. So while Deaf people are a linguistic minority and term themselves as such, society has for so long refused to accept what Deaf people have always known – that BSL is a full and complete language. Instead, hearing people have preferred to attempt to normalize Deaf people, thinking they should speak and be as much like hearing people as possible (see the discussion in chapter 2 on education). Deaf people's experience, therefore, includes the dual oppression of being a cultural-linguistic minority group, whose language society has only just recognized, alongside the treatment of Deaf people as a disabled group who should be normalized.

Issues in Deaf Culture

Having examined the nature of the Deaf community in relation to disabled people and cultural-linguistic minority groups, I now aim, under the title of what many Deaf people refer to as 'Deaf culture', to reflect more deeply on the nature of the Deaf community. The phrase 'Deaf culture' itself raises important questions. Studies on culture cover a diverse spectrum of perspectives[66] and it signifies many different things to different people. While some describe 'culture' as being closely associated with a particular (usually affluent) perspective on the arts, others refer to culture as anything connected with a group's expression of their identity. There are many other perspectives on 'culture' and this diversity of definitions can lead to confusion as to what exactly is being referred to by the word 'culture'. The term 'Deaf culture', however, is widely used by the Deaf community and is generally used as an umbrella term for anything that is distinctively 'Deaf'. Whether Deaf culture is the right term to use for this is debatable, but as it is the term used by Deaf people, it is the term that will be employed here.

Other phrases signed by Deaf people and used more or less synonymously with Deaf culture are highlighted by Paddy Ladd – namely, 'Deaf World' and 'Deaf Way'[67]. Ladd also suggests that a phrase translated literally from BSL as 'Deaf-His'

---

[63]   Ladd, P., *Understanding Deaf Culture*, p.1.
[64]   British Deaf Association, *British Deaf News*, (London, 2003), p.6.
[65]   British Deaf Association, *BSL Recognition*.
[66]   See the discussion in Ladd, P., *Understanding Deaf Culture*, pp.196–231.
[67]   Ladd, P., *Understanding Deaf Culture*, p.237.

predates what Deaf people now call Deaf culture[68]. This third phrase is not one used in Birmingham by Deaf people with whom I have come into contact while 'Deaf-Way' is commonly used. While 'Deaf culture' may be a term developed by hearing people[69], it is widely used as a concept by Deaf people and points towards what is unique to the Deaf community.

I think it is important to be aware that Deaf culture or the Deaf Way is not the opposite of hearing culture. Deaf and hearing people share the same geographic space, in many instances work together, use the same hospitals, courts, and are governed by the same parliament. Issues need to be thought through with great care, however, as hearing people exercise much greater power and control in society than Deaf people both because hearing people are the majority and have historically held more power than Deaf people. Many hearing people are either not aware or do not care that Deaf people have a different culture while others remain convinced that BSL is not even a proper language. At some point, however, the two cultures engage with each other. Finger-spelling, for example, is used by Deaf people to describe many proper nouns such as the names of places and people. Finger-spelling involves using the hands to spell out words using English spelling[70]. Another example of the influence of hearing culture is the sign in Birmingham for 'Bristol' which is the same as the sign for 'pistol'. This is because, Deaf people tell me, Bristol and pistol sound similar and because the lip patterns created by the two words are identical. This kind of 'hearingism' is frowned upon by some Deaf people, though I fail to understand why. That is perhaps my problem, but languages and cultures borrow from one another all the time, making use of different nuances of culture and understanding and re-appropriating them for a new situation. Most of the English language is made up from other languages – Anglo-Saxon, French, Latin and Greek, and continues today to borrow words from other languages such as 'safari', 'palaver', and 'karaoke' all now a part of common parlance.

So cultures and languages overlap. They do not and cannot live in a vacuum from one another. That is especially true in our increasingly globalized world but also when two cultures like Deaf and hearing exist alongside each other.

Deaf History

History is an important aspect of the identity and culture of any community. Most work on the history of Deaf people has focused on issues in education, which is discussed in the next chapter. However, I will outline a brief history here, as much as it is possible to do so, as the final part of this discussion on the Deaf community, their culture and identity in the UK.

As a minority group in Britain and having always been so, it is inevitable that the history of the Deaf community is not well documented. There is mention of Deaf people in texts from early Classical Greek literature such as Socrates and in the Bible

---

[68]   *Ibid.*, p.237
[69]   *Ibid.*, p.233
[70]   Sutton-Spence, R. and Woll, B., *The Linguistics of British Sign Language: An Introduction* (Cambridge, 1999), pp.16–19.

itself. The visual and tangible world of Deaf people is witnessed to when Socrates talks about those who communicate with their hands[71]. In the Old Testament, Deaf people are referred to in Leviticus 19.14, where there is warning given not to 'revile the deaf'. Commenting on this passage from a Jewish perspective, Sacks explains its significance: 'If we treat disrespectfully those who are deaf or disabled, even if they are unaware of it, we diminish their humanity and thereby *our* humanity'[72]. In Isaiah 43.8, 'deafness' is used as a metaphor for not understanding or 'listening' to the Lord. The story of the healing of the Deaf man in Mark 7.32–37[73] is the only place in the New Testament that a d/Deaf person appears.

In the medieval era, Banham has illustrated how a silent religious order of monks in Anglo-Saxon Britain developed a system of sign language for communicating with each other. The system of language became quite complex and, it would seem, almost meant that talking became unnecessary anyway. Arguably, the development of such a signing system makes a vow of silence irrelevant. While this does not say anything about the history of Deaf people, it demonstrates well how, when speech is not available as an option for communicating, signs are the most natural alternative[74]. However, despite a few random references to Deaf people and sign languages in texts from earlier historical periods, most of what can be said about Deaf history begins with developments in the eighteenth century.

Harlan Lane's seminal and highly influential survey of Deaf history[75] begins with the story of Deaf people in eighteenth-century France at the school in which sign language was used to educate Deaf children, run by Charles, Abée de l'Epée. There is little point in repeating much of the story of this school here as Lane has more than adequately done this already. From these beginnings of Deaf education through sign language in France, Lane traces how this led to key Deaf people moving to America and the establishment of the first and still only Deaf University for the Liberal Arts at Washington DC: Gallaudet University[76]. While Lane's book says little about Deaf history in the UK, it has had an important conscientizing influence in Britain, having far-reaching effects as Deaf people have begun to claim this history as a major part of their own identity and heritage.

Although there is little of significance that has been written about the history of Deaf people in Britain, more recent memories are kept alive and transmitted from one generation to another through a 'signing tradition'. One of the most important aspects of Deaf culture is the use of story-telling. In this tradition stories are told about what the Deaf community was like, how it was managed by Missioners[77], and what life was like at school. Many older Deaf people have told me harrowing stories

---

[71]   See references in Ladd, P., *Understanding Deaf Culture*, p.91.

[72]   Sacks, J., *Faith in the Future* (London, 1995), p.218.

[73]   This particular text is examined in more detail in chapter 5.

[74]   Cf. Banham, D. (ed.), *Monesteriales Indicia: The Anglo-Saxon Monastic Sign Language* (Hockwold-cum-Wilton, 1991).

[75]   Lane, H., *When the Mind Hears*.

[76]   Rochester Institute in New York has a considerable number of Deaf students, though the focus of study there is more focussed on the fields of technology than the arts.

[77]   Many Deaf centres were founded by Anglican dioceses and were managed by a 'Missioner' who was invariably hearing. See Ladd, P., *Understanding Deaf Culture*, pp.139–44.

about how their hands would be tied or they would be made to stand in a corner at school if they were caught signing. The horrors of the past are made present in stories and remind those of us in the present (Deaf and hearing) of the need to keep fighting for better rights properly protected in law, and practised in such spheres as education.

Birmingham Deaf Church

The focus of this research has been the Deaf community as I have discussed it above. Most of the research for this project has been carried out specifically among the Deaf community in Birmingham, and particularly the Anglican Deaf church there. While what is above relates to the Deaf community in Birmingham as much as anywhere else, below is an outline of some of the unique dimensions the Deaf community in Birmingham that has been central to this research project.

The Deaf Community in Birmingham

It is not clear how many Deaf people live in Birmingham. The main organization working with Deaf people, Birmingham Institute for Deaf People (BID), estimates that there are in the region of 2,000 profoundly Deaf BSL users in the city[78]. Birmingham City Council estimate that there are about 5,000 BSL users (though it does not specify whether that includes hearing BSL users) in Birmingham, but this figure is derived from the 'predicted' percentage of BSL users in the population nationally and that same percentage is applied to the population of Birmingham[79]. The Council suggests, however, that this figure may be higher[80]. The Council asserts that 'there is a strong and vibrant Deaf Community in Birmingham'[81] and a visit to the main Deaf Club in Birmingham would confirm the Council's statement. It is rich and varied in terms of religion, ethnicity, sex, and social class and, as you would expect in the Deaf community, includes Deaf and hearing people working and socializing alongside one another, communicating in the first language of the community, BSL. Those people using Birmingham Deaf Club as a place to socialize are generally older as, following national trends, younger Deaf people are choosing to socialize with other Deaf and hearing people elsewhere[82]. The Deaf Club, however, is active in Birmingham and includes women's groups, an OAP club, bingo, presentations on issues pertinent to the Deaf community, sports groups, a bar with a pool table, facilities to buy food and is the place where the Anglican Diocesan Deaf Church is based. The Deaf Club shares a building with BID which also provides social services, interpreting services, an information service, a chaplaincy office, a regular

---

[78] See Birmingham Institute for Deaf People (BID). *Did You Know?* (Birmingham, 2004).

[79] Birmingham City Council, *Scrutiny Report to the City Council: Review of Signing Services* (Birmingham, 2003), pp.7–8.

[80] *Ibid.*, p.8.

[81] *Ibid.*, p.8.

[82] Ladd, P., *Understanding Deaf Culture*, p.47.

newsletter and works with the council to provide services to Deaf people across the city[83].

The Deaf Church of Christ the King, Birmingham

The Deaf church in which I conducted the vast majority of the research for this project is based at the Deaf Club in Birmingham. The chaplain at the church is funded by the Anglican Diocese of Birmingham. When I began the research for this project, the chaplain was working full time with Deaf people, but this has since been cut to a half-time post. Because the Deaf church's chaplain is funded by the Church of England, and thus the chaplain is himself Anglican, the church would identify itself as a part of the Anglican Church. However, a survey of the members of the Deaf church showed that members attend the church who would identify themselves as Anglican, Baptist, Methodist and Roman Catholic (though many Roman Catholics attend the church funded by the Roman Catholic Archdiocese of Birmingham). The church meets every week on a Wednesday evening at 6:00pm and on the first Sunday of every month at 5:00pm. On a Wednesday, there is an average of 40–50 regular members and on Sundays, about 15–25 who attend[84]. Previously, all services had taken place on Sundays, but the main service was moved to Wednesday because that is the day when the OAP club meets. This change meant that the number of people attending the church weekly more than doubled.

Birmingham Deaf Church includes both men and women. However, from a weekly count of the number of men and women attending over a period of three months, about 70 per cent of the regular congregation is women. There are a number of hearing people who attend the church on a regular basis and make contributions at the request of the chaplain and Deaf members of the church. The regular congregation is all white with most being over the age of 60. Inevitably, the timing of the service excludes those who are employed from attending on a Wednesday and the limitations of public transport stop many people from attending on Sundays. This difficulty is one that is currently being addressed. My research has shown that the vast majority of members of the church (c.90 per cent) have lived in Birmingham for the whole of their lives and have attended the Deaf club and church since they were children. Outside of worship, the church also met for a variety of social events.

The church is managed in a different way to many hearing churches. There is no parochial church council because Deaf churches are not part of the parish system. During the period I was attending the church, there were two male chaplains, both of whom were hearing. The chaplain worked alongside a committee which was made up of Deaf people, including a Chairperson, Treasurer and Secretary. This committee took responsibility for all decisions relating to the church, including furnishings, finances, social events and decisions about worship. The Committee was elected annually by members of the Deaf church.

Two people were trained as Pastoral Workers who assisted the chaplain in the leading of worship and were licensed by the diocesan bishop to assist with the

---

[83]   See the BID Website: www.bid.org.uk, 2007.
[84]   Figures obtained from the church's register between 1998 and 2004.

administration of the chalice. During the time I spent with the church, one Deaf member was selected to train for ordination and was ordained as a stipendiary deacon in 2001 in the Diocese of Wakefield. Two Deaf priests from other dioceses also attended the church and led worship at occasional intervals. When the worship is led from the front, it is usually led in English using Signs to support the English word order[85]. The liturgy is based on Anglican liturgical texts meaning that the worship reflects English hearing culture. However, as I will discuss in chapter 6, there are elements of Deaf culture in the worship and those elements are increasing in significance. For example, sermons are increasingly led in BSL as are the intercessions. Fixed prayers, however, like the Confession, Creed, Eucharistic Prayers and the Lord's Prayer continue to follow English Word order.

International Comparisons: Zimbabwe

I explained in the Introduction to this book that while the majority of the research I conducted to inform this project was carried out in the United Kingdom, I should also mention that much literature on the Deaf community itself emerges out of the USA. Where appropriate, I have indicated when I have used such literature and discussed its relevance to the British context. In addition, I spent a much shorter period of time working with Deaf people in Zimbabwe and the findings of that research have informed the argument here to a lesser degree. Little work has been done on the Deaf community in Zimbabwe, and the resources available on theology in Zimbabwe generally were scarce when I visited in 1999, except for some key texts by Canaan Sondido Banana and books and papers by one or two other theologians including Ezra Chitambo[86], Isabel Mukonyora[87] and Jim Cox[88], but their work is not as well known outside of Zimbabwe as other Africa Theologians like John Mbiti and Mercy Amba Oduyoye.

It is my contention, as argued later, that the ways in which BSL is used to express theology offers some interesting parallels with vernacular theology formulated among some groups in Africa. It seemed appropriate to analyse, therefore, the experience of Deaf people within such a context as this and to consider how they thought and expressed themselves theologically. I would have liked to return to Zimbabwe to gather more data for the purposes of this project, but the political stability of the

---

[85]   This form of communication is called Sign Supported English (SSE).

[86]   Chitambo, Ezra., 'What's in a Name? Naming Practices among African Christians in Zimbabwe', in Fiedler, K. et al. (eds), *Theology Cooked in an African Pot* (Zomba, Malawi, 1998), pp.106–19, and 'Fact and Fiction: Images of Missionaries in Zimbabwean Literature', *Studies in World Christianity*, 7/1 (2001), pp.80–94.

[87]   Mukonyora, I., 'Women's Readings of the Bible', in Mukonyora, I. et al. (eds)., *'Rewriting' the Bible: the real issues* (Gweru, Zimbabwe, 1993), pp.199–216 and 'The Dramatization of Life and Death by Johane Masowe', *The Journal of Humanities of the University of Zimbabwe*, XXV(ii) (1998), pp.191–207.

[88]   Mukonyora, I. (eds), *'Rewriting' the Bible: the real issues* (Gweru, Zimbabwe, 1993).

country and tensions between the governments of Zimbabwe and the UK have made this impossible.

Conclusion

In this chapter, I have described the Deaf community in Britain and I have outlined and discussed some of the issues that are important to them and help to form their Deaf identity. I have argued that Deaf people should not be homogenized together with either disabled people or linguistic minority groups, but that any discussion about their experience should recognize that Deaf people have particular needs and a particular identity that will share some experiences with some other groups, but as a group, have an identity that is, in its entirety, unique. In the next chapter, I will look at two related issues of particular significance to the Deaf community: British Sign Language and Education. That chapter will complete this first part which aims to introduce and discuss the experiences of Deaf people and their identity as a community before moving on to look in detail at how I conducted my research and how Deaf experience informs and shapes Deaf theology.

Chapter 2

Talking with your Hands:
Issues in British Sign Language

Introduction: BSL The 'Natural' Language of Deaf People?

Many Deaf people in Britain and around the world argue that sign languages are the 'natural languages' of the Deaf community[1]. Such a notion, however, needs further clarification because 'which language or languages they (infants) actually learn depends on which language they have access to'[2]. In this sense, therefore, no language is acquired naturally but is in fact determined by the context of a child's parents and the community in which an individual is born and grows up in. However, many leading linguists have argued that, while the language we learn is determined by culture, our capacity to learn language is instinctive. Pinker argues,

> Language is not a cultural artefact that we learn the way we learn to tell time or how the federal government works. Instead it is a distinct piece of the biological makeup of our brains. Language is a complex, specialized skill which develops in the child spontaneously, without conscious effort or formal instruction, is deployed without awareness of its underlying logic, is qualitatively the same in every individual, and is distinct from more general abilities to process information or behave intelligently. For these reasons some cognitive scientists have described language as a psychological faculty, a mental organ, a neural system, and a computational module. But I prefer the admittedly quaint term 'instinct'. It conveys the idea that people know how to talk in more or less the sense that spiders know how to spin webs[3].

Pinker demonstrates this point by drawing on research from Noam Chomsky and others and using examples from the encounters between different cultures. He argues that if 'speakers of different languages have to communicate to carry out practical tasks but do not have the opportunity to learn one another's languages, they develop a makeshift jargon called a pidgin'[4]. Evidence shows that when children who are at the right age to learn a language (no later than 5 years old) are exposed to a 'pidgin', the fragmented words of the pidgin take on a greater grammatical complexity,

---

[1] See for example, Lane, H., *The Mask of Benevolence: disabling the Deaf Community.* New Edition (San Diego, 1999), p.46. This is a commonly used phrase in the Deaf community

[2] Woll, B., 'Development of Sign and Spoken Languages', in Gregory, S. et al. (eds), *Issues in Deaf Education* (London, 1998), p.59.

[3] Pinker, S., *The Language Instinct* (London: 1994), p.18.

[4] *Ibid.*, p.33.

'... resulting in a brand-new, richly expressive language'[5]. Thus the pidgin, within only one generation, can become a native tongue and is called a creole. Lane et al. describe this as the 'nativization hypothesis'[6]. Pinker provides the following example to show how this works.

By examining how language has developed among Deaf people in Nicaragua, Pinker explains that until 1979, Nicaraguan Deaf people remained isolated from each other. Following the introduction of an education act in 1979, new schools for Deaf children were created. While an oral approach to education was pursued in schools, Deaf children developed a 'pidgin language' that they used outside of school. When young Deaf infants were exposed to the pidgin signing it was noted that 'their signing is more fluid and compact, and the gestures are more stylized and less like a pantomime'[7]. In other words, the pidgin signing developed into a creole using a more complex grammar. The point that is most important to note is that while the particular words and grammar used in a language are acquired through nurture, one's general ability to master and use – and if necessary create – grammar is a natural instinct.

Of course, the grammars of BSL, English, French, Japanese, are all different, so to what degree can it be argued that one's ability to use grammar is an instinctive ability? In English, for example, we are familiar with using the phrase 'red wine' so the adjective comes before the noun. In French, one would say, 'vin rouge' so the adjective comes after the noun. It is not at this level at which it is argued that language is instinctive, however. The crux of the argument is that children cannot learn by rote from their parents every instance in which, for example, a verb ends with a certain suffix; Pinker uses the example of the verb 'to walk' noting that in the third person singular, 'walk' becomes 'walks'. This same rule is applied to hundreds of other verbs such as think, speak, look and so on. Research on a child of pre-school age has shown that in 90 per cent of the instances in normal speech where the 's' suffix should be applied to a verb, the suffix was applied correctly[8]. Therefore, a particular rule is learned and then applied instinctively. Even mistakes support this thesis; where the verb was not used correctly, 'He's a boy so he *gots* a scary one'[9], this further demonstrates that the rule is applied instinctively, rather than learned, because such anomalies would not have been learned from a parent. Few, if any, parents sit with their child explicitly teaching them rules of grammar as is evident in the way so few children in Britain explicitly understand how English grammar works. They just use it.

Pinker's argument is further developed by drawing on the work of neuropsychologist, Howard Gardner[10]. Gardner interviewed a man who, three months previously, had had a stroke and was living with a linguistic problem not present prior to the stroke. Pinker notes, 'Obviously, Mr Ford had to struggle to get speech out, but

5   *Ibid.*, p.33.
6   Lane, H. et al., *A Journey Into the Deaf World* (San Diego, 1996), p.49.
7   Pinker, S., *The Language Instinct*, p.36.
8   *Ibid.*, p.44.
9   *Ibid.*, p.45.
10   Gardner, H., *The Shattered Mind* (New York, 1974), pp.60–1.

his problems were not in controlling his vocal muscles. He could blow out a candle and clear his throat, and he was as linguistically hobbled when he wrote as when he spoke. Most of his handicaps centered around grammar itself'[11]. One's linguistic abilities are governed by a specific part of the brain. Mr Ford's ability to remember individual words was not impaired and nor was, as Gardner notes, his intelligence[12]. However, his ability to put together words using a grammatical structure was affected by the brain's impairment. What the interview with Mr Ford, and other research has shown is that linguistic capacity and intellectual ability are not the same. A person can be quite able to think intellectually, but not express herself linguistically (e.g. Mr Ford), and visa versa (i.e. a person with an intellectual impairment such as Down's Syndrome may have relatively good speech). Pinker concludes, 'Your parents need not bathe you in language or even command a language. You don't need the intellectual wherewithal to function in society, the skills to keep house and home together, or a particularly firm grip on reality. Indeed, you can possess all these advantages and still not be a competent language user, if you lack just the right genes or just the right bits of brain'[13]. If one's ability to acquire language therefore is comparable to the spider's capacity to spin a web – it is an instinct – what does this mean for Deaf people and the acquisition of BSL – is it their natural language?

The Significance of Sign Languages: The Evidence

It is essential to emphasize at this point that BSL is a language. Pinker explains, 'Contrary to popular misconceptions, sign languages are not pantomimes and gestures, inventions of educators, or ciphers of the spoken language of the surrounding community'[14]. Oliver Sacks suggests that as early as the 1870s the anthropologist E.B. Tylor, through his experience of Deaf people, had 'fascinating insights into signed language'[15] and, had the Milan conference of 1880 (described shortly) not taken place, he may have initiated a study into sign languages over one hundred years ago. The first major study to suggest that sign languages are languages in their own right and for that to make an impact on linguistic study came from William C. Stokoe in 1960. Pursuing research into American Sign Language, he argued that sign language was not, as Pinker explains, pantomimes or gestures but a complex language with a structure and grammar[16]. Since then, numerous studies have been published in the UK arguing and demonstrating that BSL is a complete language with a complex and detailed structure and grammar capable of conveying

---

[11]   Pinker, S., *The Language Instinct*, p.47.

[12]   Gardner, H., *The Shattered Mind*, p.61.

[13]   Pinker, S., *The Language Instinct*, pp.53–4.

[14]   *Ibid.*, p.36.

[15]   Sacks, O., *Seeing Voices* (London, 1991), p.76.

[16]   Stokoe, W.C., *Sign Language Structure: An Outline of the Visual Communication System of the American Deaf*, University of Buffalo – Studies in Linguistics, Occasional Paper 8, 1960.

information on a par with any spoken language[17]. Linguistic study shows, therefore, that sign languages have a distinct grammar. Pinker's reference to the Deaf children in Nicaragua shows how sign language there developed quickly from a pidgin to a creole. Just as hearing people instinctively communicate with speech, so do Deaf people with their hands, face and bodies. For the Deaf community, that naturally uses visual gesture to communicate with one another, their language instinct is manifest in the development of a sign language grammar.

Cerebral Activity

Sutton-Spence and Woll explain, 'The brain is divided into left and right hemispheres: the left is known to be more important for language and the right is more important for spatial skills. Even though sign languages are visual languages, they are still primarily located in the left hemisphere'[18]. The evidence that sign languages engage the same part of the brain as spoken languages helps to reinforce the position that BSL is a language which is acquired instinctively. BSL does not make use of another side or part of the brain but the same side as spoken languages. This position is reinforced by the pioneering work conducted by Poizner et al.,[19] demonstrating how the brain and language are connected and examining the similarities between spoken and signed languages.

Ability to Learn English as Opposed to BSL

The way that sign language and the brain interact to demonstrate that BSL is a natural language is further reinforced by comparative research between the acquisition of spoken languages and sign languages among Deaf children. Drawing on research from Gregory and Mogford (1981) on six severely Deaf children, Kyle and Woll show that by the age of 34 months, a Deaf child's average spoken vocabulary included about 100 words. In a hearing child, this level of vocabulary has been acquired by about 20 months[20]. In a more recent study, Woll argues, 'Hearing children generally have a lexicon of about ten words by fifteen months and fifty words at 20 months; studies of ASL report that children learning to sign have similar-sized lexicons'[21]. Such research shows that Deaf children clearly acquire sign languages much more easily than spoken languages. If language is an instinct in response to the sounds a child hears – their language environment – a child who cannot hear will not acquire spoken language in the usual way. However, placing Deaf infants in a BSL language

---

[17]   See especially, Kyle, J.G. and Woll, B., *Sign Language: The Study of Deaf People and Their Language* (Cambridge, 1985); Sutton-Spence, R. and Woll, B., *The Linguistics of British Sign Language: An Introduction* (Cambridge, 1999); and Brennan, M., 'The Visual World of British Sign Language', in Brien, D. (ed.), *Dictionary of British Sign Language/ English* (London, 1992), pp.1–133.

[18]   Sutton-Spence, R. and Woll, B., *The Linguistics of British Sign Language*, p.130.

[19]   Poizner, H. et al., *What the Hands Reveal About the Brain* (Cambridge, Massachusetts, 1990).

[20]   Kyle, J.G. and Woll, B., *Sign Language*, p.63.

[21]   Woll, B. 'Development of Signed and Spoken Languages', p.60.

environment is not straightforward because, as explained earlier, Deaf people do not live in isolation from hearing people and indeed the majority of Deaf people are born to hearing parents. But the advantages of creating such environments are obvious in terms of language acquisition and the potential advantages in education that brings. Despite the evidence, however, those with power over Deaf people, in government and education, still insist on speech as the first language for Deaf children, though the recognition of BSL as a national minority language may change things manifest in new policies to 'mainstream' Deaf children[22].

Introduction to British Sign Language

British Sign Language is a language of movement and space, of the hands and of the eyes, of abstract communication as well as iconic story-telling, but most important of all, it is the language of the Deaf community in Britain[23].

British Sign Language is a language in its own right which follows a particular set of grammatical rules and principles. While BSL may share certain characteristics with other languages, the grammar which it follows, in its entirety, is unique to BSL. A common misunderstanding concerning sign languages has traditionally been that they are not languages at all, but rather involved nothing more than a few gestures which anyone, who tried, could understand. This error must immediately be rectified, as I have already tried to do, by stressing that a hearing person who has never learned BSL could no more comprehend that language than an English-speaking person who has never learned Dutch could understand a person from the Netherlands. Although BSL is particular to the Deaf community in Britain, deaf people are more able to move between different sign languages than hearing people are able to move between different spoken languages. While each country has a sign language which is particular to that nation, following very specific and particular grammatical rules – not to mention local dialects within nations – Deaf people tend to be able to cross these barriers of language with Deaf people from other nations. Indeed, American Sign Language and BSL are quite different, yet when Deaf people from both countries meet, they can often communicate with few problems after a very short space of time. The same has been observed by me between a British and a Korean man who met in London by chance and were able to communicate with each other, at first with difficulty, but quickly with ease[24]. When I was in Zimbabwe, some communication with Deaf people was possible within a short period of time. Again,

---

[22]   Ladd, P, *Understanding Deaf Culture*, pp.157–8.

[23]   Kyle, J.G. and Woll, B., *Sign Language*, p.5.

[24]   There can sometimes be cultural problems when particular concepts are being used. For example, time in the West is understood in terms of the past being behind and the future in front. People say, 'look ahead' in reference to the future. Among the Urubu Kapoor people of Brazil, in their sign language the opposite is true where the past is understood as that which can be seen and is therefore placed in front and the future is behind (see Kyle, J.G. and Woll, B., *Sign Language*, p.143–4). As cultural concepts are expressed through language this may cause some barriers. Once explained, however, communication would probably become possible again.

this is not to say that sign languages are merely systems of gestures. However, this does illustrate something of the visual dimension of sign languages in contrast to the arbitrary nature of many spoken languages.

Below I would like to attempt to try and outline some of the basic principles involved in the grammar of the visual world of BSL. However, there are three things which ought to be considered before continuing. Firstly, because I am not Deaf, the insights and explanations given below come from reading studies, personal observations and the practical use of a person for whom BSL is a second language and from a person who is still very much a student of this language. Secondly, the author is not a linguist but a theologian. The account, therefore, while drawing on personal experiences and observations, relies to some extent on experts in the field of linguistics; namely the works of Kyle and Woll, *Sign Language: The study of Deaf people and their language* (1985), Mary Brennan in 'The Visual World of British Sign Language: An Introduction', in Brien, D. (ed.), *Dictionary of British Sign Language* (1992) and Rachel Sutton-Spence and Bencie Woll, *The Linguistics of British Sign Language – An Introduction* (1999). BSL also has a number of 'dialects' so that a significant number of all signs are different in the various regions of Britain[25]. This work, therefore, focuses primarily on BSL and its use in the Birmingham area. Thirdly, as anyone who has studied languages will know, it is impossible to explain all of the rules and intricacies of a language in such a brief few pages as this and further detail should be sought from the books listed above. Indeed, problems have arisen, not by trying to find material to include, but in determining what must be omitted. Therefore, this is intended to be a basic overview of the language of BSL for the person who knows nothing, to help in understanding why it is so difficult for sign language to be written down, and to aid with understanding the rest of this work.

There are three sections to the outline given below. Firstly, a brief history of the language will be given so that the reader may know both where and how sign languages emerged and how BSL has developed into a language in its own right. Secondly, to show how the human body is used as both an object for producing signs, and how the individual signs become a language through outlining some of the basic principles of grammar. Thirdly, to look at more theoretical aspects of the language and the implications this has for theology.

The History and Development of British Sign Language

Records of the history and development of BSL are in less abundance than the history of Deaf people. As with most oppressed groups, there is very little history written either by Deaf people – because both education has been denied, and sign languages cannot be written down – or by those who have marginalized Deaf people – because they have not been interested in the particularities of the Deaf community. With so little general history on Deaf people, it is virtually impossible to find much on the history of sign languages specifically.

---

[25]   Sutton-Spence, R. and Woll, B., *The Linguistics of British Sign Language*, p.29.

It is perhaps true to say (although there is little evidence to support such a claim) that sign languages have always existed where there has been a need for Deaf people to communicate. Reference has already been made to Socrates' mention of Deaf people and to the use of sign language by hearing people in Benedictine monasteries in the previous chapter. Laurent Clerc, a Deaf pioneer of sign language in both France and America was sent to the first school for Deaf people in Paris in the late eighteenth to early nineteenth century. Harlan Lane explains how strange Clerc found the normal signs used there in comparison to the 'home signs' he had used with his family[26]. What seems clear, however, from the signs used by the monks and the 'home signs' employed by Clerc and his family, is that whenever speech is not an option for communication, sign languages are the first alternative. This arguably implies, therefore, that sign languages are as natural a form of communication as spoken language.

However, throughout the ages Deaf people have been excluded from and ignored in education and thus, sign languages were, for a long time, never formalized. In 1755, following the foundation of the first recorded school for Deaf children, by Charles Michel Abbé de l'Epée in Paris this began to change. This became the 'first public school for the Deaf in the history of the world'[27]. As the school developed so did French sign language, which slowly became more formalized and Epée also perfected a manual alphabet which enabled Deaf people to spell out words using French spelling constructions. At this time, Epée's methods did not favour the natural forms of communication for Deaf people, but rather signs followed French grammar. This, claimed Laurent Clerc, a pupil of Epée, was a 'distortion of language'[28]. Thomas Braidwood in Britain was developing systems similar to those of Epée in Scotland, which is where the manual alphabet developed in Britain[29]. As an increasing number of schools for Deaf children emerged it meant that Deaf people were able to come together more in a communal way. Despite the educationalists using the grammar of spoken languages within the schools, in private, Deaf people, so their traditions inform them and me, have always controlled their own language and expressed themselves in a way which is natural for them. After all, languages arguably cannot be artificially created as such, but rather they evolve. These developments saw the beginnings of formal sign languages – particularly in Europe and later in North America, which are now used by Deaf people. The unique sign language used in Britain is called British Sign Language. These natural languages of Deaf people have constantly been ridiculed and oppressed by hearing people, yet they have never been able to stop Deaf people fulfilling the most basic of human needs: communication, in a way that is most obvious to them; sign language[30].

---

[26]   Lane, H., *When the Mind Hears*, p.10.

[27]   *Ibid.*, p.6.

[28]   *Ibid.*, p.15.

[29]   Dimmock, A.F., *Cruel Legacy* (Edinburgh, 1993), pp.17–24.

[30]   In my conversations with Deaf people, many tell stories of how they were banned from using sign language in schools but always used in it in secret to communicate with one

Basic Features of British Sign Language

Having explained how BSL has developed, it is helpful to try to explain how it works as a language today, conscious that as I write, it continues to change and develop. Signs are produced in BSL by using four dimensions of the human body: the hands, the face, the upper body and the space around the upper body. All four together work to create individual parts of signs, the signs themselves and with the order they are signed in, parts of the grammar.

Hands

Hands are tools that are able to create a multiplicity of shapes, which when used in a particular way and in a specific context, become signs. Although the hands are the central part of communication in BSL, many hearing people who learn BSL often believe that the hands themselves are the only part of the body used in the communication process. However, it is true to say that only when the face, body and space are used in a supporting role, do many of the signs take on meaning and the individual signs form a language. It may be suggested that in comparison to spoken languages, the hands play the same role as the individual words produced by the speaker. Without any of the dynamic of different expressions used in spoken language, and the grammar which holds them together, the words would be nothing more than a series of meaningless sounds. For example, meaning is created firstly by the order in which words are spoken thus determining who or what is the object or subject of the sentence. Secondly, in French (and to some extent in English) a phrase is understood to be a question when the voice goes higher at the end of the phrase. This peculiar dynamic of French helps the person to know immediately that a question had been asked as opposed to someone making a statement. So it is with BSL, the hands need some other kind of expression to support and consolidate the meaning: the face, the body and space.

Another of the hands' functions is that of spelling out words using a manual alphabet which uses English spelling constructions. This is normally used as a last resort in BSL but can be a useful resource for parts of language, such as proper nouns, where there may be no particular sign. The relationship of speech to written language depends on each letter being associated with a sound. When these symbols for sound are arranged in a particular order, the voice is able to express those sounds. This phonetic dimension to speech is obviously alien to a visual language and this is why fingerspelling is used in BSL. Invariably once a proper noun, such as someone's name, becomes familiar to Deaf people, they will often develop a sign to replace the fingerspelling.

---

another. See also accounts of Deaf experiences at school in Taylor, G. and Darby, A., *Deaf Identities* (Coleford, 2003), p.41.

Face

The face has a more subtle, yet nevertheless an important role to play in the process of communication. When the face and/or the body is used in BSL, they are together called 'non-manual features'[31]. Patterns made by the lips help to clarify what the sign being used is actually referring to. It should be explained that lip patterns are generally *not* the same as patterns which would be made by 'mouthing' words. The face is also used in an adjectival way. For example, a short queue would be expressed through a short sign, a lip pattern, with very little other facial expression, while a long queue would extend the sign while puffing out the cheeks in an exaggerated way. There would be a slow release of air through the mouth during the sign and the brow would be tense. Facial expression is often greater depending on the intensity of the situation. If a person was expressing a small amount of pain, the face would support the sign by showing some pain – but not very much. Extreme pain would use exactly the same sign (expressed more intensely), while the expression on the face would be increased. The face is also used to determine whether a phrase is a question or not. For example, the phrase transliterated as 'car – you – have' with a relaxed facial expression and particular lip patterns, would be translated into English as the statement, 'you have a car!' This phrase becomes a question when the face shows an inquisitive expression and is thus translated as 'do you have a car?' These are just some of the basic uses of the face in BSL.

Body

The parts of the body used in BSL are the arms, the head and the upper body. The body sometimes acts in a similar way to the face in that it can be used in an adjectival way. For example, when the phrase translated as 'a little tired' is used, the face and body look fairly relaxed. When one wants to express 'extreme tiredness' the sign remains the same (although it may be repeated more) while the cheeks are puffed out and air is quickly released through the mouth. The body is involved by 'slouching' as if it has no strength to support itself thus showing the *extent* of the tiredness. In other situations the body may be used to clarify the meaning of the sign. For example, in spoken English, the words 'there' and 'their' sound exactly the same whilst having quite different meanings. In English, the context in which the word is used is often sufficient to determine which version is intended. The same is usually true in BSL as well, although the body can be used so as to leave less doubt.

Space

How the space around the body is used is equally as important as what the body is doing itself. An invisible cube is created around the body from the waist up and the head down. In formal BSL, the signer is restricted in the use of this area although many Deaf people use all the space around them and the whole of their

---

[31] Sutton-Spence, R. and Woll, B., *The Linguistics of British Sign Language*, p.31.

body if necessary. This space is used not only as an area in which to create the picture, it also has a more formal grammatical purpose. A line from behind the right shoulder to beyond the front of the signer is used to express time. Behind is the past, immediately in front of the signer is the present and further in front is the future. While not being a formal tense structure, this helps with the basic understanding of when something took place. Another line runs in a continuum in front of the signer from left to right, which expresses a continuous event. A further line is also drawn from the base of the cube upwards and relates to the specific context of growing up from childhood to adulthood. More will be explained about verbs along with the concepts of 'placement' and 'direction' later.

Further Grammatical Features[32]

Classifiers

Classifiers are a group of handshapes which do not refer to any one piece of vocabulary specifically but are used and adapted by the signer for their own purposes. For example, a closed hand with the thumb pointing up generally indicates something is good while the small finger, protruding alone from the hand, indicates bad or evil. Individual fingers may represent a person or people when they point up, so, if one person of the Trinity was being referred to, only one finger is used, for all three persons, three fingers are used. An activity may also be shown through the use of classifiers. For example, when the activity of Jesus is being described, the sign for Jesus is given and then one finger stands erect. If Jesus is going into heaven, heaven is signed and the finger simply moves up vertically towards where heaven is placed. If he is coming from heaven to earth, the opposite occurs. If Jesus is walking about on earth, the finger moves around on the horizontal plane. If Jesus lies down, the finger may then lie flat, and so on. Classifiers are one of the most creative aspects of BSL. They are a series of handshapes which represent something. Once that 'something' has been signed and changed to a classifier, the possibilities of what that something can do are considerable (this forms part of the productive lexicon described later).

Placement and Case and Role

In English, the case of the nouns within each sentence is determined by the word order. BSL, however, being a visual language, does not use the order of the signs to determine case but rather what Deaf people call 'placement'. An example should help to clarify what is meant here. Luke 23 tells the story of when Jesus was brought before Pontius Pilate just before his crucifixion. The story is well known enough for it not to be quoted here. However, this is useful to explain the concept of placement, case and role. Imagine that Jesus is standing in a courtyard and Pilate is standing on a balcony above and this is the context of the interrogation of Jesus by Pilate. This

---

[32]   Much of what is explained in this section draws on the work of Kyle J.G. and Woll, B., *Sign Language*, pp.131–61, and also from personal experiencing of using and seeing BSL.

story would be signed as follows. Firstly, the building on which Pilate is standing and which surrounds Jesus must be shown. Walls forming a circular shape, for example, may be signed. Next, Pilate is placed on the building and Jesus on the ground. Both Jesus and Pilate become classifiers represented by a single forefinger pointing upwards on each hand. For the sake of this example, let us assume that Jesus is the finger on the left hand and Pilate is on the right hand. The hands would be set a distance apart and the right hand would be higher than the left, showing that Pilate is standing on a higher surface than Jesus. To determine who is the object and subject in the interrogation (which switches depending on who is speaking) the signer must take on the role of both Pilate and Jesus, depending on who is speaking at any one time. Having put everything in context, the interrogation begins: 'Pilate asked him, 'Are you the King of the Jews?' (v.3). To show that Pilate is the subject here, the signer faces left, looks down and begins, 'Are you the King of the Jews?', without any introductions like 'Pilate asked him'. When Jesus replies, the signer turns round and looks up to where Pilate was originally placed and signs, 'You say so'. Thus the subject and the object are changed by the signer taking on different roles.

This concept of placement is also important in terms of verbs. Kyle and Woll identify three types of BSL verbs: directional, invariant, and reversing[33]. Directional verbs in BSL are those verbs which change direction depending on who or what is the object or subject. The verb 'to give' is such a directional verb. If Jesus gave Pilate something, the sign would start with Jesus and move towards Pilate, and the reverse is true if Pilate gave something to Jesus. However, if the signer continues in the role of Jesus and Jesus says, 'Pilate gave me something' (the passive voice in English), the signer would begin by facing where Pilate is placed, locating the sign near to Pilate and then they would move it down until it rests by the signer still in the role of Jesus.

Invariant verbs ignore this rule and can only move in one direction. Reversing verbs start with the subject, move towards the object and then reverse back in the direction of the subject. The most common form of verbs, however, are directional. The use of placement and case and role will be important in discussions that come later concerning the Deaf use of placement for God, humans and the devil using the Jewish and Christian idea that God is above us, and the devil below us. Much interaction and movement between God and us makes use of this placement and is also particularly important in terms of the Deaf perspective on the theology of the incarnation in signs such as that for 'Emmanuel'.

Vocabulary: Two Lexicons

Brennan outlines two types of vocabulary used in BSL[34]. These are namely: the 'established lexicon' and the 'productive lexicon'. The established lexicon includes those signs which could be put into a dictionary, and are thus a standard set of vocabulary. It is a finite and indeed limited resource of vocabulary which

---

[33] Kyle, J. and Woll, B., *Sign Language*, p.140.
[34] Brennan, M., 'The Visual World of British Sign Language', pp.86–96.

does, however, form the foundations of BSL. The productive lexicon is a much more creative dynamic in the language which allows BSL to have almost infinite possibilities. The boundaries between the two are not always that clear as sometimes the productive lexicon becomes part of the established. For example, 'believe' has been produced from two signs within the established lexicon: 'think' and 'true'[35]. Together these signs have been combined to become one action and, over time, this sign has become a part of the established lexicon.

The productive lexicon also develops signs through a 'process of association'. For example, there is no sign that is in standard use for the town of 'Bethlehem'. To save fingerspelling this every time it is used, a sign has been developed which expresses something which is associated with Bethlehem. Traditionally, Bethlehem has been called the 'City of David' (Luke 2.4) and is a place linked with Kingship through both David and Christ. Thus the sign developed for this place, in Birmingham at least, is a combination of two signs: 'King' and 'City'. Another way in which the productive lexicon is used is by taking established signs and altering the action involved to create new meaning. For example, the sign 'God' is placed above the right eye with the forefinger of the right hand pointing upward and the rest of the hand closed. To sign 'Emmanuel', this sign for God makes a movement down to be with the people and suggests that God is still in the hearts of people today[36]. In the productive lexicon, there is the potential to have a totally creative dimension which may include forms of signs which have never been used before. By using such techniques as classifiers, placement and case and role, these can create a new picture which uses particular rules of BSL in a totally new way. It must again be stressed that BSL is not simply a system of spontaneously made-up gestures but is a language which follows particular grammatical principles. The productive lexicon can only be used, and thus understood, within the boundaries of these principles.

The Use of BSL for Theology: Theological Vocabulary

Until recently, it is arguably fair to say that most religious sign language has developed as a result of Deaf and hearing people using the grammar and various types of lexicon to develop signs which convey the concepts of God which Deaf people have. Today, however, it is increasingly becoming the business of Deaf people to formulate and construct signs which express their theological ideas and this will be discussed later. However, the important point is, that as theological language has been developed, it has normally been done on a communal level beginning with a discussion of the meaning of biblical and theological concepts in conjunction with the grammar of BSL, to try to convey those concepts in a visual way – in the natural language of the Deaf community in Britain. In this sense, theology is a community activity, similar

---

[35]   This is so in Birmingham. In other parts of the country, the sign used involves the two signs 'know' and 'true'. This arguably reflects a theological difference among Deaf people concerning what it means 'to believe'.

[36]   This same sign is often used to translate 'Messiah' but not 'Christ', which is used more as a proper noun for second person of the Trinity, as it is in English.

to many of the oral theologies of Africa[37]. The rest of this book is concerned with the results of this process – of both how Deaf people think about God and how they have chosen as a group to express that.

Acquiring BSL and its Use in the Education of Deaf Children

History of Deaf Education

The history and education of Deaf people has been rife with oppressive practices and procedures, which have, arguably, arisen from the reality that medical, educational and social services for Deaf people have been, and in many instances continue to be, dominated by hearing people. Lane argues that the hearing person generally makes an '… extrapolative leap: to imagine what deafness is like, I will imagine my world without sound'[38]. Most Deaf people have had no experience of being able to hear and so the sense of horror at the *loss* of sound felt by hearing people is simply not present in the Deaf community. Being Deaf does not mean struggling through life regretting not being able to hear because the very concept of 'hearing' is alien.

Having argued that BSL is a full and complete language, learned more easily by Deaf people than English, and explained in brief how it works, it would seem logical that educational policies would at least make use of the natural language of Deaf people. Many Educationalists, however, have colluded with proponents of the medical model of Deafness in pursuing an approach to education which has focused on the 'normalization' of Deaf children. As early as the mid-eighteenth century, approaches to Deaf education in Paris showed that the use of sign language was a highly effective means of education[39]. While this worked with considerable success, the famous conference of (mainly hearing) Deaf educators held in Milan in 1880 agreed that oralism was the best system and should be the primary method of education for Deaf children[40]. The ramifications of this conference spread quickly and dictated Deaf educational policy in many parts of the world for more than a hundred years. The oral method involved teaching children to speak, read and write with a complete ban on the use of sign language, usually to the ultimate detriment of other areas of academic study[41]. Since the 1880 conference in Milan, BSL has been banned in many British schools and only in more recent years have policies

---

[37] See the discussions throughout Healey, J. and Sybertz, D., *Towards an African Narrative Theology* (Nairobi, 1996).

[38] Lane, H., 'The Medicalization of Cultural Deafness in Historical Perspective', p.481.

[39] See Lane, H., *When the Mind Hears*. Much of this work is dedicated to detailing the story of the origins of Deaf education using sign language in eighteenth-century France following its movement to the USA.

[40] Lane, H., *When the Mind Hears*, p.387.

[41] Svartholm, K., 'Second Language Learning in the Deaf', in Ahlgren, I. and Hyltenstam, K. (eds), *Bilingualism in Deaf Education: International Studies on Sign Language and Communication of the Deaf* (Hamburg, 1994), pp.61–70; and Tucker, I. and Powell, C., *The Hearing Impaired Child and School* (London, 1991), p.80.

begun to change[42]. For this reason – the suppression of BSL – educational policy has become one of the most significant issues which Deaf people are involved in trying to change today.

The Milan Conference of 1880 was one of the most important events to determine the shape of Deaf history in the twentieth century[43]. While the significance of this event is present in the minds of many ordinary Deaf people in the UK, it would be difficult to find any book on the Deaf community that does not make reference to this event at some point. Following the foundation of the first modern-type school for Deaf people in Paris in the eighteenth century, the use of sign language as a means for education had become increasingly widespread over the following decades[44]. The Milan Conference changed this considerably[45]. To summarize, the conference was convened to discuss the value of the use of sign languages and speech as the primary medium for the education of Deaf children. Those who were not present at this meeting – virtually no Deaf people – was as significant as those who were – the proponents of oral education. Lane comments: '… the Milan conference amounted to two dozen hours in which three or four oralists reassured the rest of the rightness of their actions in the face of troubling evidence to the contrary'[46]. The action resulting from this event was a decision to ban sign language in education and this decision was followed in many countries around the world as policy makers took notice of the views of the so-called 'experts' at Milan.

The consequences for Deaf people were devastating, as Deaf people's first language ceased to be used in education, so excessive amounts of time were spent learning to speak while the rest of Deaf education suffered. The implications of this conference for Deaf people are summed up well by Lane: 'The suppression of sign, the firing of deaf faculty, the retrenchment of educational goals, and the medical model of the deaf as defective all conduced to Milan's last catastrophic effect: the infantilizing of deaf young men and women'[47]. The suppression of sign language for education continued for about a hundred years, and only in more recent times have practices started to change in some places[48].

Recent Developments in Deaf Education

In more recent times, many (though by no means all) schools in Britain now use a 'total communication'[49] approach to education which is a mixture of BSL and

---

[42]   Watson, L. et al., *Deaf and Hearing*, p.35.

[43]   See Ladd, P., *Understanding Deaf Culture*, p.89 and Alker, D., *Really Not Interested in the Deaf*, p.41.

[44]   Ladd, P., *Understanding Deaf Culture*, p.105.

[45]   Lane, H., *When the Mind Hears*, extensively documents the proceedings of the conference, pp.386–401.

[46]   Lane, H., *When the Mind Hears*, p.387.

[47]   *Ibid.*, p.401.

[48]   For example, in Sweden, bilingualism in Deaf Education has been significant for about 30 years. See Ahlgren, I., 'Sign Language as the First Language', p.55.

[49]   This is a form of education which is used with children who may have learning difficulties, deafblindness, or deafness and is, very crudely, a way of trying to get information

English. Practices, however, vary nation-wide[50] and despite these developments, the emphasis on teaching [English] literacy remains predominant. Since its launch in 1996, the *Journal of Deaf Studies and Deaf Education*[51] has sought to lead the way in publishing research on Deaf education. This international journal, published quarterly, however, has dedicated in most years at least one of its editions to questions surrounding teaching literacy. Other editions also have a scattering of papers on the same subject. Most books on Deaf education[52] have traditionally been dominated by the theme of improving literacy among Deaf children. This presents and raises important questions and ambiguities.

The value of being literate in the twenty-first century cannot be underestimated. In Western society at least, but in many other parts of the world as well, much knowledge and information is accessed through the written text. Literacy gives knowledge, and knowledge gives power and so literacy must, generally speaking, be one of the primary aims of education. However, the emphasis on teaching literacy in an academic journal claiming to be about Deaf *education*, almost to the total exclusion of other areas of tuition, is disturbing. Where, for example, is the research being published on teaching Deaf children about British Deaf and hearing history? Where is the research on teaching science, religious studies and the arts in a way that is culturally relevant using appropriate linguistic approaches? There is very little at all[53]. It has long been recognized that education should not just be about the traditional 'three Rs' and nothing else, but also about personal development and the ability to use knowledge creatively and in practical situations. In other words, a child's education, both at home and at school should be holistic.

A number of issues complicate the use of BSL in education, however. Gregory and Knight explain that 'Ninety per cent of Deaf children are born to hearing families'[54]. As Gallaway highlights, 'Children learn the language they hear – or see – around them ... However, for infants with a severe or profound prelingual hearing

---

across in as many ways as possible. So for example, touch, sign language, speech, the use of tangible objects and art, etc., are all used as methods of education; some will be used at the same time (such as speech and sign). See Baker, R. and Knight, P., '"Total Communication" – current policy and practice', pp.77–87.

[50]   A variety of approaches that involve various levels of signing in education are discussed in Watson, L. et al., *Deaf and Hearing*, pp.35–6. Oralism is, however, still the approach of at least one Deaf school in Britain.

[51]   *Journal of Deaf Studies and Deaf Education* is published quarterly by Oxford University Press.

[52]   Webster, A., *Deafness, Development and Literacy* (London, 1986), p.80, although more recent work considers a variety of issues in education – See Ahlgren I. and Hyltenstam, K. (eds), *Bilingualism in Deaf Education*, and Gregory, S. et al. (eds), *Issues in Deaf Education*.

[53]   Watson, L and Parsons, J., 'Supporting Deaf Pupils in Mainstream Settings', in Gregory, S. et al. (eds), *Issues in Deaf Education* (London, 1998), note that Wolverhampton Metropolitan Borough Council (1996) and Bromley Borough Council (1994, 1997) produced sign language dictionaries for specific curriculum areas to aid teaching. See p.140.

[54]   Cf. Gregory, S. and Knight, P., 'Social Development and Family Life', in Gregory, S. et al. (eds), *Issues in Deaf Education* (London, 1998), p.4; Ladd, P., *Understanding Deaf Culture*, p.36; and Kyle, J.G. and Woll, B., *Sign Language*, p.48.

loss, ... ensuring that they experience enough language to activate their natural language acquisition processes can be a problem'[55]. For a hearing child, therefore, a first language is learned from parents who use that language in everyday situations but for the Deaf child of hearing parents, learning language in this way is far from straightforward.

In light of this, Kyle and Woll explain, 'The question is simple: do children who cannot hear effectively acquire, through lip-reading and residual hearing, their parents spoken language or the language of their peers (i.e. other Deaf people) as a first language? If one is a believer in the oralist philosophy then the answer is the former, and if one is a profoundly deaf person the answer is the latter'[56]. As I argued earlier, Deaf people acquire sign languages at a similar rate to hearing people acquiring speech. It is true that Deaf people believe passionately that BSL should be the first language of profoundly Deaf children and this conviction has mostly emerged out of the experience of being taught orally and living with its consequences. If the hearing parents of a Deaf child do not use BSL, and Deaf people cannot, as I have already argued, easily learn spoken language through lip-reading, language acquisition can be severely impaired.

It is generally accepted that the crucial years for language acquisition are in the first three years of life.[57] Woll further argues that 'Children who have not acquired fluency in a first language by the age of 5 do not subsequently catch up, either in a signed or spoken language'[58]. In light of the arguments put forward earlier that BSL is learned at a much faster rate by Deaf children than English, and the first five years of life are crucial for language acquisition, then hearing parents need to expose their children to as much sign language as possible. The medical model's approach to Deafness is used by many advisors to Deaf parents by which parents are advised to pursue using technology and teaching speech, instead of teaching Deaf children BSL. The consequence can be that language acquisition is impaired[59]. If, as Ladd argues, language is the means by which reality and identity is shaped and understood, then not using BSL with Deaf infants has potentially far more serious consequences[60].

Reflecting on the situation of Deaf children born to hearing parents, Gallaway suggests, 'First, human beings have an overwhelmingly strong drive to communicate and are capable of adapting to unusual circumstances. Secondly, it should be possible for adults to tinker with and rearrange the learning environment in ways that facilitate language acquisition for young Deaf children'[61]. Pinker argues that

---

[55]   Gallaway, C., 'Early Interaction', in Gregory, S. et al. (eds), *Issues in Deaf Education* (London, 1998), p.49.

[56]   Kyle, J.G. and Woll, B., *Sign Language*, p.58.

[57]   Kyle, J. and Woll, B., *Sign Language*, p.64; Lane, H., *The Mask of Benevolence*, p.224; and Ahlgren, I., 'Sign Language as the First Language', pp.55–7, argue that the crucial age by which language should be acquired is actually 3–4 years old.

[58]   Woll, B., 'Development of Signed and Spoken Languages', p.65.

[59]   Ahlgren, I., 'Sign Language as the First Language', pp.55–7.

[60]   Ladd, P., *Understanding Deaf Culture*, p.84.

[61]   Gallaway, C., 'Early Interaction', p.50.

to acquire a language, you do not need to be constantly bathed in that language[62]. Gallaway suggests using 'attention management strategies' and allowing signing adults to be a part of the child's environment[63]. The 'language instinct' described by Pinker works in favour of Deaf children being able to learn BSL, even if they have hearing parents. It may be time consuming and involve considerable effort to ensure that Deaf children are exposed to Deaf adults, but no more than the time and effort invested in trying to get Deaf children to speak. This evidence that BSL should be the first language of Deaf education in order to benefit Deaf people is overwhelming

At school and beyond in education, BSL can be an effective means of teaching and learning for Deaf people[64]. I have worked alongside a number of Deaf adults in Higher Education as a BSL communicator and Deaf people have been able to learn effectively through this means – including a subject like theology. In 2006, at the University of Chester where I now work, we launched a level one programme in theology for Deaf students in which all learning, teaching and assessments took place in BSL[65]. There were teething problems, but this approach to education worked and five students received an award in September 2007. Some schools for Deaf children now also use BSL for communication, though none use it exclusively, but rather as a part of the total communication method. However, Deaf people argue for a 'bilingual' approach to education which Miranda Pickersgill defines thus: 'Sign bilingualism is an approach to the education of deaf children, which uses both the sign language of the Deaf community and the spoken and written language of the hearing community. In the UK, this is British Sign Language (BSL), English and, for some families, other spoken languages'[66]. This approach supports the early exposure of Deaf children to BSL but uses BSL and English throughout school life. Further research has also demonstrated that acquiring and learning sign language in the very earliest years of life has advantages for Deaf children in learning a second language such as English[67]. The value of this approach, bilingualism, therefore is significant for the future of Deaf people in Britain.

Conclusion

In this chapter I have introduced some of the basic rules of BSL grammar and I have argued through what appears to be overwhelming empirical evidence, that BSL is the natural language of the Deaf community. It is a language with a richness of expression comparable to any spoken language. It will also be evident from this and the previous chapter that issues in Deaf education play a key role in the Deaf community and I have presented a case for why BSL should be the first language

---

[62]　Pinker, S., *The Language Instinct*, pp.53–4.

[63]　Gallaway, C., 'Early Interaction', p.50.

[64]　Watson, L., *Deaf and Hearing*, pp.33–41.

[65]　See Morris, W., 'Learning, Teaching and Assessment with Deaf Students', *Discourse: Learning and Teaching in Philosophical and Religious Studies*, 6/1 (2006): 145–73.

[66]　Pickersgill, M., 'Bilingualism – current policy and practice', in Gregory, S. et al. (eds), *Issues in Deaf Education* (London, 1998), p.88.

[67]　Lane, H., *The Mask of Benevolence*, pp.170–1.

of Deaf children in education. Having defined what I mean by the Deaf community, examined their language and discussed the issues that concern Deaf people alongside their experiences, I would now like to move on to discuss how I went about discovering some Deaf people's perspectives on theology.

PART II
In Search of Deaf Theology

Chapter 3

Developing Appropriate Research Methods

Introduction

In addition to using data and research from theological, educational, linguistic and sociological texts, it was clearly important to carry out field research in order to gather the evidence that has formed and informed the argument of this book. The nature of this field research was inevitably qualitative rather than quantitative. While it may have been interesting to survey how many Deaf people believe in God in Birmingham or even in England, that would not provide any detailed material concerning what Deaf people think that God is actually like and how they relate to God from and through their Deaf experiences. What was needed was extensive information gathering accompanied by close examination, assessment and interpretation of that information. This chapter describes how methodologies were employed from the social sciences, reflecting how the material for this book was gathered and argues for a methodology that combines social science research methods with theological perspectives in order to formulate an appropriate and holistic method for researching the theology of Deaf people.

There is a small, but increasing amount of literature which has focused on the experiences of Deaf people and has provided some foundations for the research needed for this book, much of which has been referred to in the previous two chapters. There are many strong and opposing arguments from different perspectives today about the role and place of Deaf people in society and increasingly these arguments are diversifying as Deaf people more clearly articulate their own perspectives and experiences. This has inevitably moved the debate away from education, science and medicine alone to include in addition such disciplines as linguistics, anthropology, sociology and theology. What is most noteworthy about Deaf people is that their identity has been significantly defined by their struggle for a means by which to express themselves freely as Deaf people and not as sorry imitations of hearing people.

Deaf Theology in Print

In terms of the theology of Deaf people, there is relatively little material available at all in published text form. Whilst the theology of disability has been growing and diversifying, the experiences of Deaf people specifically have tended to be ignored by theologians. This is probably because of the barriers of language between hearing/ deafened people and Deaf people. The most influential and well-known work completed on disability and theology in Britain and Europe has been done not by people with disabilities but by carers or family members of people with learning difficulties[1]. The influence of such texts is arguably due to the contributions to developing spirituality more generally that the authors have made in their reflections concerning people with learning disabilities. John Hull, whose influence has also been significant, has published two important books on the experience of blindness, one of which is a biblical hermeneutic from the perspective of a blind person[2]. Nancy Eiesland's, *The Disabled God* (1994), has been a highly influential and controversial contribution from the United States. Eiesland writes out of her experience as a wheelchair user. Will Morrey has written on the experience of being deafened[3], but there is relatively little on the experience and theology of the Deaf community per se.

A number of unpublished MA and BA dissertations have been written on Deaf theology primarily by Deaf people training for ordination or by hearing people working as chaplains among Deaf people[4]. A collection of papers in the book, *Ephphatha* (1996) reflects some Deaf Catholic perspectives including an important paper on the Bible and BSL by Peter McDonough. Kathy Black, in *A Healing Homiletic* (1996), also reflects on the experiences of Deaf people and the preaching practices of the Church with particular reference to Mark 7.31–37[5]. Hannah Lewis of Birmingham University has completed a PhD on Deaf liberation theology focusing on issues concerned with the Deaf church, which is undoubtedly the most important contribution to this field as it is the only text of its kind and length to be written by a Deaf person[6]. Another book published in 2004 also discusses the Deaf church in relation to the ecclesiology of Jörgen Moltmann[7]. The most significant published work (before Lewis) on Deaf theology was by Mary Weir, which was a short paper appearing in a book with fairly limited circulation: *The Place of Deaf People in the Church* (1996)[8]. This paper discussed briefly the idea of God as Deaf and what that could mean for the Deaf community.

---

[1]   Theological Reflections concerning people with learning difficulties include, Pailin, D., *A Gentle Touch* (London, 1992); Young, F., *Face to Face* (Edinburgh, 1990); Young F. (ed.), *Encounter with Mystery* (London, 1997); John Swinton, *A Space to Listen* (London, 2001), and *Why Are We Here?* (London, 2004). Works such as Nouwen, H.J.M., *The Wounded Healer* (London, 1994) and Vanier, J., *Made for Happiness* (London, 2001), have been significant in terms of the contributions these authors have made to contemporary Christian Spirituality more generally, being read by a wide audience.

[2]   See Hull, J.M., *In the Beginning there was Darkness* (London, 2001).

[3]   Morrey, W., *Seeing is Hearing: Reflections on Being deafened* (Bangor, 1994).

[4]   For example, Shrine, R., *The Language and Culture of Deaf People*, Unpublished MA Thesis (St John's College, Nottingham, 1997).

[5]   Black, K., *A Healing Homiletic: Preaching and Disability* (Nashville, 1996), pp.88–103.

[6]   Lewis, H., *A Critical Examination of the Church and Deaf People: Towards a Deaf Liberation Theology*, Unpublished PhD Thesis (University of Birmingham, Birmingham, 2002). This thesis has now been published as Lewis, H., *Deaf Liberation Theology*, (Aldershot, 2007).

[7]   Hitching, R., *The Church and Deaf People* (Carlisle, 2003).

[8]   Weir, M., 'Made Deaf in God's Image', in International Ecumenical Working Group, *The Place of Deaf People in the Church* (Northampton, 1996), pp.1–10.

From among the texts on Deaf people's theology, what is available tends to have emerged out of and been informed by the individual experiences of the Deaf theologian (e.g. Weir and Lewis) and her reflections on that experience in relation to the Deaf community. They have then used that as a basis for talking generally about Deaf people. Rarely have the perspectives of the wider Deaf community been taken seriously and reflected upon in depth. I do not make any criticism of the method of doing theology which develops theological arguments based on the theologian's own experience of God and the community she belongs to. This is a perfectly valid approach to theology employed by feminist and black theologians among others[9]. As long as they own up to their methods and perspectives and do not make any universal claims as white, Western patriarchal theology has traditionally done, their theologies are useful. Criticisms have been raised against, not the methods, but the conclusions of early black and feminist writers who made generalizations about their respective communities, which in fact did not represent the experiences of everyone or even the majority of those about whom they were writing. For example, James Cone has been heavily criticized for totally ignoring the experiences of black women in his earlier works[10]. Nancy Eiesland similarly talks about disabled people and the 'Disabled God'[11] in terms which suggest they have meaning for all disabled people. In contrast, John Hull's idea of Christ as blind[12], and therefore by implication disabled, contrasts considerably with Eiesland's image demonstrating the differences between the theology of someone who has a physical disability and someone who is blind.

Thus, to understand the complexities and ambiguities of Deaf theology, and to avoid universalist claims, my qualitative research approach with varying individual Deaf people was necessary in order for the aim of this work – to understand Deaf theological perspectives – to be fulfilled. A further and paramount reason for using field research was that I, as the researcher, am hearing. In order to try to avoid paternalistic statements about what Deaf people do or should think theologically, I have tried to relate and discuss only those things I have been told and observed from the Deaf community although I have inevitably selected and interpreted that material. Methods of qualitative research from the social sciences provided a helpful framework and guidance for conducting the necessary field work in the first instances.

---

[9]   See for example the methodologies of Cone, J.H., *A Black Theology of Liberation: Twentieth Anniversary Edition* (Maryknoll, New York, 1990); and Brock, R.N., 'Dusting the Bible of the Floor', in Schüssler-Fiorenza, E., *Searching the Scriptures: A Feminist Introduction* (London, 1993), pp.64–75.

[10]   James Cone acknowledges this himself in Cone, J.H., *A Black Theology of Liberation*, pp.197–8. Likewise, Fabella and Torres refer to the statement from the Sixth EATWOT conference which claimed: '... those [women] from the Third World were not always comfortable with First World feminists' definition of the issues and strategies for change'. See 'Doing Theology in a Divided World: Final Statement of the Sixth EATWOT Conference', in Fabella, V. and Torres, S. (eds), *Doing Theology in a Divided World* (Maryknoll, 1985), pp.179–93.

[11]   See Eiesland, N., *The Disabled God: Toward a Liberatory Theology of Disability* (Nashville, 1994), Especially pp.89–105.

[12]   See Hull, J. M., *In the Beginning*, especially pp.127–48.

Questionnaires

To Whom Were They Sent and What Was Asked?

I will dedicate only a short space to this section because (as will be demonstrated below) questionnaires quickly proved to be a highly inappropriate method of information gathering from Deaf people. Following a sample of five short interviews and a series of informal conversations to guide me on how to phrase questions, 100 questionnaires were sent out to a random selection of Deaf people linked with Birmingham Deaf centre and a further 100 to Deaf contacts in and around Britain. It is usual for only a small minority of questionnaires to be returned in field research. However, out of the 200 questionnaires I sent out with stamped envelopes for return, I received back only nine (4.5 per cent). I had wrongly assumed that Deaf people would be able to engage with questionnaires, but I had not fully understood Deaf people's abilities in literacy in the early stages of my research over against their preferences to express themselves in BSL.

Had this research method been successful I would have been able to conduct a wide and diverse survey of Deaf people's theology although the questionnaire method would not have yielded the rich individuality of a more qualitative approach. In the questionnaire, I asked respondents to comment on:

- If they believed in God

And if so:

- What they thought God was like.
- What words or signs they would use to describe God.
- How they would describe God to another person.
- How did their Deaf experience impact on their ideas about God.
- What was their experience of going to and participating in churches.
- What does the Gospel have to say to Deaf people and how can Deaf people contribute to a better understanding of the Gospel?
- What words, pictures, dramas, images have communicated something about God to them?
- Is God Deaf or hearing, and if so, what does that mean?
- Does God understand sign language?

To What Extent Were Questionnaires Useful?

The few responses I did receive and the many which I did not, said something very significant about this method of research with the Deaf community. While questionnaires would have been an effective way to survey a lot of hearing people, they proved to be quite inappropriate for Deaf people. One questionnaire came back saying, 'Deaf people do not relate too well, or at all, to pen and paper questionnaires.' This person was right. When I asked Deaf people in Birmingham about doing questionnaires, many did not feel confident enough to answer them. Others said, 'we cannot express our ideas properly in English, only in BSL'. In order to understand the theology which emerged out of Deaf experiences, it was clear that the research would need to be conducted in BSL and not English. I anticipated that there may be problems with English (although not to such a large extent) on the questionnaires, and so I tried to ensure that questions used uncomplicated English and were short. However, the result was that answers were also short using sometimes only one word such as 'yes' or 'no'. These were clearly insufficient to get a thorough understanding of Deaf theology. The second, more effective and in-depth method I used involved conducting a series of interviews in BSL.

Interviews

Pole and Lampard define an interview as, in essence, 'a verbal exchange of information between two or more people for the principal purpose of one gathering information from the other(s)'[13]. Immediately, this definition poses problems for interviews with the Deaf community, because a 'verbal exchange' suggests an exchange of words. In the Deaf community, this is rarely possible, and even when Deaf people can speak, for the purposes of finding out about their theology, it is never desirable, because language itself is such an important indicator of the way in which a community thinks about God. Many Deaf people indicated that when they think, they do so in BSL or in pictures, rather than in English.

It is widely accepted in social research that there is a basic spectrum on which varying types of interviews take place. At one end is the structured interview and at the other end is the unstructured. Hammersley and Atkinson argue that all interviews to varying degrees are a mixture of the two[14]. The purpose of the structured interview is to do with greater levels of objectivity. In a structured interview, the interviewer would ask the same questions in the same way to each interviewee in order to extract from them a response, which is influenced equally as much by the interviewer in each instance. However, as Moser and Kalton explain, '… interviewers are not machines. Their voices, manner, pronunciations and inflections differ as much as looks, and no amount of instruction will bring about complete uniformity in technique'[15]. Complete objectivity, therefore, may be the goal of structured interviews, and a useful goal to have even if it is ultimately beyond the reach of human interviewers.

For this project, a highly structured approach seemed inappropriate for at least three reasons. 1. Sometimes an interviewee was unsure about a question and would ask for clarification. This meant that I often needed to elucidate and express the question in a different way. 2. Because of the nature of BSL and its productive lexicon, it would be virtually impossible to phrase a question in exactly the same way to each interviewee without writing the question down. As BSL cannot be written down,

---

[13]   Pole, C. and Lampard, R., *Practical Social Investigation: Qualitative and Quantitative Methods in Social Research* (Harlow, 2002), p.126.

[14]   Hammersley M. and Atkinson, P., *Ethnography: Principles in Practice*. Second Edition (London, 1995), pp.151–5.

[15]   Moser, C.A. and Kalton, G., *Survey Methods in Social Investigation*. Second Edition (Aldershot, 1971), p.276.

this is impossible. 3. I was interested not only in the content of Deaf theology, but where their ideas had come from and why. This necessitated asking a considerable number of probing questions, which meant that the conversation could go in all sorts of directions and at times I would allow the interviewee to determine that direction.

Of course I had some structure to the interviews. I knew the general subject areas I wanted to ask about and the interviews took place in the overall framework of wanting to find out about the theology of Deaf people. However, on the whole, I followed a conversational or casual method for interviewing. This enabled the Deaf person to be more relaxed and converse freely. Most of the Birmingham interviews took place in Birmingham Deaf Club. All other interviewees chose where they wanted to be interviewed and I travelled to them. The interviewee was able to relax, therefore, in a familiar and safe environment. Pole and Lampard note that feminist commentators have 'questioned the attribution of clear cut roles of interviewer and interviewee, believing that successful and more ethical interviews are about an exchange of information rather than a unidirectional transfer of data'[16]. Likewise, in this research, a more informal conversational approach yielded better results, in which I was seen more as a friend than a researcher, to those whom I interviewed.

What questions were asked?

Following the preliminary introductions, the nature of the interviews involved asking questions about three broad areas:

1. What was the Deaf community and Deaf culture. In this area, I tried to probe what Deaf people thought the Deaf community and culture was, who was involved in it, and what the significance of it was for them. This has informed much of the previous two chapters and was crucial to understanding Deaf people's theology, recognizing that theology is inseparable from culture.
2. What was Deaf people's experience of Church and theology, such as levels of access and participation in both, and how their own contributions had been received by hearing people.
3. How did their experience shape the way they understand God, and how did their perception of God shape their perspectives on their experiences.

I was particularly interested in whether Deaf people thought that God could be perceived of as in any way Deaf. This question triggered a number of different responses and usually entailed a lengthy discussion about what this actually meant. Further discussion on this topic can be found in chapter 7.

The Informants

I began this research by conducting a series of in-depth interviews of about one hour with members of the Deaf community. I have interviewed 40 Deaf people from the Deaf community in Birmingham and 20 Deaf people from other locations in Britain.

---

[16]   Pole, C. and Lampard, R., *Practical Social Investigation*, p.146.

I also interviewed 20 people from Zimbabwe. I have also interviewed 16 hearing people from Britain who have extensive experience of the Deaf community either as chaplains, as family members of Deaf people or as those who work with Deaf people in other secular contexts. The breakdown of the interviewees in terms of age, sex and ethnicity in the larger British sample is shown in Table 1:

Table 1

Deaf people in:	Birmingham	Other Britain
Women	22	10
Men	18	10
White	32	16
Black	4	3
Asian	4	1
Age 16–20	2	1
Age 21–30	5	2
Age 31–40	6	2
Age 41–50	3	4
Age 51–60	3	3
Age 61–70	11	4
Age 70+	10	4
Hearing people in:	**Birmingham**	**Other Britain**
Women	2	8
Men	2	4
White	4	12
Black	0	0
Asian	0	0
Age 16–20	0	0
Age 21–30	0	1
Age 31–40	0	2
Age 41–50	1	3
Age 51–60	3	4
Age 61–70	0	1
Age 70+	0	1

Table 1 shows that from among the Deaf people interviewed, the biggest majority were white men or women over the age of 60 years old, reflecting the make up of the church in Birmingham. There are two main reasons why this is so. Firstly, the Deaf clubs where many Deaf people tend to meet, are attended by a majority of older people. Deaf people are increasingly meeting each other in pubs and at other social places and can communicate using various technological means. Hence there is a significant decline in the number of people attending Deaf clubs. Because Deaf people meet in many different places, they are more difficult to locate for a researcher. It would not be correct to say that younger Deaf people do not attend the Deaf clubs at least in Birmingham, simply that some are less inclined to do so. Secondly, there are fewer younger Deaf people generally in Britain as many of the causes of hearing loss in younger children, such as measles or meningitis about 50 years ago, no longer have the same impact.

The ethnic mix, as I have categorized it in the figures above, is very crude. In Birmingham, the Asian population is extremely diverse with people living there whose origins can be traced from practically every Asian country from Japan in the East to Turkey in the West and from Kazakhstan in the North to Indonesia in the South. Indeed, many people whose origins were in Asia were born in Britain and identify themselves as either British Asian, fully Asian or somewhere in between. The cultural, ethnic and religious diversity of these people is considerable and it is arguably wrong to homogenize them together under one category. No Deaf Asian Christians could be located for this research. Those who did participate were either Hindu or Sikh. I felt it was important to include these four people of Asian origin in order to understand some of the diversity of the Deaf community, although this research has not addressed itself to issues of religious pluralism. The category of black people is similarly very crude. In Birmingham again, there are black people whose origins are West Indian, North American and African to name but a few. Some black Deaf people did have Christian beliefs, but again it was more difficult to locate them.

I endeavoured to interview an equal number of men as women although the statistics show that slightly more women participated than men overall. This was because of a slightly greater willingness among women to respond than men and because in the church in Birmingham, in the region of 70 per cent of regular members are women.

How useful were the interviews?

Despite being advised by some Deaf people to conduct interviews, I did not find this to be a wholly adequate way to obtain the information I needed. Recording interviews with hearing people is much easier than recording interviews with Deaf people. A conversation between two people who communicate using sound can be recorded in a non-intrusive way and a literal transcription of the content of the dialogue can be produced on paper as long as the interviewee is happy for the interviews to be recorded. This is possible because both the interviewer and the hearing interviewees communicate primarily by using English which can be audibly recorded and later written down[17]. This is not possible with Deaf people. Some Deaf people may speak English, but in order to understand their perspectives on God more fully in terms of the culture and context in which it arises, it was important that

---

[17]   This does not take into account the role of non-verbal communication, however, which is much more difficult to record and interpret.

Deaf people expressed themselves in BSL because the language in which an idea is expressed carries with it its own nuances and meaning which can be lost or changed in a different language. However, some of those interviewed did not have English as a first or second language so in such instances this issue did not arise.

The problem then is, how to interview a Deaf person and keep a record of the interview. One solution would be to use a video camcorder. I used this option for five of the interviews with Deaf people. However, when the video camcorder was used, it changed the atmosphere of the interview. Some found it to be intimidating and felt nervous about signing anything, while others when answering questions would ask me 'is that right?' This suggested that they were not so much expressing what they thought as much as what they thought I wanted them to say. It also became obvious that using one camcorder was unhelpful. Because the interviews were conversational, it was important that what I expressed was also recorded. Either the camcorder needed to be moved to focus on the interviewee or me, depending on who was signing, or a second camcorder could have been used. However, even this would have involved a lengthy editing process, which I as the researcher would have not been capable of doing. Consequently, after five interviews, I abandoned the use of a camcorder.

Some social researchers have explained that when the interviewee has refused to allow an interview to be recorded, they have taken abbreviated notes during the course of the interview and written up what was said at the earliest possible time afterwards[18]. Again, this system has limitations with Deaf people. In order to be able to write notes, the interviewer needs to be able to see what she is writing. If you are conducting an interview with a Deaf person and taking notes, you will be watching BSL, interpreting what they are saying into English and writing it down all at the same time. This is quite an impossible task to perform adequately. I was also not able to employ a third party to take notes during the interviews, and felt that this would make the interview more formal and intimidating. Nevertheless, I did take brief, shorthand notes at frequent intervals at the end of responses on what I thought was significant for the purposes of this project. I then wrote up a record of what was discussed, in all instances, within 24 hours of the interview taking place. Whilst this relies on my selection of what is significant, it was difficult to find any other way of recording the necessary information. In the inclusion of material for my purposes here, an inevitable further amount of selection by me was necessary and unavoidable. When I had written up these interviews, I always discussed what I had written with the interviewee at a later date (usually one week later) to clarify the details and that I had understood them properly. This process of clarification was only possible with those I interviewed in Birmingham whom I saw regularly, but not with Deaf or hearing people in other parts of Britain.

Still, even without any equipment, some felt intimidated by the formality of being interviewed which made the situation feel very artificial. Whilst some useful information and insights into Deaf theology could be gleaned from interviews with Deaf people, it quickly became apparent that this methodology was an inadequate way – on its own – of researching this thesis. It should further be noted that some

---

[18]   See, for example, Pole, C. and Lampard, R., *Practical Social Investigation*, p.83.

Deaf people welcomed the opportunity to express some of their ideas about their faith and God and to explore those issues with someone else. For some, it was probably one of the first opportunities they had had to do that.

Participant Observation

Although little information was gathered from the questionnaires and some more significantly from the interviews, the most useful method for gathering information was through a process of what the social scientists may call 'participant observation'[19]. Over a period of five years, I attended the Anglican Church among Deaf people in Birmingham every week, excluding holidays. The worshipping life of the Deaf community was inevitably a rich resource for discerning something of their theology. At the beginning of my visits to the church, Sign Supported English was mostly used, although now, BSL is increasingly the language used. Sermons and prayers led by Deaf people provided numerous insights into the ways Deaf people in Birmingham thought about God. Also the behaviour of Deaf people in churches (often very relaxed) indicated some of the ways in which Deaf people thought about God, confirmed in conversations later. For example, God was seen more as a friend than as someone to be feared. Some Deaf people often like to sign the words of hymns, while others are opposed to Deaf people signing to music[20]. The choice of hymns used, the way they are signed and the way that odd words are changed to be of meaning to Deaf people all indicated theological perspectives particular to Deaf people. I have also visited churches among Deaf people in other contexts including the Diocesan churches in Lichfield, Hereford, Exeter, an ecumenical church in North-East Wales and the Roman Catholic Church in Birmingham.

As well as attending the Deaf church, I also attended the Deaf club every week. This provided the opportunity to be alongside Deaf people in their main social lives together. I have also been on a number of trips arranged by Deaf people, including a three-night holiday, another part of the social lives of Deaf people. These provided ways of entering into informal conversations about experiences and ideas, which would happen spontaneously. I have further participated in protest marches to gain recognition of British Sign Language as a national language and been alongside Deaf people in other contexts. I was able to attend a number of funerals for Deaf people at the invitation of the chaplain among Deaf people and with the agreement of the families concerned. I was able to go with Deaf people to other social events and activities as a friend.

---

[19]   See, for example, Moser, C.A. and Kalton, G., *Survey Methods*; Neuman, W.L., *Social Research Methods: Qualitative and Quantitative Approaches*. Second Edition (Massachusetts, 1994), also refers to this as 'Field Research' (see pp.330 ff.).

[20]   In my research, some Deaf people have strongly argued that this is part of the attempt to 'normalize' Deaf people. Others enjoy being part of a Deaf signing choir and they have often been important in terms of building bridges between Deaf and hearing people. The debate continues.

For a total of three years during this research project, I worked part-time with Deaf people in various contexts. I was a communication support worker[21] for three years for a Deaf ordinand in Birmingham. I also spent three months as a care worker with Deafblind adults and fifteen months supporting Deaf students in Higher Education at the University of Central England. So for three years, I spent an average of more than twenty hours a week with Deaf people in varying situations.

Kathleen Pitcairn, in a paper outlining research conducted with people with learning difficulties describes, 'we were able to immerse ourselves for two years in the institutions and communities during the data collection phase which meant that we collected data in many informal ways in addition to those using the formal instruments'[22]. They later go on to talk about how this was a means of building trust between themselves and those they were researching. I have found similar such immersion to be most beneficial. To be with a group only at pre-arranged times can only provide limited resources which may be controlled by the person with whom the arrangements are made. Being immersed in a community, not only allows trust to develop, but opens up to the researcher much wider possibilities of observing people who are not always 'on their guard' because they are conscious of being observed. Thus the researcher will witness spontaneous events and enter into conversations which provide more depth than a formal interview.

Using a Journal

Throughout this research, I have maintained a journal[23] of my experiences and encounters which has extended to many volumes. In the journal I have both recorded the events of the experiences and encounters themselves, as well my own reflections on them. I have endeavoured to include a series of events which were of both great and little significance as soon as possible after they have taken place, along with my own initial response. At later dates, I have also recorded my own further reflections. This has proved to be a most useful record of events from my research as records of experiences are freshly outlined and can be referred to much later. In all contexts in which I have been with Deaf people, I have been open about the work that I have been doing. Whenever a person has indicated that they did not want to have any

---

[21]   A communication support worker is someone who assists a Deaf person in a hearing environment – usually education. They may use a variety of methods for communication such as BSL and note taking. Usually a communication support worker is not a registered BSL interpreter. See RNID, *Working with a Communication Support Worker in Education* (London, 2004).

[22]   Pitcairn, K., 'Exploring Ways of Giving a Voice to People with Learning Difficulties', in Humphries, B. and Truman, C. (eds), *Re-thinking Social Research: Anti-discriminatory approaches in research methodology* (Aldershot, 1994), p.63.

[23]   Keeping a research journal is recommended by Pole, C. and Lampard, R., *Practical Social Investigation*, p.249. They also recommend writing separate, more formal field notes of events. I included both my formal notes and my personal responses to each event or experience I observed in the same journal. Keeping two sets of notes involved unnecessary repetition of describing events. The journal was kept separate from the notes taken during interviews.

experience included in this research, I have respected their wishes. This happened only twice. Again, however, any system which attempts to record what has been expressed through BSL into English is inadequate. This problem is something which I had to learn to accept if I was to produce a publishable academic study and has not been overcome. However, no communication is free from both the interpretation of the one communicating something and the one receiving the communication[24]. I have tried to record stories, events and insights as objectively as possible, but I make no apology for being prone to the very human characteristic of expressing and interpreting from my own context. No person is free from this. My bias to be in solidarity with Deaf people inevitably means that much of my interpretation has been coloured by this.

The journal involved recording and reflecting on experiences encountered in my work among the Deaf community. The methodological framework I applied for engaging with and interpreting the experiences was Green's 'pastoral cycle'[25] developed from the work of Paolo Freire[26] and elaborated by other practical and pastoral theologians[27]. The pastoral cycle is a well-established and used method of reflecting theologically and critically analysing experiences in communities in the fields of pastoral and practical theology[28]. The journal consisted of a series of A5 books in which each set of two pages was divided into four sections as illustrated in Table 2. Each section was then given a heading as follows: Experience, Exploration, Reflection and Action/Response. Under each of these headings, I applied a series of questions to the experience, and Table 2 also shows the types of questions I used to examine each experience or encounter gathered from my work with Deaf people and recorded in the journal. I have constructed these questions based on the Pastoral cycle with further reference in particular to some of the developments to the cycle proposed by Lartey[29].

---

[24]   See the discussion about '*differance*' in chapter 4 of this book.

[25]   Green, L., *Lets Do Theology: A Pastoral Cycle Resource Book* (London, 1990).

[26]   Freire, P., *Pedagogy of the Oppressed* (London, 1972).

[27]   For example, Ballard, P. and Pritchard, J., *Practical Theology in Action: Christian Thinking in the Service of Church and Society* (London, 1996), and Lartey, E., 'Practical Theology as Theological Form', in Woodward, J. and Pattison, S. (eds), *The Blackwell Reader in Pastoral and Practical Theology* (Oxford, 2000), pp.128–34.

[28]   For example, Ballard, P. and Pritchard, J., *Practical Theology in Action*, and Lartey, E., 'Practical Theology as Theological Form', pp.128–34.

[29]   Lartey, E., 'Practical Theology as a Theological Form', pp.128–34.

Table 2

Experience:	Exploration:	Reflection:	Action/Response:
1. What exactly is the experience?	1. How and why has this experience happened?	1. What do Christian traditions have to say to this situation? Use the tools of the Bible, Doctrine, Other Church Traditions (from ancient to contemporary)	1. Having completed the first three stages, am I equipped to help in this situation?
2. Identify who is involved	2. What other experiences have I had both inside and outside of the Deaf Community to help me understand this experience?	2. What is the situation in which these Christian traditions arose: contextual analysis?	2. What am I going to do or how do I respond?
3. What are the stages that have led to the experience happening?	3. How can I understand the situation more fully?	3. Can these Christian traditions help me to understand the experience better?	3. What am I not going to do? Ministers are not super-heroes. You will not always be the best person to deal with a situation.
4. What are the stages of the experience itself?	4. How can other disciplines inform my understanding of the experience? e.g. Psychology, Education, Politics, Linguistics, History, Sociology, Cultural Studies, Deaf Studies, Disability Studies.	4. Is there any point of conflict between Christian traditions and the experience?	4. How have my beliefs and understandings been changed?
5. What are the main issues, questions or problems involved?	5. Having done the above, how do I now understand this situation?	5. Can Christian traditions help me to understand and interpret a situation better?	5. Be practical and realistic about what can be done and make a plan of action
			6. What are the wider implications of my actions on local, national and global levels?
			7. How will I monitor my actions to see if they are helping? How will I ensure I build in further theological reflection?

Using the Pastoral Cycle

Experience

In relation to this aspect of the cycle headed 'experience', Lartey explains that, 'The main point is that it involves an encounter with people in the reality of life's experiences'[30]. It is essential in trying to understand any experience, that will later be analysed, that time is taken to understand the situation that has been experienced whether it is worship, conversation, observation or participation in an event, for example. Ballard and Pritchard argue that there are three processes involved in analysing an experience:

- gathering information and attending to experience;
- recording information and experience;
- shaping information and experience for presentation[31].

Attention to detail in understanding an experience is important not only so that the record of the experience is useful to the researcher at a later date, but also because the analysis that comes later is dependent upon an accurate and detailed account of the experience. The information that is gathered needs to be recorded in an objective way, as much as that is possible, and that information and impressions of the experience need to be ordered in such a way as to be useful for the purposes of being able to make use of them in the construction of an argument about them.

Exploration

Once the experience has been recorded, the next stage is to begin analysing that experience. Lartey labels this stage as 'situational analysis' and describes this stage as follows: 'What it can and must do is to bring selected perspectives from relevant disciplines to bear on the situation, in the hope of gaining a clearer understanding of what is going on'[32]. Elsewhere, in a discussion of pastoral care, Lartey argues that 'Counselling and psychotherapy occupy a central place in Western approaches to pastoral care'[33] and the role of other disciplines in pastoral care and practical theology are growing in significance. Lyall explains that 'the pastoral ministries of the Christian Church have themselves drawn to varying degrees upon their [counselling and psychotherapy] insights and practices'[34]. However, he emphasizes the 'integrity of pastoral care' and affirms the 'particular and peculiar contribution' of pastoral carers, as distinct from professionals from other disciplines[35].

---

[30]   Lartey, E., 'Practical Theology as a Theological Form', p.132.
[31]   Ballard, P. and Pritchard, J., *Practical Theology in Action*, p.88.
[32]   Lartey, E., 'Practical Theology as a Theological Form', p.132.
[33]   Lartey, E.Y., *In Living Colour: An Intercultural Approach to Pastoral Care and Counselling* (London, 1997), p.55.
[34]   Lyall, D., *Integrity of Pastoral Care* (London, 2001), p.5.
[35]   *Ibid.*, p.5.

In addition to counselling and psychotherapy, pastoral care draws upon a number of other disciplines to inform praxis and theological understanding and Lyall demonstrates this in a number of case studies of experiences of people involved in pastoral ministry[36]. Similarly, in my quest for understanding theology in the Deaf community, other disciplines were needed to inform my understanding of Deaf experiences, though not counselling and psychotherapy. These have included the disciplines of Deaf history, linguistics, education, community and cultural studies and the social sciences, all of which are crucial to understanding how the theology of the Deaf community has developed, which is the reason for including a detailed discussion of the Deaf community and the issues that affect them at the very beginning of this book. As with pastoral care, this thesis is interdisciplinary and this is reflected in the research methods I have employed. However, I agree with Lyall (above) that, as with pastoral care, an approach that aims to understand the theology of the Deaf community, while making use of other disciplines, must use a distinctively theological approach. Hence I discuss later in this chapter the limitations of other disciplines in trying to understand the theology of the Deaf community and the need to use methodologies from contextual and practical theologies. And so, in exploring each situation, I have used other disciplines to inform my understanding of the situation and experience, but most important has been the role of specifically theological reflection.

Reflection

In using the pastoral cycle as an analytical tool to interpret experiences with the Deaf community, the third stage of the cycle looks at theological reflection. Lartey explains that this is '… the point at which faith perspectives are allowed to question the encounter as well as the situational analysis'[37]. In Lartey's model, he distinguishes between firstly, 'theological analysis' and secondly, the 'situational analysis of theology'[38]. The theological analysis is the process of using faith perspectives to help the theologian to understand a situation. The situational analysis of theology is the process of questioning faith perspectives. To my mind, these two aspects of theological reflection should not be separated out. From a Christian theological perspective, it seems illogical to apply faith perspectives to the reflection on an experience before opening them up to critical questioning. Conversely, the questioning of theological perspectives may occur as a result of the process of engaging them with the experience. They are each a part of the same process and mutually inform each other.

In using the Christian tradition to inform my understanding of the theology of Deaf people, care was clearly needed. Because Deaf people have such limited access to the written text, the entire role of the Bible and other Christian texts is brought into question. Clearly, sacred and other texts of the Christian tradition play a key role in the identity of many Christian people, but to use them in analysing the theology of

---

[36] *Ibid.*, pp.132–53.

[37] Lartey, E., 'Practical Theology as a Theological Form', p.132.

[38] *Ibid.*, p.132.

the Deaf community could result in imposing a hearing literary form of Christianity onto Deaf Christian theological perspectives. Further discussion of the role of the Bible can be found in Chapter 5. In addition to the texts of the Christian tradition, the corporate Christian experience of which I, with Deaf people, am a part, and the tradition handed down to me and to Deaf people were also used to critically engage and understand Christian theological perspectives from the Deaf community.

Action/Response

The final stage of the cycle is to act or respond to an experience in light of the exploration and theological reflection that has taken place. Lartey explains that it is to '…explore what response options are available to me in the light of what has gone before and make decisions as to the preferred one'[39]. In this thesis, it has been the response that has been the most important result of the whole process rather than how to act. I have been convinced from the beginning, that it is not up to me to *do* anything as a result of my analysis of Deaf people's theology, other than to record and discuss it here. It has long been a criticism from Deaf and disabled people that non-disabled and hearing people have considered it to be their duty to care for Deaf and disabled people and to act on their behalf, while disabled people are the passive recipients of that action[40]. This has been particularly so in the way charities have been run leading disabled people to cry, 'rights not charity'[41]. It has been my role, therefore, to engage with Deaf theological perspectives, and to analyse them and respond to them. This book is the product of that response and is in itself an act of solidarity with the struggles of Deaf people for greater rights.

Criteria for Selecting Material Relevant to the Thesis

The purpose of this work is to investigate the theology of the Deaf community and this became the primary criterion by which I selected material that was relevant to the investigation and discarded that which was not relevant. Though many theologians would have a very broad definition of theology and would want to be ambiguous about what would count as theology and what would not, my primary focus was narrowly defined in terms of what Deaf people thought about God. Early on in the research, however, it became clear that not only the question of what and how Deaf people thought about God was important to Deaf people themselves, but also how that theology was explored and expressed and the context in which that theology is done. Hence there are three parts of Deaf theology that are presented in this thesis: Deaf people's tools for exploring and expressing theology, their ecclesiological and liturgical context for that, and some of their understandings and perspectives of God. Because these three issues were also recurring themes in both my interviews and observations as well as my own reflections, these three elements of Deaf theology

---

[39]   *Ibid.*, p.133.

[40]   Swain, J. et al., *Controversial Issues in a Disabling Society* (Buckingham, 2003), pp.90–2.

[41]   *Ibid.*, p.92.

are used as the framework for the remainder of this book and also act as the criteria for the selection of relevant material.

Researching as a Hearing Person

In a discussion about social research methods, Humphries and Truman explain that 'a researcher may locate herself within the research process as black, but it is rare for someone to locate themselves within research as a white, able-bodied, Euro-centric, heterosexual woman *and then explore the implications of those aspects of identity*'[42]. This is an important and serious point to make. From the outset, I have tried to be open about doing this research as a hearing person and in order to understand Deaf theology more fully, I have needed radically to question some of the traditions and ideas about God which have been handed to me and which are embedded in British culture. For example, as a hearing person, to become Deaf would be a traumatic experience. To deny this reality would be dishonest. At the same time, however, to impose this perspective on to the Deaf community might be tempting and much easier, but it is highly inappropriate because Deaf people rarely think of their Deafness as traumatic. Therefore in order to understand Deaf theology it has been important to explore and be open about my own identity and background. It is only in an open dialogue, and some struggle, with my own experiences and those of Deaf people, that I would be able to begin to understand not only the content of their theology but also how it developed and why.

Further, as with all theologies, the theology of Deaf people has not emerged independently of other movements both theological and secular. The Western Christian tradition has emerged out of a Jewish heritage, heavily influenced by Greco-Roman culture. It has developed throughout the Middle Ages, remnants of which are still prevalent today[43]. Some areas of Ethics are still greatly influenced by Victorian values and so on[44]. Likewise, Deaf theology has emerged alongside of and through all of these traditions, as well as emerging as a result of Deaf history, education, the use of a visual language, and through positive and negative engagement with hearing peers. To ignore these influences would be to fail to understand much of what Deaf theology is about. And so, I have tried to be open about my experiences and perspectives as a hearing person and to engage creatively with the experiences of Deaf people.

As mentioned earlier, however, the social sciences only offer helpful guidelines in exploring the theology of a community. Social Research literature encourages researchers to maintain distance from the researched and to find ways of leaving the group once the research is finished[45]. This is useful to some extent. The time I spent

---

[42] Truman, C., 'Feminist Challenges to Traditional Research: Have They Gone Far Enough?', in Humphries, B. and Truman, C. (eds), *Re-thinking Social Research: Anti-discriminatory approaches in research methodology* (Aldershot, 1994), p.32.

[43] Church architecture is evidence of a continuing medieval influence today as some buildings constructed in the twentieth century have followed medieval designs. For example, Liverpool's Anglican Cathedral.

[44] For example, many popular views on sexual morality.

[45] For example, Neuman, W.L., *Social Research Methods*, p.362.

in Zimbabwe was easy to fit into these criteria. I was only there for one month which enabled my research to have a clear beginning and a clear end. I will also not be able to sustain the kind of level of involvement with the Deaf community in Birmingham for the rest of my life that I have had whilst doing this research. Nevertheless, as feminist researchers point out, for example in interviews, the relationship between the researcher and the researched should be seen as much more equal[46]. Indeed, I would suggest that the most information and most honest responses were achieved in my research much later on, when my relationship with Deaf people was more like that of mutual friends. Of course, as with any relationship, boundaries are important but many of the friendships made will outlive the time taken to do the research.

In a project on a community's theology, the social science methodologies are helpful but not sufficient as a model for conducting theological research. The learning journal has also been used as a critical tool for reflecting on experiences during my participant observation. However, theological research needs to be committed and involved. Being too distant, rather than being a participant in the struggles of the community and their developing theology is inadequate. Theology calls for solidarity in the struggles of those about whom you are writing, and participation in the fight for liberation. For some this will be a life-long commitment. For others, they will simply not be able to distance themselves from the group they are researching. And so I turn, to complete the outline of my methodological framework, to the theologies of culture and liberation, most notably, those from Africa and Latin America.

Using the Methodologies of the Theologies of Culture and Liberation

In an inaugural lecture as Professor of Historical Studies at Birmingham University, John Parratt commented on the significant growth of Christianity in the non-Western world saying, 'If numbers count, it should no longer be possible to do Christian theology adequately today, or indeed to study it adequately, without taking into account the way theology is done in the Third World.' He goes on to observe that, 'It is still the case that in some erudite theological circles … the mention of Asian or African Christian theology will still be greeted with an ironic raised eyebrow or with blank incomprehension'[47]. In contrast to Parratt, John Mbiti writing on North American black theology purports, 'As an African one has an academic interest in Black Theology just as one is interested in the "water buffalo theology" of Southeast Asia or the theology of hope advocated by Jürgen Moltmann. But to try to push much more than the academic relevance of black theology for the African scene is to do injustice to both sides'[48].

Parratt and Mbiti exemplify two apparently contrasting themes in theology, which might be labelled as the tension and relationship between theology in the

---

[46]   See Pole, C. and Lampard R., *Practical Social Investigation*, p.146.

[47]   Parratt, J., *The Globalisation of Christian Theology*, An Inaugural Lecture given by John Parratt as Professor of Historical Studies at the University of Birmingham, February 26th, 2002.

[48]   Mbiti, J., 'An African Views American Black Theology', in Cone, J.H. and Williams, G.S. (eds), *Black Theology: A Documentary History Volume One: 1966–1979* (New York, 1993), p.383.

global context and theology in the local context. The criticism raised in practically any theological book which has been written from a non-Western perspective is that in the Western missionary activity which accompanied colonialization, 'The western construction was superimposed on other peoples to show western culture as the norm and inherently superior'[49]. Christianity had been so deeply immersed in Western intellectual, political and cultural frameworks that the Western peoples had no reason to question whether their version of Christianity was free from historical-contextual influences or not. They assumed that it was free from such influences and could be transplanted into any other historical context without much difficulty. This notion of the singular universality of Christianity was not borne out by experience. Canaan Banana comments, 'It was this simplistic approach and failure to recognize and respect African culture that created a serious tension between the Christian practice and African spirituality ... Christianity needs to be liberated from the garbage of Western mythology and traditional values and be presented to Africa in its original purity'[50]. Universalist claims to express God in ways meaningful for all humanity have proved themselves to be inadequate and irrelevant, but whether it is possible to present Christianity in its 'original purity' is also debatable.

To see theologies which emerge out of a context other than one's own as having little or no relevance to you, as Mbiti does, other than for academic interest, is a grave mistake. For example, the impact of liberation theology on Western theological thinking has been significant and the interest roused in it provided the methodologies to such theologies as black theology which has had political as well as academic and theological ramifications, not to mention the political impact in places such as South Africa. Liberation theology was influenced by Western socio-economic theory, namely Marxism, again showing the value of studying and engaging with theories from all over the world. In a world which is increasingly experiencing the effects of globalization, theologians anywhere cannot ignore what is going on in other parts of the world. As liberation theology has influenced other theological and ecclesiastical developments, so African, Asian and other cultural theologies are gaining momentum and significance. Each have experiences and insights that others can learn from. Theologies from various contexts can take note of these global theologies without compromising the historical contextual particularity of their own thinking. The most constructive theological world does not opt for the universalism of the nineteenth century nor the theological tribalism which Mbiti suggests, but of particularized theologies which can be mutually enriching and informative on a global scale. For these reasons, this theology from among Deaf people has drawn on the insights and experiences of global theologies with particular reference to Latin American liberation theologies and African theologies. I also believe that Deaf theology has much to contribute to other areas of theological thinking.

Non-Western theologians often use the phrase 'Western theology' as synonymous with the theologies of nineteenth-century missionaries or twentieth-century academics. Musopole, for example, argues, 'In western theological tradition, theology has been understood as the critical reflection upon God's revelation and understanding. At the

---

[49] Kwok Pui-Lan, *Discovering the Bible in the Non-Biblical World* (New York, 1995), p.9.
[50] Banana, C.S., *The Church and the Struggle for Zimbabwe* (Gweru, 1996), p.20.

heart of critical thought is the principle of non-contradiction resulting in objective knowledge'[51]. The quest for objective, universal knowledge about God is a post-enlightenment approach to theology followed by those who were educated to use it, with such as Schleiermacher being influential in the development of this theology. As theology is not globally the same, however, it must be recognized that there are varying theologies in the West as well. It is just that the theologies of the poor, of women, of disabled people, of gay people and of course Deaf people have rarely been written down. There are many yet untapped theological insights even in Britain which can contribute and enrich the understanding of God in other local contexts on a global scale. It just needs members of these groups to break free from the shackles of the white, male, traditional theology.

Below, I will demonstrate how I have borrowed the notion of 'solidarity' from liberation theology as a model for conducting the research for this book. I will also explore how the theologies of Deaf people in Britain have more in common methodologically with some African theologies than with some British theologies. By employing these theologies from particular situations, I will simultaneously provide myself with a completed research methodology and evidence of the significance of particularized theologies, like Deaf theology, for other contexts of the world.

Using Liberation Theology: Solidarity with Deaf People

Liberation theology gives a voice to those who are poor. Stephen Pattison comments: 'It [liberation theology] must be undertaken by the poor themselves, as they seek to become the subjects of their own history. It cannot be done on their behalf, although people from other social classes can opt to join the poor in their struggle to bring about change'[52]. Liberation theology in its oral form may be undertaken by the poor, but the medium through which it is read by us in the West is not written by the poor, but by men and women from other social groups with a different type of education who have opted to join the poor in their struggle.

Academic theological texts – even liberation theology – are inevitably written by those who are educated and one step removed from the theological perspectives and actions of those who live on the margins. Jürgen Moltmann asks of Gutierrez's *A Theology of Liberation*, 'But where is Latin America in it all?'[53] because of his use of European theologians and philosophers in analysing the Latin American situation. In response, however, I would ask, 'to whom is Latin American Liberation Theology addressed?' which is the same question I asked myself in the Introduction to this work. Whilst liberation theologians would be unlikely to own up to it, their theology is not really for an audience of grassroots groups in Latin America. Liberation theology is a political-economic theology seeking liberation from Euro-American oppression as much as from the oppressive regimes in their own country. They

---

[51]   Musopole, A., 'Needed: a Theology Cooked in an African Pot', in Fiedler, K., Gundani, P. and Mijoga, H. (eds), *Theology Cooked in an African Pot* (Zomba, Malawi, 1998), p.9.

[52]   Pattison, S., *Pastoral Care and Liberation Theology* (London, 1997), p.29.

[53]   Moltmann, J., 'An Open Letter to José Miguez Bonino', in Hennelly, A.T. (ed.), *Liberation Theology: A Documentary History* (Maryknoll, 1990), p.198.

write, perhaps unintentionally, in a medium which their oppressors will recognize and understand. It is effective because of this as it at least helps to 'afflict the comfortable'[54] and challenge the powerful by challenging the West in a language they understand. Someone wanting to be liberated from oppression would hardly go about it by spending two or three years writing an academic theological book about it. These observations are not meant as a negative criticism of the work of liberation theologies which have had such an impact on theological and ecclesiastical thinking around the world. Such books have given a very important and much needed voice to many who struggle to make their needs known.

Deaf people are increasingly finding their own metaphorical 'voice' in society and the Church, and I aim here to help their views to be understood by using the skills of one who has opted to join the Deaf community in their struggle to bring about change. Sometimes this is welcomed by Deaf people and frequently it is viewed with suspicion that a hearing person is writing about Deaf people's theology. But this project has emerged out of a desire to be alongside Deaf people, to help to give them a theological voice, and not to tell them how to think theologically. Like liberation theology, this book is addressed primarily to hearing people, in the hope that they will see how their own behaviour and attitudes have worked to marginalize and oppress the Deaf community in this country, but also to demonstrate the rich and varied theological perspectives of members of the Deaf community both individually and collectively, in the hope that the Church and theology will open their eyes to see the contributions which Deaf people can make.

Solidarity with Deaf People

Boff and Boff argue that in liberation theology, 'we need to have direct knowledge of the reality of oppression/liberation through objective engagement in solidarity with the poor'[55]. Solidarity is defined by Sobrino and Hernandez Pico as being like a 'neighbour' who gives of herself not in charitable benevolence but by participating in and being in meaningful relationship with the poor[56]. Gutierrez echoes this notion: 'A spirituality of liberation will center on a conversion to the neighbor, the oppressed person, the exploited social class, the despised ethnic group, the dominated country'[57]. Boff and Boff suggest that there are three forms of commitment to (or ways of being in solidarity with) the poor. One can:

i)   regularly visit communities and be involved with them;
ii) alternate periods of scholarly work with pastoral work;
iii) live permanently among the poor[58].

---

[54]   See Pattison, S., *Pastoral Care and Liberation Theology*, p.54.
[55]   Boff, L. and Boff, C., *Introducing Liberation Theology* (Tunbridge Wells, 1987), p.23.
[56]   Sobrino, J. and Hernandez Pico, J., *Theology of Christian Solidarity* (New York, 1985), pp.2–3.
[57]   Gutierrez, G., *A Theology of Liberation* (London, 1988), p.118.
[58]   Boff, L.. and Boff, C., *Introducing Liberation Theology*, p.23.

In terms of the way I have used the method of solidarity for this research project, I will deal with these three forms of commitment in reverse order.

Living Permanently Among the Poor

Firstly, living permanently among the Deaf community is not really an option for a Deaf or hearing person in Britain. Apart from one or two very small, isolated places in the world, Deaf people do not live in close proximity to one another. As argued in chapter 1, Deaf people live in the midst of hearing communities like a Diaspora community. It is thus impossible to live permanently among the Deaf community as Deaf people only meet together at frequent intervals. Liberation theologians live permanently amidst the communities about which they write because it enables them to participate more fully in the struggle of the poor and to experience the lives of those who are poor. A hearing person can never experience what it is like to be Deaf because one cannot give up hearing as one can give up money and material possessions. The solidarity of a hearing person with Deaf people must, therefore, take a different form and recognize this limitation.

Alternating Periods of Scholarly Work with Pastoral Work

Neither have the arguments presented here emerged out of alternating periods of scholarly work with pastoral work. The purpose of this book is to try and understand Deaf perspectives on God and is not meant as my own personal reflection on pastoral experience. Whilst this thesis and my involvement with the Deaf community may be interpreted by some as pastoral acts, I have deliberately tried to avoid being seen in the role of a 'pastor' in the Deaf community, which for many Deaf people will be the ordained leader[59]. This has not been particularly difficult, as I am not ordained[60]. Further, whilst certain boundaries are always necessary in any relationship, being seen as a pastor may alienate certain people from you. 'Pastors' in the Anglican Church are licensed, they receive authority to exercise their ministry from both the Church structures and the people to whom they minister. This authority brings with it formal boundaries and develops a relationship which is appropriately distanced in many respects from the people. My solidarity with the Deaf community has aimed to go deeper than the distanced relationship of a professional pastor and their flock, to a solidarity based on mutual friendship and trust. Thus it has been necessary that this field work has been carried out over an extensive period of time and has involved much time and commitment from me.

---

[59]   In chapter 6, I discuss models of ministry in the Deaf community, where I argue that pastoral care is a community activity and not just the work of an ordained leader.

[60]   In churches it is generally held that Pastor is the ordained or authorized minister to a congregation. I recognize that many Pastoral Theologians and many ordinary church members argue that pastoring is not just the activity of qualified, authorized ministers. See for example, Lyall, D., *Integrity of Pastoral Care*, pp.1–3.

Regularly Visiting Communities and Being Involved With Them

The methodology most appropriate for me to employ was regularly to visit communities of Deaf people and be involved with them. While Deaf people do not live in close proximity to one another, they do meet regularly in certain locations. In Birmingham, the gathering place for the Deaf community is the Deaf Club. It is not the only place, however. Other clubs and organizations exist exclusively for Deaf people, such as churches, fellowship meetings, youth groups, OAP clubs, football teams, gay and lesbian groups as well as through the varying employment I had. These Deaf groups exist as distinct from hearing groups because they use as their first language, BSL. Because of these places and times of meeting it has been possible regularly to visit gatherings of Deaf people to communicate with them and discuss their experiences and/or their ideas about God. As described earlier, this enabled mutual trust and friendships to grow.

Solidarity with Deaf People

Liberation theology provides a useful framework from which to write in terms of exploring the types of solidarity and commitment a theologian can exercise who is not from that group, and the way in which the theologian can authentically write theologically with reference to the life stories and experiences of those about whom they write. This form of solidarity has provided the context in which the participant observation work and critical reflection on it, described earlier, took place. However, I would suggest that liberation theology on its own would fall short of providing an adequate theological methodological framework in the writing of a theology from among Deaf people, because of its focused emphasis on socio-economic and political issues and its employment of Marxism as a critical tool. Socio-economic and political factors impact on Deaf theology considerably, but I would argue that what is at the foundation of such socio-economic and political thinking, and what shapes their particularly Deaf theological understanding, is also the significance of culture. Because of this in addition to the social sciences, theological reflection, and liberation theology's model of solidarity with Deaf people I have also employed much of the methodological framework that can be found in some African theologies.

African Theology and Deaf Theology: Making Connections

Politics, Economics and Culture

African theology is not unique in terms of addressing culture. Other areas of the world in which theology is done increasingly recognize the importance of culture and this insight is spreading. However, I have chosen to use the methods of African theology in particular because of some of the work done on the role of oral tradition and theology. This also is not unique to Africa, but is gaining in significance there, arguably more so than elsewhere.

John Mbiti argues that African theology,

> ... emerges out of our joy in the experience of the Christian faith, whereas Black Theology emerges from the pains of oppression ... African Theology is concerned with many more issues, including all the classical theological themes, plus localized topics, such as religious dialogue between Christianity and African Religion and between Christianity and Islam. Relations between Christianity and African culture, between Church and State, together with innumerable pastoral and liturgical problems, give African Theology a very full agenda for the years ahead[61].

Like African theology, Deaf theology is not concerned with the more narrow socio-political agendas of liberation theologies such as those which emerge from Latin America or black theology from North America. Later in the same paper, Mbiti goes on to argue, 'African Theology has no interest in coloring God or Christ black, no interest in reading liberation into every text, no interest in telling people to think or act "black"'[62]. In contrast, Desmond Tutu in South Africa writes, 'I contend that Black Theology is like the inner and smaller circle in a series of concentric circles ... I and others from South Africa *do* Black Theology, which is for us, at this point, African theology'[63].

The situation in South Africa has now changed since the end of Apartheid and the political focus of their theology is perhaps changing. The theology about which Desmond Tutu was speaking, however, was a theology concerned with the socio-economic and political division of people based on their skin colour and not on which continent those people came from. The fact that the black theology of South Africa emerges in Africa is surely sufficient to make it an African theology. Academics, whatever their calibre, such as John Mbiti, should not think of themselves as having a bird's eye view of a continent such as Africa and think themselves able to label what should be considered African and what should not. Any theology which is done by Africans must surely be African theology. The use of labels such as 'African theology', while useful in terms of identifying theologies with some common concerns, have an homogenizing dimension to them which can suggest that all theology in Africa has the same concerns. It would be nonsense to suggest that the Masai of Kenya, Zulus in South Africa, Ndebeles in Zimbabwe, Hutus in Rwanda and Egyptian Coptic Christians all have the same concerns and theological perspectives.

Mbiti may be right that African theology – and perhaps all theology – 'emerges out of our joy in the experience of the Christian faith'. This should not mean, however, that theology ignores the difficult questions which it faces, about for example, 'the pains of oppression'. Clearly many African theologians have addressed such difficult questions. In Zimbabwe, Canaan Sondido Banana has been a leading theologian who has written about socio-political concerns. His book, *The Church and the Struggle for Zimbabwe* (1996), offers an historical account and analysis of

---

[61]   Mbiti, J., 'An African Views American Black Theology', p.383.

[62]   *Ibid.*, p.383–4.

[63]   Tutu, D.M., 'Black Theology/African Theology – Soul Mates or Antagonists?', in Cone, J.H. and Williams, G.S. (eds), *Black Theology: A Documentary History Volume One: 1966–1979* (New York, 1993), p.391.

the Church's involvement in the struggle of Zimbabweans for independence from the repressive colonial government. Similarly, Mercy Amba Oduyoye, writing from the perspective of African women explains that, 'Women's theology is crafted in the midst of the ongoing life in Africa, overshadowed by economic exploitation, political instability and militarism'[64]. Their concern is also for liberation.

God's 'blackness' is also a concern for many African theologians and people. Increasingly, God is seen as an African and this is represented for example, through artistic impressions of a black Christ. This was true in Zimbabwe at least. The colour of God's skin in Africa is as important as in North America. If it was irrelevant, the white, Western image of Christ would not have been removed from many churches to be replaced by black images[65].

Deaf theology like African theology contains a multiplicity of strands. It has concerns for the political and socio-economic dimension to life and yet it is concerned also with engaging Deaf culture and experience with the Christian tradition which has been formed and expressed in a Western, hearing theological framework. Deaf theology is diffuse and variegated and any theological thinking done by Deaf people, I will consider to be Deaf theology. Deaf theology is concerned with freedom and liberation from unfair structures which favour the hearing in both secular and religious spheres of life. At the same time, it is concerned with (to echo Mbiti) the classical theological themes, plus localized topics, such as relations between Christianity and Deaf culture, between Church and State, together with innumerable pastoral and liturgical problems. As God's blackness has become a concern in Africa, so in the Deaf community, God's Deafness has become a significant issue (see chapter 7 for a full exploration of this). As in Africa, Deaf theology is diverse and fluid and cannot be homogenized as one unified perspective because it reflects the varied and rich lives of the Deaf community. Yet Deaf people are also community orientated and what concerns many Deaf individuals usually concerns also the community. Such issues include education, BSL recognition and how to develop and nurture a Christian faith which is particular to Deaf people and free of hearing dominance.

Deaf Theology and African Oral Theology

An area which is growing in significance, especially in Africa, is that of 'oral theology'. Parratt explains that oral theology, 'consists of theological reflection which takes place in sermons, addresses and hymns, and in the personal discussions and reflections of Christian believers'[66]. Such theology, Parratt elaborates, 'is usually

---

[64]   Oduyoye, M.A., *Introducing African Women's Theology* (Sheffield, 2001), p.23.

[65]   E.g. In Zimbabwe, especially in the Roman Catholic and Methodist Church, Christ was Black in painting and in sculpted crucifixes. In the Anglican Church, this was not so frequently found – especially in affluent white areas. However, in the poorer Black areas, Christ was also Black. In the African Independence Churches – such as Johane Masowe – there were no visual representations of Christ used. See Mukonyora, I., 'The Dramatization of Life and Death by Johane Masowe', pp.191–207.

[66]   Parratt, J., 'Conclusion: Current Issues in African Theology', in Parratt, J. (ed.), *A Reader in African Christian Theology* (London, 1997), p.139.

done in the vernacular, rather than a European language such as English or French'[67]. He also explains that, 'African theologians are beginning to take such grass-roots theologizing seriously and to use its insights, especially in identifying particular areas which are of spiritual concern to African Christians'[68]. Healey and Sybertz also say, 'the artist, the painter, the carver, the creator of liturgical symbols, the film or video maker can be theologians in their own right'[69].

Oral theology has always been a part of Christian believers thinking and theological expression even if it has not traditionally been acknowledged or recognized in academic or clerical circles. Mercy Amba Oduyoye explains that 'African women's theology remains a story that is told, a song that is sung and a prayer that is uttered in response to experience and expectation'[70] because written theological literature from African women has been non-existent and has mostly, if not all, appeared in the last thirty years in a more public arena. Investigation into oral theology is sparse. Those among whom oral theology is rife often do not have the skills or capacity to write it down. Parratt identifies a study by Harold Turner in Nigeria, but laments that it 'has been little used with regard to the mainstream churches'[71]. The study by Healey and Sybertz, *Towards an African Narrative Theology* (1996) examining narrative traditions in Kenya and Tanzania has also had little impact on the churches.

Oral theology is not unique to Africa. It occurs wherever Christians are. For some non-literate groups such as the Dalits of India, it is the primary theology in their context[72]. Some people from the Western context also value oral theology. Laurie Green, a bishop in the Church of England, has dyslexia – an impairment which can alienate people from books. He argues that, 'In our theological education, in our book-ridden worship, in our abstracted thinking about God, the Church needs a spirituality of the Word – and from oral cultures we may learn more of what that can be'[73]. The theology of Deaf people is much more akin to oral or narrative theologies than to written theologies. 'Oral theology', however is an inappropriate term for describing Deaf people's theology. 'Narrative theology' (Healey and Sybertz, 1996) is also unhelpful as it suggests theology is transmitted through stories, which would describe only part of Deaf theology. Rather I have opted for the phrase 'non-written theology' or 'non-literary theology'.

Investigating non-written theologies as Parratt points out is difficult. It involves the type of solidarity with and participation in the community of Deaf people, which was outlined earlier in order to learn how Deaf people communicate and express themselves and to observe the theology which is done in this way. Deaf theology is always active: 'The written word is an abstract thing. The spoken word is an

---

[67]   *Ibid.*, p.140.

[68]   *Ibid.*, p.140.

[69]   Healey, J. and Sybertz, D., *Towards an African Narrative Theology*, p.23.

[70]   Oduyoye, M.A., *Introducing African Women's Theology*, p.22.

[71]   Parratt, J., 'Conclusion: Current Issues in African Theology', p.140.

[72]   See Clarke, S., *Dalits and Christianity: Subaltern Religion and Liberation in India* (New Delhi, 1999), pp.4–5, and Parattai (J. Theophilus Appavoo), 'Dalit Way of Theological Expression', in Devasahayam, V. (ed.), *Frontiers of Dalit Theology* (Madras, 1997), pp.283–9.

[73]   Green, L., 'Oral culture and the World of Words', *Theology*, CII(809), (1999): 335.

event'[74]. It is also communal and so requires the theologian to be involved in that community. Theological expression usually involves dialogue and involvement from the expressers rather than the distance a book gives. It is rare, therefore, for a non-literary theologian to do theology in the isolation of, for example, an academic's office. Oral theology is also something that is not fixed but is in constant change. That makes it much more difficult to grasp and explore the theology of communities who use the oral method in theology, as will be seen in chapter 4.

Conclusion: Drawing the Research Methods Together

In quantitative research, it is much easier for other researchers to check the findings claimed in a thesis. Collecting statistics such as a group's age, sex, ethnicity and disability using the same criteria for data collection should yield the same results for each researcher, presuming the group's make up does not alter. This is not so in qualitative research of a theological nature as I have described it. Theology deals with ideas, perspectives, feelings and opinions, which are shaped by a continuous dialogue between the experiences of individuals and communities and the Christian tradition as it is handed down. Theology is thus never fixed but is dynamic and constantly changing, especially oral theology. It is also particular to a time and situation. A different researcher looking into this same topic could potentially produce a quite different exploration of the theology of Deaf people than will follow here. My own experience has shown that the Deaf perspective on God is different in Zimbabwe to Britain. I have no doubt that it is also different in Cornwall, London, Liverpool, Edinburgh or North Wales. However, there is much which Deaf people share in common with each other that is different from that of hearing people. Deaf people around the world share in common such things as a visual language, and a culture that is based on vision, touch and relationship. Hence it is possible to talk about a Deaf community in national and international terms. How that language and culture is manifest and expressed, however, will vary from town to town and country to country, as in the United States, American Sign Language is different to BSL.

So, while there is diversity, there will also be similarities between the many Deaf theological perspectives and for those who know anything about the Deaf community, I hope that they will recognize at least some of what is contained here. It is this recognition that I hope will provide validity to this research. Throughout, I have consistently been involved in the Deaf community and have acted in solidarity with them wherever possible. There is nothing which I have said in what follows which does not come as a direct result of what a Deaf person has expressed to me, or my own reflections on an individual or set of experiences and this is integral to what follows. The theology which follows is concerned with socio-economic-political issues as well as with culture. It would be dishonest and pointless to deny that my own perspectives and reflections have influenced what I have included and excluded. I am not the proverbial machine that Moser and Kalton (1971) refer to

---

[74]   *Ibid.*, p.331.

earlier, and the purpose of a theology such as this is not to list information but to put forward an argument.

Chapter 4

*Deaf*ining and Doing Theology

Introduction

What theology is and how it is done are two central issues which need to be addressed when thinking about the ways in which Deaf people do theology. This involves considering what theology is on an abstract, philosophical level, as well as trying to define who does theology, what resources are needed in order to engage in the theological enterprise, what the purpose of theology is, and how theology is communicated. Those who have traditionally been called theologians inevitably have used the resources and experiences which they have at their disposal to define and do theology. Unfortunately, as they have defined who should engage in the theological enterprise and how it is undertaken, they have done so by creating boundaries which have historically led to the exclusion of many groups of people, including Deaf people[1]. A result of addressing these issues is, therefore, that traditional definitions of theology will need to be transformed and new tools for both formulating and expressing theological ideas need to be introduced, in order to fulfil the aim of this chapter, which is to consider from the perspectives of Deaf people what theology is and how they do it.

The consequence of this will be that this argument must turn to issues concerning theological language, but with a slightly unusual approach to such classic authors on the subject as Sallie McFague and Ian Ramsey among others. Whilst the questions and challenges which they offer are important and relevant to this thesis, from the perspectives of Deaf people the question concerning language needs to be much more pragmatic than those above, because the primary issue which relates to Deaf people and theology is concerned with the very *means* they have at their disposal to talk, or rather sign, about God in the first place. And so, the argument focuses not on metaphor and analogy[2] or 'logically odd' language[3], but on the use of books in contrast to non-literary means for expressing theological ideas.

---

[1] Theology as a minority activity in the church is argued for by Castle, B., *Unofficial God?: Voices from Beyond the Walls* (London, 2004), p.16, and many feminist theologians such as King, U. (ed.), *Feminist Theology from the Third World* (London, 1994), pp.4–5.

[2] The subject of McFague, S., *Models of God: Theology for an Ecological, Nuclear Age* (London, 1987).

[3] The subject of Ramsey, I., *Religious Language* (London, 1957).

Hearing Theology: What and How?

Faith Seeking Understanding

Anselm's famous phrase, 'Faith Seeking Understanding' is a classic description of what theology tries to do. It implies that theology is to do with people of faith who try to discover and understand something of the nature of God and the relationship which exists between God and humankind. As O'Collins argues, Barth would also agree with this notion that theology is done by people of faith as Barth understands dogmatic theology to be 'essentially ecclesiastical'[4]. Traditionally, both of these perspectives have been interpreted to mean that 'ecclesiastical' or 'people of faith' means Christian academics or clergy; in other words, people with academic training and literary abilities. Jones points out that the word 'understanding' is vital to theology as it cannot be about 'faith seeking knowledge'. This is because the act of revelation is always accompanied by concealment. Therefore Anselm's phrase is important for theology because, 'implicit within (it) is his (Anselm's) awareness of the mysterious origins of faith'[5]. Theology, therefore, can never reach a final conclusion, but is a continuous and dynamic activity.

Before leaving this point, it is worth asking 'Why does faith want to seek understanding?' It would seem that there are a number of possible reasons and some are discussed here. The first is that understanding is sought for purely academic or intellectual reasons so that it becomes an end in itself with no ulterior motive other than it being an interesting cerebral exercise. Alternatively, Barth would suggest that understanding is gained by the revelatory Word of God given by God to the Church which by implication makes theology much more serious in terms of human existence. This perspective makes theology an ecclesiastical affair, but with the Church in a passive role as messengers, and God in an active role, providing the message. A final purpose in seeking understanding is that understanding is a means to an end for people of faith. For example, in liberation theology, seeking to gain a deeper insight into the God who is on the side of the poor, aims to heighten awareness concerning the evils which lead to poverty[6]. Such a theology thus has important social and political ramifications as it is a theology which incites action. Deaf people's awareness of God's love and care for them, as many conversations with Deaf people have indicated, has provided many Deaf people with a sense of self-worth, empowering them to challenge the evils that lead to discrimination against Deaf people.

---

[4]   O'Collins, G., 'Dogmatic Theology', in Richardson, A. and Bowden, J. (eds), *A New Dictionary of Christian Theology* (London, 1983), p.163.

[5]   Jones, G., *Critical Theology* (London, 1995), p.7.

[6]   Hennelly, A.T. (ed.), *Liberation Theology: A Documentary History* (Maryknoll, 1990), p.xx.

Theos ... Logos

It is useful to be briefly reminded that the word theology derives from the Greek words meaning God and discourse / account / language[7]. Words such as 'discourse' and 'account' have usually been interpreted to mean that an important aspect of theology is reason and logical argument (discussed later in this chapter). This particular aspect of theology, which has been given pride of place for hundreds of years, has become a measure by which an idea about God can be considered to be 'true' or not. The prefix 'systematic', which is placed before theology by many university departments, emphasizes the centrality of reason in theological debate – especially if one's aims for understanding are purely academic.

The Postmodern Influence on Theology

The rise of postmodernism over the last thirty years and before has had a major impact on theology and no contemporary analysis of theology is complete without considering this impact. The poststructuralist approach to linguistics, as argued by Derrida (among others) helps us to understand this impact. Derrida argues that an object's, thought's or relationship's meaning can never be fixed and universally comprehended in exactly the same way by everyone or even by two different people, because as meaning is presented or written down, it will always be interpreted differently by each person to whom it is presented. The equivocality of meaning which comes as a result of individual interpretation is named by Derrida as *differance*[8]. Thus Chris Weedon argues that, 'its (poststructuralism's) founding insight, ... is that language, far from reflecting an already given social reality, constitutes social reality'.[9] Weedon goes on to explain that this 'theory implies that the meaning of 'woman' or the qualities identified as womanly, are not fixed by a natural world and reflected in the term 'woman', but are socially produced within language'[10]. For example, 'The meaning of the signifier 'woman' varies from ideal to victim to object of sexual desire, according to its context'[11]. The result of this is that what one person means by the word 'woman' is never fixed, but the word's meaning will be different, however small, from person to person.

Postmodernism thus suggests to theology that anything it says about God and God's relationship to humanity is never universal, can never be fixed, and that we can never grasp 'truth', because the meaning given to any theological expression will always be influenced by *differance* and thus is confined within the limits of language. Such a notion directly challenges literal approaches to theology. Many

---

[7] Schüssler-Fiorenza, F., 'Systematic Theology: Tasks and Methods', in Schüssler-Fiorenza, F. and Galvin, J.P., *Systematic Theology: Roman Catholic Perspectives* (Dublin, 1992), p.5.

[8] Garver, N., 'Preface', in Derrida, J., *Speech and Phenomena: And Other Essays on Husserl's Theology of Signs* (Evanston, 1973), p.xxiv.

[9] Weedon, C., *Feminist Practice & Poststructuralist Theory.* 2nd Edition (Oxford, 1997), p.21.

[10] *Ibid.,* p.25.

[11] *Ibid.,* p.25.

theologians have resisted such ideas in theology, but the influence of postmodernism cannot be ignored. The theological slant given to postmodernism is most apparent in the understanding of theology as 'contextual' though I recognize they are not precisely the same approaches to theology.

Theology is Contextual

The notion that theology is contextual is a point that hardly needs to be made as it has been argued for and modelled by hundreds of theologians for the past thirty to forty years among whom are Paul Tillich[12], Laurie Green[13], and key black[14], feminist[15], liberation[16], disabled[17], African[18] and Asian[19] theologians among many others. Like Barth, these theologians argue that theology is an ecclesiastical affair. Parratt explains the role of context when he argues, 'Theology ... is not something which exists eternally in the heavens and descends to earth untouched and unmarked by the human condition[20]. On the contrary, it is something which emerges from that condition and it cannot avoid reflecting the historical and cultural context in which it is done'[21]. Parratt also argues that theology is 'reasonable communication about God'[22].For communication to be possible, a minimum of two people are needed and, if communication is an important part of theology, then theology cannot be done individually but only in a community of two or more people. However, contrary to Barth's approach to theology, which places the proclamation of theology with 'the Church', contextual theology places thinking about God with churches in the original meaning of the word (ekklesia: an assembly of citizens[23]). Thus theology is no longer considered to be only the activity of academics and clergy but of all people of faith. Theology then is a community activity, but because of the impact of *differance*, discussion and debate are continuous and meaning is always dynamic.

---

[12] Tillich, P., *Theology of Culture* (London, 1964).

[13] Green, L., *Let's Do Theology* (London, 1990).

[14] Cone, J.H., *A Black Theology of Liberation* (London, 1990).

[15] Oduyoye, M.A., *Introducing African Women's Theology* (Sheffield, 2001).

[16] Gutierrez, G., *The God of Life* (London, 1991).

[17] Eiesland, N.L., *The Disabled God* (Nashville, 1994).

[18] Banana, C.S., 'The Case for the New Bible', Sugirtharajah, R.S. (ed.), *Voices from the Margin* (London/Maryknoll, 1995).

[19] Sugirtharajah, R.S., *The Bible and the Third World: Precolonial, Colonial and Postcolonial Encounters* (Cambridge, 2001).

[20] This notion contradicts Barth's understanding of Theology as given directly by God to the church which proclaims it. See Barth, K., *Church Dogmatics*. Vol I.ii (Edinburgh, 1956).

[21] Parratt, J., *A Guide to Doing Theology* (London, 1996), p.17.

[22] *Ibid.*, p.13.

[23] See Abbott-Smith, G., *A Manual Greek Lexicon of the New Testament* (Edinburgh, 1994), p.138.

The Tools or Resources for Doing Hearing Theology

Various groups of theologians use different tools or resources in order to develop their thinking about God, as will be illustrated below by an examination of a selection of theologies from around the world. This selection should give us an idea about the types of resources available to theologians, which will then enable us to further clarify the place of Deaf people in the wider theological arena. The examples which are presented below have been chosen because they represent a wide variety of key areas of contextual theology (which all theology is), as it has emerged over the past thirty years or so.

In American black theology, James Cone identifies six contributory factors which help to make up black theology. These include: black experience, black history, black culture, revelation, scripture, and tradition[24]. Similarly, Basil Moore in South Africa argues that what contributes to black theology in his country includes the analysis of the black situation in South Africa and 'then Black Theology will be able to turn to the Scripture and tradition'[25]. Further, Augustine Musopole argues that in African theology 'the ingredients would include: the Bible, theological traditions, African religions and philosophies, life of the church, culture, and history'[26]. Stanley Samartha has a similar set of ingredients when he argues that, 'in a religiously plural world, the interplay among the scripture, tradition and reason has to be far more dynamic and theologically imaginative than ever before'[27]. The Latin American liberation theologian, Gustavo Gutierrez, also has a model for doing theology which by now will look familiar: 'Our starting point is our faith: we believe in the God of life. We aim to think this faith by going ever deeper into the content of biblical revelation. And we do this while taking into account the way in which the poor perceive God'[28]. Similarly in their book, *Introducing Liberation Theology* (1987), Leonardo and Clodovis Boff explain, 'When invited to do so by the group, liberation theologians will then from other points of view try to ponder, deepen and criticize the questions raised, always relating them to the word of revelation, the magisterium, and the normative tradition of the church'[29]. For Mercy Amba Oduyoye, 'the sources of African women theologians are whatever uphold women's and men's humanity in the Bible, in African traditional religion and in African culture'[30].

---

[24]   Cone, J.H., *A Black Theology of Liberation*, pp.23–35.

[25]   Moore, B., 'What is Black Theology?', in Moore, B. (ed.), *Black Theology: The South African Voice* (London, 1973), p.6.

[26]   Musopole, A., 'Needed: A Theology Cooked in an African Pot', p.19.

[27]   Samartha, S.J., 'Scripture and Scriptures', in Sugirtharajah, R.S. (ed.), *Voices from the Margin* (London/Maryknoll, 1995), p.32.

[28]   Gutierrez, G., *The God of Life*, p.xvii.

[29]   Boff, L. and Boff, C., *Introducing Liberation Theology* (Tunbridge Wells, 1987), p.20.

[30]   Explained in Isabel Apawo Phiri, 'Doing Theology as African Women', in Parratt, J. (ed.), *A Reader in African Christian Theology* (London, 1997), p.49.

Summarizing Hearing Theology

What is Hearing Theology?

What is hearing theology as it has been understood historically and as it is widely understood today? Firstly, it endeavours to seek understanding of and not knowledge about God. Thus theology is a continuous activity which never reaches any final conclusions about God. Theology for some is a purely intellectual exercise, but for others it is a means to an end, such as socio-economic and political liberation. Secondly, discussion or speech about God is vital, but should be engaged with reason. Thirdly, theology has traditionally been understood to be the job of academics and clergy, but this is increasingly changing so that theology is done as the activity of communities of faith (although academics can reflect on this theology). Finally, theology is contextual but should never be individual. Theology is always dependent on a particular time and culture, but it should always be the project of communities of individuals engaging with one another. Because of issues of interpretation, postmodernism suggests that there is nothing which can be said about God that is universal and timeless.

How is Hearing Theology Done?

The examples of theologians and the models they use for doing theology that have been presented above are models which on the whole share the same tools for doing theology. These tools include, revelation, the analysis of a situation or context, the Bible, tradition and/or magisterium, reason, and culture. All of these tools somehow or other are engaging and interacting with each other to do and create theology, although the starting point and emphasis placed on each resource will usually be different. It is interesting to note that despite the protestations of many writers of theology, and the arguments of contextual theology, that while theology is done by communities of faith, both Boff and Boff (above) call *themselves* theologians rather than the groups with whom they work. This highlights an important issue, which will be discussed later, that theologians are still often perceived to be only those who have academic training and literary abilities. Thus we have a loose definition of what hearing theology, for many, is about as well as an awareness of the tools which are used by hearing theologians in order to formulate their theology.

Assessing the Role of Literature in Hearing Theology

Among the resources of theology which were listed above, it is evident that for most areas of contextual theology there are resources used which are both written and unwritten. Among the unwritten resources are culture, experience, the skills to analyse a context, and reason. These are not always unwritten, as culture, for example, may include a group's literary heritage. The skills of analysis and reason may also be abilities which have derived from ideas expressed through literature. However, in many contexts traditions, culture, experience and so on will be part of the 'non-written traditions'. Literature also provides important resources for hearing theology in the format of the Bible, as well as Church traditions and magisterium which are ultimately expressed in written formats. Let us briefly consider the significance of written texts for theology.

Firstly, in most if not all Christian traditions, the Bible is important for doing theology in however many different ways it may be used. Some theologies measure the extent to which a theology is Christian against the Bible, others argue that the Bible is only useful for theology inasmuch as it supports the liberation of oppressed peoples[31]. Barth stresses the importance of the Bible as a key witness to God's revelation[32]. Canaan Banana on the other hand would seem to prefer that the Bible be amended and rewritten in order to be relevant to particular times and places[33]. In contrast, Patrick Kalilombe would go so far as to argue that without the Bible doing theology is in vain[34]. Whatever the point of view, the significance of the Bible cannot be underestimated for theology as it powerfully evokes responses from many different theologians and these perspectives are discussed in more detail in chapter 5.

Similarly, the traditions and teaching of the Church generally are significant written texts which play a key role in theological debate. The exact wording of the creeds has caused controversy throughout the ages when a difference of opinion has arisen or a slight change in understanding has emerged. The famous controversy over the idea of the Filioque, for example, was significant in the split between the Church in the East and the West. Other important texts are those which form the Magisterium of the Roman Catholic Church or, in the Church of England, the Thirty-Nine Articles of Religion which priests still assent to at their ordination[35].

Finally it is invariably true that most contextual theologies, even if they initially occur orally among the ekklesia, are thought out and given wider validity in the context of books. For whatever these writers say about theology actually taking place in the community with which they are engaging, it would seem that it is only in the format of literature that this theology gains significance. It was explained earlier that Leonardo and Clodovis Boff identify the theologians as those who relate what people in the community are saying to the magisterium, scripture and tradition, rather than calling the grass-roots groups theologians. Still, therefore, even though unwritten resources have a role to play in theology, written resources as well as the written texts of theology still are held in higher esteem and are given a greater validity and status as theology than unwritten theology.

---

[31] Examples include, Oduyoye, M.A., *Introducing African Women's Theology*, p.12; and Schüssler-Fiorenza, E., 'Transforming the Legacy of *The Woman's Bible*', in Schüssler-Fiorenza, E., *Searching the Scriptures: A Feminist Introduction* (London, 1993), p.5.

[32] See for example, Barth, Karl, *Church Dogmatics*. vol I.i (Edinburgh, 1975), pp.99–110.

[33] Banana, C.S., 'The Case for a New Bible' (Gweru, 1995), pp.69–82.

[34] Kalilombe, P.A., 'A Malawian Example: The Bible and Non-literate Communities', in Sugirtharajah, R.S. (ed.), *Voices from the Margin* (London/Maryknoll, 1995), p.434.

[35] Church of England, *Common Worship* (London, 2000), p.xi.

Literature and Theology: Deconstructing the Written Word

Jacques Derrida has taken the opposite view to me by arguing that greater emphasis has traditionally been placed on speech over writing, at least in relation to Western metaphysics. Stephen Moore summarizes Derrida's understanding with the phrase, 'The Garden is Speech, The Desert is Writing'. Moore expands this phrase by arguing that for Derrida, 'in mainstream Western thought, speech has always been the paradigm not only for every form of presence but also for every truth'.[36] These suggestions form part of Derrida's arguments that in the West, philosophy has been dominated by dichotomies between certain ideas, concepts or objects, for example, light and darkness, white and black, masculine and feminine, and speech and writing. The former in each case, Moore explains, has always been privileged over their opposite. The histories of many blind people, women, and black people would suggest that Derrida has made a correct analysis of Western metaphysics by presenting these dichotomies as a part of it.

He argues in *Speech and Phenomena* (1973), that speech has been privileged because it is as though, 'My words are "alive" because they seem not to leave me: not to fall outside of me, outside my breath, at a visible distance; not to seem to belong to me'[37]. Thus according to Derrida, the myth has been that because speech takes place in the present, and the utterance can be controlled by the speaker then it can be assumed that one is nearer to 'truth' or 'meaning' in speech, and misinterpretation is less likely to happen. When something is written down, it can be interpreted in a greater variety of ways because the author is unable to control it.

Derrida aims to challenge this notion of the superiority of speech over writing by arguing that speech can potentially be interpreted in as many different ways as writing and that *differance* must apply equally to both. Andrews explains that for Derrida, 'A writer's intentions cannot be the same as that which he actually writes because writing is representative'[38] and the same is arguably true for speech in terms of what the speaker intends to say and what she actually says. The person who reads or hears what is being communicated by another person, can also never fully know what the communicator intends because they only hear or read a representation of the intentions. Each person who hears someone's speech will also interpret what they hear differently to another person as well. And so, because intended meaning can never be understood in its entirety, we all have to make do with a mediated interpretation whether an intention is represented by speech or by writing.

Derrida has, therefore, been instrumental in trying to break down a dichotomy which privileged one mode of communication over another. The equality of speech and writing, and the understanding that interpretation and meaning will be different in every context is welcome. Such an understanding opens up a way to value the diversity which can be discerned from person to person and culture to culture in

---

[36]   Moore, S.D., *Poststructuralism and the New Testament: Derrida and Foucault at the Foot of the Cross* (Minneapolis, 1994), p.29.

[37]   Derrida, J., *Speech and Phenomena* (Evanston, 1973), p.76.

[38]   Andrews, I., *Deconstructing Barth: A Study in the Complementary Methods in Karl Barth and Jacques Derrida* (Frankfurt, 1996), p.27.

terms of how they express their ideas. However, it is not Derrida's conclusions which are problematic in relation to Deaf people as much as his argument. Is it so that in the West, it has been thought that speech is a superior form of communication to writing in which one is nearer to true meaning? The experiences of Deaf people among other marginalized groups help provide an alternative perspective on this issue.

The Garden is Writing, the Desert is Speech? Signing and Speech on the Margins

Hart has pointed out that 'Derrida's text reveals that he is concerned solely with the metaphysics in theology, and would be sympathetic to those theologies, if any, that do not "appropriate the resources of Greek conceptuality"'[39]. Of course there are many theologians in third world countries who by no means apply Greek conceptuality to their theology. For example, in India, entirely different philosophical frameworks are available for and used by theologians[40]. However, as will be suggested later, it is not just non-Western theologians who are left on the margins of theology by the dominance of Greek conceptuality, but many groups within the West as well, and none more so than Deaf people.

In her book, *Feminist Theology from the Third World*, Ursula King writes: 'Feminist Theology anywhere, whether in the First or the Third World would never have come about without women's full access to theological education up to the highest academic level'[41]. I would like to suggest that women, right from the earliest years of Christianity's history, have always done theology. However, like Deaf people and like many people in Africa, their ideas and experiences of God have been ignored and suppressed by the academy and church. Bearing this in mind, therefore, feminist theology happened without women's access to theological education. It was only when women started to be educated, and could thus read and write and were able to engage with male theology on patriarchal terms that feminist theology began to be taken seriously and to find a place within the academy and church. Access to literacy, therefore, is one way in which an oppressed group can empower themselves. History suggests, then, that written texts have been used by those with access to them to exclude and oppress those without access, and history shows that this includes Deaf people, women, disabled people, black people in the West and Africa, and those from lower social class groups. It is difficult to see, therefore, how Derrida is able to argue that speech has been privileged over writing when written texts have been used as a source of oppression over those whose only mode of communication is speech.

Mukonyora quotes the Ghanaian Theologian, Bediako, who writes, 'Taking the vernacular seriously then, becomes not merely a cultural but also a theological necessity. For it is only through the vernacular that a genuine and lasting theological

---

[39] Hart, K., 'Jacques Derrida (b1930): Introduction', in Ward, G. (ed.), *The Postmodern God: A Theological Reader* (Oxford, 1997), pp.161–2.

[40] Alternative frameworks are described in Kim, K., 'India', in Parratt, J. (ed.), *An Introduction to Third World Theologies* (Cambridge, 2004), pp.48–60.

[41] King, U. (ed.), *Feminist Theology from the Third World* (London, 1994), p.5.

dialogue with culture can take place'[42]. In an interview with Mukonyora, she explains how in the Johane Masowe ekklesia, oral communication is given priority over written books – including the Bible – which are regarded with suspicion[43]. Speech is not given priority in the ecclesiastical context because Apostles (members of the Johane Masowe church) believe that they are closer to meaning and truth when they are speaking, but because literature is regarded as idolatrous. Healey and Sybertz spend a significant part of the beginning of their book, *Towards an African Narrative Theology*, arguing for the validity of a theology which takes place in the realm of orality and they quote the African theologian Mbiti who says, 'African oral theology is a living reality … This form of theology gives the church a certain measure of theological selfhood and independence'[44]. John Parratt in the conclusion to his, *A Reader in African Christian Theology*, argues that African oral theology has been 'claiming increasing attention'[45] by theologians.

Evidence suggests, therefore, that African theologians are endeavouring to establish an agenda in which oral theology, which takes place among ordinary African Christians, can be of benefit to a wider understanding of African theology(ies). Mukonyora explains that, 'for the last two decades at least, African theologians have been trying to face up to the challenge of post-colonialism by drawing attention to traditional African religions and to questions of liberation and the political control of churches'[46]. This process of inculturation both of the Church and theology has been a necessary agenda to establish as African people have attempted to construct an identity which had been marred by over a hundred years of colonial rule. The model of a white imperial Christ, and the theology of *Imitatio Christi* justified an oppressive regime on African people in both theological and ecclesiastical contexts (not to mention social, economic and political contexts). The imperial Christ and his followers took with them as a part of their baggage to Africa, languages, theologies and social ideologies which were based on Western metaphysical frameworks of thought. Inculturation and the process of trying to break free from that baggage involves an increasing attention to oral theology which the theologians above are urging. How, therefore, is Derrida able to claim that speech has been privileged over writing? How does he reach the conclusion that people in the West have always assumed that they were closer to truth and meaning in speech? If this were the case, surely this would be true in theology which is concerned with questions of ultimate truth and ultimate meaning? How can it be that in Africa a methodological framework is only just being set up to include oral theology as an equal partner to written theology if speech has priority already? After all, for a people who communicate orally, if speech was privileged, why would they ever have bothered to try to break free from Western theology written in books and Western metaphysical frameworks

---

[42]   Mukonyora, I.,'The Dramatization of Life and Death by Johane Masowe', 1998, p.192.

[43]   I interviewed Mukonyora while I was in Zimbabwe.

[44]   Healey, J and Sybertz, D., *Towards an African Narrative Theology* (Nairobi, 1996), p.22.

[45]   Parratt, J. (ed.), *A Reader in African Christian Theology*, p.139.

[46]   Mukonyora, I.,'The Dramatization of Life and Death by Johane Masowe', p.191.

of thought? Could Derrida's analysis of Western metaphysical history be wrong? I would like to argue that he most certainly is wrong and I would like to argue this point further with reference to the experiences of Deaf people.

Literacy is Power!

It is necessary to ask that if Derrida argues that Western metaphysical frameworks privilege speech over writing, about whom is Derrida himself writing? The arguments in this chapter show that it is an elite group of people with access to literary abilities, abilities which give power which has been abused[47]! For people who find access to literacy and spoken language difficult, Deaf people's theology has thus been marginalized in the churches and by the academy. Unlike the women whom King describes, Deaf people cannot access theological education as it is currently delivered, in order to empower themselves, because such education is only available for those with high levels of literacy. Whilst women have the capacity to learn written languages equally with men, Deaf people are not able to do so on an equal level to hearing people. Theology then must free itself from the confines of literacy and embrace other methods of communication such as British Sign Language. Begbie also argues this in relation to the arts[48] and the point is relevant also to such groups as the church of Johane Masowe in Zimbabwe. The result can only be that theology will be richer with greater insights gained into the God who is the subject of theological enquiry.

Reconstructing Deaf Theology from Deaf Perspectives

Deaf Church as the Context of Deaf Theology

In chapter 1 I explained that Deaf churches are usually a part of some other Church denomination and in chapter 6, I will be focusing on Deaf perspectives on ecclesiology. However, I would like to argue here that Deaf churches as ekklesia is the context from which Deaf theology emerges. In attempting to understand the nature of Deaf churches it is necessary to understand firstly what we mean by 'Deaf' and then what is meant by 'churches'. The first of these has been dealt with in the first and second chapters of this book as well as elsewhere throughout. But what is 'the Church'? Dulles offers a variety of models of what the Church is and he argues that despite being Catholic himself, his arguments draws on an ecumenical approach[49]. One of the models he discusses is that of the Church as institution. While recognizing some of the limitations of this model, he argues, 'The Church of Christ does not exist in this world without an organization or structure that analogously resembles the

---

[47]   Chadwick argues that one of the contributing factors to the Reformation as Christians struggled to free themselves from Roman power was the greater availability of books and the increased knowledge that followed. Chadwick, O., *The Reformation* (London, 1964), pp.29–30.

[48]   Begbie, J., *Beholding the Glory* (London, 2000), pp.xi–xv.

[49]   Dulles, A., *Models of the Church: A Critical Assessment of the Church in all its Aspects*. Second Edition (Dublin, 1987), p.11.

organization of other human societies'[50]. This perspective is debatable as one could challenge his assumption that the Church is a human society resembling others societies. Some may argue that this is part of the Church's problem of operating effectively because it has power structures and hierarchies open to the same abuses as secular institutions when the Gospels speak of Jesus founding a kingdom that is different from the powers of the earth (John 18.36). It is often the power structures of churches that have left Deaf people on the margins and continue to patronize Deaf people by asking 'what can we do to help and include them in our church' rather than empowering Deaf people to be a church in culturally appropriate ways. As we will see when I discuss liturgy (also in chapter 6), access to worship for Deaf people has often been on hearing people's terms using hearing people's ways of worshipping.

In both Britain and Zimbabwe, Deaf People congregate as churches for worship, prayer, discussion, and fellowship. As Deaf people of faith meet together in this way, they thus become an 'ekklesia' which will here be referred to as a Deaf church. In Britain and Zimbabwe these Deaf churches are usually a part of a wider network of churches. In Britain, Deaf churches are a part of either the Roman Catholic Church, the Anglican Church or are part of a series of independent groups which make up the Hands Together Network. As Deaf people think about God in their own situations and contexts and how he relates to them, then Deaf People are doing theology and are thus theologians. Deaf people also often engage with other theologies and critique them from their own perspective. This occurs, not from the academic reading of theological texts, but as they interact with other Deaf churches as well as with hearing churches and the theological perspectives that develop and emerge from them.

Deaf Theology: An Academic Enterprise?

To suggest that theology for the Deaf Community is an academic undertaking, the aim of which is nothing more than purely academic understanding, would be to suggest nonsense. Due to the unhelpful educational approaches used by Deaf schools and the arts faculties of most universities in Britain, few Deaf people have been able to secure a place at university to study an arts subject. Among those who do get to university, many will choose to study science or engineering subjects undoubtedly due to the reality that intelligence does not necessarily need to be complemented by a good standard of English[51] – a skill less important in some other disciplines[52]. It is arguable also, that the notion of seeking knowledge for its own sake is not really part of Deaf culture. The academic pursuit of theology, therefore, is irrelevant to the Deaf community as Deaf people rarely have the opportunity to obtain the skills needed for such an academic pursuit or the context in which to interact with academic theologians.

---

[50]   *Ibid.*, p.10.

[51]   Pinker, S., *The Language Instinct* (London, 1994), pp.51–3.

[52]   In four years working in three Higher Education Institutions with Deaf people, c.90 per cent of all students were studying in science or engineering faculties.

Deaf People and the Notion of Context

As Deaf churches think about God, they of course do so from their own particular perspectives. However, rather than trying to disguise the reality of this as church structures have tried to do by claiming that their perspectives were universal truths, Deaf people recognize that any viewpoint which they have about God comes out of a particular context. When a group of people is on the margins of society, with perspectives that society constantly rejects (for example, the idea that God is Deaf), the recognition that ideas are based on and emerge out of culture and experience is inevitable. The fact that sign language cannot be written down also means that once an idea is formulated, it can never be 'set in stone' for all time and so theology in the Deaf community is always contextual.

Deaf Theology: Faith Seeking Understanding?

Theology, as it is done by most Deaf churches, is often not a conscious activity. Sometimes organized discussions or retreats take place which include only Deaf people. However, Deaf people's understanding of God does not always emerge out of the conscious decisions of Deaf people to think about God and come up with a solution to an issue or problem, in the same way in which many of the Creeds of the Church were formulated, for example. Rather, theology as the activity of Deaf churches, as with most hearing churches, is a process which emerges with no specified prior agenda. Thus Deaf churches are people of faith, but their 'seeking' occurs in response to given situations which will result in unplanned discussions and thinking. This is Theos ... Logos, discussion and debate about God for Deaf people. The consequences for those who digress from the views of the majority in the Church today are not as serious as they were for the so called 'heretics' after the councils of the early Church. However, there are clear parallels with the way theology emerged and developed in the early churches, as it does among Deaf people now, out of the experiences and debate of the community.

I would like to suggest also that Deaf people's theology is not necessarily an activity which desires 'understanding' either, although this again may be part of Deaf theology. In looking at theology through the arts, Jeremy Begbie rewrites Anselm's phrase as 'faith seeking deeper wisdom' and he goes on to say that theology has 'typically been dazzled by a kind of intellectualism, where the mind is effectively divorced from other parts of humanity and forced to work at a high level of abstraction with a very restricted set of tools'[53]. Begbie argues that this has led to the exclusion of the arts from theology, but this is not all that is excluded. Deaf people are a people of vision and touch. The very idea that Christian faith and theology could possibly be divorced from everyday life is thus inconceivable to Deaf people. It is no wonder then, if Begbie's analysis of theology is correct, that Deaf people have been marginalized in theology for so long. Theology for Deaf people, as for people in many other contexts, cannot be only about understanding but about moving deeper into relationship with God as a result of life and experience.

---

[53] Begbie, J., *Beholding the Glory*, p.xii.

The Role of Reason in Deaf Theology

To what extent does the communication of the experience of, and thinking about God need to be 'reasonable'? Parratt has suggested that, 'there will always be something of the transcendent about the theological task'[54]. He goes on to argue, however, that 'it [theology] has to present a "reasonable" account of Christian belief and convictions'[55]. Of course Deaf people's theology is not based on beliefs which they cannot reasonably accept, but the significance of reason cannot be so prominent for Deaf people's theology. An example from a different group of people helps to demonstrate this point.

A few years ago, I spent three months working with adults who were from birth Deafblind with multiple learning disabilities. These adults had no learned rational capacities with no linguistic capabilities, other than being able to sign a few gestures. Part of the responsibility given to those of us who acted as carers was to help with their spiritual development. As a part of this programme, these adults sometimes went with their carers into their local church. For some of these adults, upon entering this building, their behaviour would change quite radically in relation to what it was usually like. For example, one loved to chew wood, but made no indication of trying to chew the wood of the pews. In any other context she would always try to chew wood. In the church, did this Deafblind adult encounter something of God and respond to it? This can never be known, but if she did, it may be argued that the respect she showed for that building was a communication of her encounter. Her communication, which was part of one of Parratt's definitions of theology given earlier, was by no means a logical argument but an expression of something transcendent and in turn may inform others in their theological seeking.

Deaf people's theology as it is expressed and communicated is at times mysterious (for example, feeling God with them in a physical way) and at times reasonable (for example, considered arguments challenging discrimination in employment). I would here, then, like to suggest that theology for Deaf people is not just about giving an account of their Christian beliefs but is also about expressing something of the mysterious encounter of God. Theology for Deaf people, therefore, involves reasonable 'thinking about God', but it is also about the expression of the 'encounter with mystery'[56].

The Primary Tools of Deaf Theology: Faith Seeking Life

Parratt explains that 'all theology is a human activity, albeit done under the guidance of the Spirit of God'[57]. In this statement, Parratt poignantly reminds us again that all theology is contextual, but with it also comes a transcendent element. The Element of the Transcendent and Contextuality are arguably the two most important tools in

---

[54]   Parratt, J., *A Guide to Doing Theology*, p.7.

[55]   *Ibid.*, p.7.

[56]   These two phrases are taken from the titles of the following books: Solle, D., *Thinking about God* (London, 1990) and Young, F., *Encounter with Mystery* (London, 1997).

[57]   Parratt. J., *A Guide to Doing Theology*, p.93.

the theology of Deaf people, which can more appropriately be named, 'Revelation' and 'Experience' respectively. These two resources of Deaf people's theology are complemented by 'reflection', defined here as 'thinking about revelation and experience'. However, it is essential that reflection is differentiated from reason. As mentioned above, some Deaf people explain that at times they have felt as though God is with them in a very physical way. Whilst Deaf people reflect on this experience of the transcendent with them, it is difficult to be able to give a reasoned account and explanation of such an encounter. On the other hand, they can reflect on the experience and learn from it. Reflection, therefore, is the preferred term in relation to Deaf people's thinking about God.

There are other resources which also feed into Deaf people's theology among which are church traditions, hearing culture and hearing people's theology. For example, like Deaf people, many of those who attend hearing churches will never have read the creed formulated at the council of Chalcedon outlining Christological doctrine. However, they will have a vague understanding of this doctrine as it forms part of the faith which they confess in other creeds, hymns and liturgies and by the transmission of faith through preaching and discussion. Deaf people also are aware of church traditions, but not because they have spent time reading the creeds and Church canons in detail, but because they form part of the generally agreed understanding of God present within the Christian churches which is transmitted by, to, and among Deaf people. Deaf people are also influenced by the culture and theology of hearing people. Because Deaf people are a minority group living among a larger, dominating group, they cannot help but be influenced by the larger group's culture and theology. Being influenced by this culture and theology does not mean that Deaf people simply accept it and take it on board. Rather, they engage with it and enter into dialogue with it from the perspectives of their own experiences. Thus this dialogue contributes to their own thinking about God but it may do so by Deaf people rejecting or embracing all or part of some aspect of hearing culture and theology.

Revelation

Revelation, then, as a resource for Deaf people's theology, includes the transcendent element of theology and this incarnates itself in a number of ways which will be described below.

At a service in the Deaf church in Birmingham, the preacher signed about an experience of walking in the hills near to her home. She explained that as she was walking, the beauty of her surroundings took her breath away. She continued, 'as I was walking, I felt as though God was with me and all about me. With me in the beauty of what I could see.' This sermon evoked an extraordinary response from the congregation for, while sermons in Deaf churches usually involve interaction, those watching vigorously signed responses of recognition from their own experiences and told of those experiences. Such encounters with God in nature reveal some important insights into the God of Deaf theology.

Firstly, these people's experiences suggested that they have a strong awareness of the creative abilities of God. These abilities are used to create beauty which can be seen and felt and which have the potential to exhilarate human beings. Secondly, these experiences point towards the idea, which will be argued in detail in chapter 5 and chapter 7, that while Deaf people may believe in a transcendent God, for him to have any relevance to Deaf people, he must reveal himself in ways which Deaf people can relate to. Thus to be able to discern something of God in nature is important not only in that it reveals the creator God, but it also reveals a God who relates to, and understands the needs of Deaf people in relating to him.

Revelation is also experienced by Deaf people in prayer and worship. At the risk of repetition, Deaf people have claimed that they are able to feel something of God with them in a physical way, often in the context of private prayer. This again reveals a God who is close to and involved with his creation as shown by the recognition of God in nature. This also suggests again that God is able to relate to Deaf people, this time not through the visual but entirely through touch. Vision and touch are the primary means of communication for Deaf people and they believe that God is able to communicate with them through both.

Deaf people also suggest that revelation takes place through encounters with or stories about other people. Frequently in sermons, stories are told about people who have been significant figures in history or in society today. For example, I have often seen stories signed about such figures as Mother Teresa during sermons, as a person who revealed Christ in her care of others. Occasionally, I have seen Deaf people signing about important figures in Deaf history such as Charles Michel Abbé de l'Epée, the eighteenth-century pioneer of sign language who was Christ-like in his understanding of Deaf people's communication. In these figures, Deaf people see something of God's compassion and love for humanity and his solidarity with marginalized peoples. Meeting other people in everyday contexts can also be significant. Communication with other people, the use of touch among human beings, can create the possibility of an encounter with the Divine, and all of this resonates with Jesus' words: 'just as you did it to one of the least of these who are members of my family, you did it to me' (Matthew 25.40).

The Bible is also seen as a part of revelation. Whilst the written text of the Bible as it stands is largely inaccessible to Deaf people, it is still seen as an important expression of the Divine by Deaf people. However, I would argue that the Bible seems only to become useful when it is made Deaf. I will not address this subject in detail here as it will be addressed fully in the next chapter. Suffice to say, however, that it is believed that the Bible does help to reveal something of God because God was key in its construction, but that it is only relevant when the Gospel message is freed from the text and allowed to engage with Deaf people's experience.

Experience

Deaf experience is to some extent an ambiguous notion, as the experiences of each Deaf person differs from those of anyone else. However, some experiences are shared and it is these areas and their contribution to the formation of Deaf people's theology which I would like here to address.

The experience of oppression and discrimination are shared by most if not all Deaf people in Britain, even if the form it takes differs from person to person. These experiences very much form the ways in which Deaf people think about God. If God is involved with and present in creation then in dialogue with revelation, thinking occurs in relation to God and oppression. To think of a God who is on the side of Deaf people, who relates to their ways of expressing themselves, who is himself Deaf, is potentially liberating to Deaf people. Not only does such a notion of God ascribe value to Deaf people, if God is on their side and is indeed Deaf, then their experience of oppression and discrimination must be wrong and worth challenging.

History is also a major factor in terms of Deaf people's experiences. Much of Deaf history in Britain focuses on issues relating to education and language (see chapters 1 and 2). Not all of Deaf history is negative, however, and many refer today to Deaf and hearing French pioneers of sign language in the eighteenth century, as a foundation upon which to argue for recognition of sign languages as languages in their own rights with equal capacities for communication as spoken languages.

Deaf culture also influences theology. Sign language as the preferred language of Deaf people clearly influences the formulation and expression of theology as will be explored further later. Being Deaf in a hearing world also has the potential to isolate Deaf people. The notion of the Deaf community is therefore significant for Deaf people as they interact with each other and form relationships in Deaf clubs, churches and groups. McDonough has pointed out that he does not 'believe that a culturally deaf person is able to live purely in a hearing world for many years without experiencing the desire to be with people they can identify themselves with'[58]. Thus the notion of being together as an ekklesia, has great significance for Deaf people because as Alker has pointed out, the Deaf community find 'support, encouragement or inspiration from being part of that particular community'[59]. Thus the Deaf community is important not only as a context in which theology is formulated, but also in terms of its impact on the development of theologies which value community and human relationships.

Revelation and Experience: A Summary

Deaf Theology, therefore, is primarily shaped by the contribution of revelation, which is both received from others and encountered in prayer, nature and other people, as well as the contribution of historical, contemporary and cultural experience. Revelation and experience, and the various aspects of each, should by no means be treated as separate resources in the development of Deaf people's theology, but rather as interrelated with and dependent on each other. The encounter of God in nature, prayer and other people is always reflected on in the light of historical and cultural experiences, and consequently these experiences attach significance to and inform the encounter with the Transcendent. Thus to believe in a God who is able to engage with and understand the needs of Deaf people and who takes the trouble to

---

[58]   McDonough, P., 'The Place of Deaf People in the Church – A Deaf Priest's View', in International Ecumenical Working Group, *The Place of Deaf People in the Church* (Northampton, 1996), p.41.

[59]   Alker, D., 'The Changing Deaf Communities', in International Ecumenical Working Group, *The Place of Deaf People in the Church* (Northampton, 1996), p.178.

reveal this, expresses to Deaf people something of the nature of the God who affirms who Deaf people are and inspires their struggle for liberation. I would finally suggest that there is no given formula to Deaf people's theology. I am always suspicious of models or formulas for doing theology such as Green's pastoral cycle[60], though I use it as a reflective tool in my research methods, or those theologies which argue that they start from the ground up or visa versa. Deaf people's theology does not always start with either revelation or experience, but always involves a constant creative dialogue between the two which allows for purposeful interaction between context and the Transcendent.

Expressing Deaf Theology

Discovering Theology Through Signs

It is my view that in sign language in Britain and Zimbabwe specific signs which refer to God, or any other aspect of theology, can be divided into two categories. The first group of signs are based on visual criteria – signs which represent a visual or physical characteristic of a person, or an object associated with an idea. By visual and physical I mean here something which could be seen, touched or experienced. Examples of these signs include those which refer to Jesus, Mary, Joseph, Spirit, and Church ('Jesus' pointing to the wounds from the crucifixion in his hands, 'Mary' the image of her headwear as on many paintings, 'Joseph' in Britain is often represented by a beard, and in Zimbabwe, by a crown, 'Spirit' is represented by breath, and 'Church' representing the technique of ringing bells, and in Zimbabwe by a sign representing the congregation). The second group of signs are more conceptual in that rather than describing a visual or physical characteristic, they aim to express a particular understanding about God by visually representing an idea. This group of signs use such language techniques as classifiers and placement (described in chapter 2). For example, the sign for the Trinity is three persons becoming one. The Birmingham sign for Emmanuel is God as a person coming from heaven (located high up above the forehead) down to earth (by the lower chest).

In what ways can these two categories of signs be useful in terms of gaining an insight into the theology of Deaf people? The sign for Jesus is helpful in responding to this question which in Britain and many other contexts is a sign which points to the wounds in his hands. It is interesting that this particular feature of Jesus should be chosen as the sign for him, rather than say a beard or a blue robe, which are characteristics that appear in so many pictures of Jesus. Other images which could have been used may include Jesus as a good shepherd, a light, a crown to show him as a king, and so on. Rather, however, the sign which is used for Jesus is a sign which points to his wounds evoking images of the cross and suffering and, as Eiesland has pointed out, that in the resurrected Jesus, the wounds of the cross,

---

[60]   Outlined in Green, L., *Lets Do Theology*, pp.24–41, and expanded in the remainder of the book.

which become an impairment, remain with him and are thus glorified[61]. With this in mind, the sign for Jesus is no longer simply a visual representation of a physical characteristic, but rather it points to a Deaf understanding of a Jesus whose identity is tied up with both suffering and resurrection hope, with oppression, and glory in impairment. Jesus then becomes someone with whom Deaf people identify, as their own identity so often is tied up with Deafness, which brings oppression and hope in which their Deafness remains with them and is understood as something positive as are ultimately the wounds of Christ.

Among the conceptual signs which are used by Deaf people is that which expresses the Trinity. This sign involves three fingers standing upright on the right hand. They then move under the left hand during which the three fingers become one. The fingers here are significant, as vertical fingers are generally used as classifiers which represent persons. Deaf people thus identify the persons of the Trinity as people in human terms, arguably because, like hearing people, Deaf people only have human language and experience with which to express their ideas about God. The idea of three *persons* in the Trinity, however, perhaps also demonstrates the very tangible, physical and visual way in which Deaf people think about God, in that the notion of the persons of the Trinity as physical beings emerges out of a culture that thinks in physical and visual ways. The Deaf Trinity by no means reduces God's divinity by being expressed in a physical way, but rather it simply illustrates the influence of Deaf experience on their theology whilst recognizing the limitations of language. Begbie has pointed out that it is much harder to describe the Trinity or the two natures of Christ visually because space cannot be entirely occupied by two things at the same time[62]. I suggest that this is arguably a hearing way of thinking, as Deaf people do not think in terms of a picture being constructed as a series of parts which cannot occupy the same space. Rather, they are more concerned with and focus on the whole picture which sign language creates. In visual terms, therefore, this sign of the Trinity should not be understood as a *process* in which three *become* one at separate times. In the grammar of sign language, the use of this sign does not indicate any notion of time. Rather the sign attempts to present a whole picture which should be understood in its entirety. Thus the Deaf Trinity consists of both three people and one person in dynamic movement in one picture.

Above, then, are two examples of how signs themselves can be used to express theological ideas by Deaf people. These two examples suffice to demonstrate that the very language which Deaf people use to communicate can be and is significant in trying to get to grips with their ideas and concepts of God. The same is true in spoken languages also, as difficulties have arisen in the translation of Western concepts into the indigenous Zimbabwean language of Shona. For example, the word holiness has at least two possible translations in Shona. The first, 'Unoyera', is a word from pagan religion which indicates that what is being described is a god (which is also different to a Western concept of a god). The second is 'Mutzimo' which relates to the ancestors – those with the power and discretion to cause suffering or prosperity – and as Healey and Sybertz explain, 'those who become ancestors must have lived

---

61   Eiesland, N., *The Disabled God*, p.87.
62   Begbie, J., *Beholding the Glory*, pp.144–6.

exemplary lives'[63]. Thus because there is no direct translation from English to Shona, and consequently words which have cultural significance need to be used, the Shona understanding of God as holy, while maybe having some points of connection, will at other times be different to the English understanding. Likewise, one cannot, therefore, begin to understand the nature of Deaf theology unless one is familiar with sign language and Deaf culture.

Deaf People and Story-telling and Drama

Story-telling and the use of drama to express theological ideas are two slightly different methods of communication, but are close enough to merit discussion together in this context. Story-telling is a significant aspect of Deaf culture, and is something at which many Deaf people are particularly adept. Because of the nature of sign language, the result is that as stories are told they can often become dramatic in terms of the variety of expression used and the animation with which such stories are told. Drama is often used as a way of telling a biblical story, but this will be discussed in more detail in the next chapter.

Any meaning a story told by Deaf people may have is invariably entirely obvious. It is therefore rare that allegory and thus some of the parables are used, as these methods of telling stories often have little meaning to Deaf people. Thus in conversation with Deaf people, they implied that the parable of the sower, for example, has more to do with farming techniques than the eschatological significance which Jesus attaches to it. The meaning behind the story of the Good Samaritan, however, was obvious to Deaf people: it is about loving God and neighbour through actions. Stories then tend to be of a more literal nature with significance which needs little or no explanation.

The use of stories and drama in theology is by no means unique to Deaf people. Green explains how in Brazil, José Marins was working with base communities, which consisted of many people who were illiterate and thus unable to read the Bible. Green comments that they will 'share stories and feelings about Jesus that often turn out to be scripturally rooted although probably not precise'[64]. Other contexts in which stories are used is demonstrated by Healey and Sybertz, who show that in many parts of Africa, stories which reflect African experience are told among various groups which have deep theological meaning. One of the stories they tell is of a boy who is being suffocated by a python. No-one is able to save the boy until his mother wrestles with the python and sets the boy free. Such a feat is extraordinary and in most circumstances would be impossible, but the story concludes, 'where there is love, anything is possible'[65]. The experience used here is one of bravery for the sake of love. The theological meaning is that when a human being has love for another, there is nothing which cannot be achieved.

I would suggest that Deaf people would relate to a story such as this and that they too tell stories which have theological significance. For example, one Deaf person

---

[63]   Healey, J. and Sybertz, D., *Towards an African Narrative Theology*, p.211.
[64]   Green, L., *Lets Do Theology*, p.141.
[65]   Healey, J and Sybertz, D., *Towards an African Narrative Theology*, p.32.

who had visited India told the story in a sermon of a Deaf man who had been involved in setting up a number of Deaf churches in Tamil Nadu. This man had received no financial or other support from the mainstream Church and had thus been forced to finance the churches himself, despite having little money. She explained how Deafness in India is understood to be entirely negative and thus how Deaf people are marginalized. By creating Deaf churches, this Deaf man had enabled many other Deaf people to find a home where they felt safe and where God and others accepted them in their Deaf condition. The result of this man's actions was that many Deaf people in that region had become Christians. The significance of this story was that it is important to have courage like this Deaf man to witness to God's love, even when the rest of society constantly puts you down and makes you feel inadequate. Stories, therefore, play a key role in communicating theological ideas.

Towards a *Deaf*inition of Theology

Musopole argues that the central principle for theology in Africa is 'LIFE[66]', not reason and that for him, 'theology is concerned with what I call the with-us-ness of God in the cosmos'[67]. I suggest that for Deaf people, this is also what they are concerned with. This is why Deaf theology cannot be about Faith Seeking Understanding, nor can it be confined by reason, because in their context of oppression, LIFE in solidarity with the God who is with them is their central principle in which understanding and reason *may* play a role. Therefore, Deaf theology is better summed up as 'Faith Seeking LIFE' and life in all its abundance (John 10.10). Deaf people seek life as they share the desire to be liberated from the domination of hearing people into a new way of being, in which Deaf people can be free to be themselves and to celebrate their humanity as a part of the good creation of God. Finding creative ways of communicating this is thus an important task for Deaf theology. In line with contextual theology, Deaf churches as ekklesia, are those who do theology. Finally, because Deaf people seek life, their theology becomes concerned with relationship, with God, among themselves, and with other humans as they seek freedom in these relationships.

Conclusion

This chapter, therefore, has endeavoured to consider the place of Deaf theology within the wider theological arena, to consider ways of making that arena more inclusive, and outlined the ways in which Deaf people do theology. In doing so, I have argued for a theology which is concerned with faith seeking life which is free from the confines of reason and literacy. I have also argued that it is appropriate that literary and non-literary resources for doing and ways of communicating theology should be understood as equal partners, which can provide a context in which Deaf and hearing theology may be able to engage with each other more fully and enrich

---

[66] Musopole, A., 'Needed: a Theology Cooked in an African Pot', p.9.
[67] *Ibid.*, p.8.

each other. Without this, Deaf people's theology remains on the margins of theology and the Church, which ultimately disadvantages both Deaf and hearing people. Deaf people are by no means unique in their exclusion by the traditional definitions and practices of academic and ecclesiastical theologians, but their potential contribution to theology is unique in terms of both its content and how it is communicated. In the next chapter, I aim to examine more closely Deaf people's use of the Bible and the narratives and images it contains because this represents an important dimension of Deaf theology, albeit complex, that merits further discussion.

Chapter 5

'Anyone who has Ears, Let them Hear ...'
... But what about Deaf People?

Introduction

The chapter that follows focuses on Deaf people's use and, to some extent, hearing people's misuse of the Bible. I have chosen to look at the Bible as a source for Deaf theology in a separate chapter because, despite the Bible being a text and therefore largely inaccessible to Deaf people, the biblical narratives are to some extent important to and inform Deaf people in their theology. Their use of the Bible is somewhat complicated and ambiguous, however. In what follows I aim to address three things. Firstly, the ways in which Deaf people may feel alienated from or included by the theological language and imagery of the Bible. Secondly, to grapple with the question of whether the Bible is at all needed in theology by Deaf people or, indeed, anyone else. Thirdly, to examine, using examples, the role the Bible plays in forming and informing their theological thinking.

Deaf People's Alienation from the Bible

In his book *In the Beginning there was Darkness* (2001), John Hull has written about the different way he began to read the Bible after he became blind from the way he read it when he was sighted. He explains, 'When I was sighted, I read the Bible as a sighted person because I was embedded in the sighted world. It did not occur to me that I was sighted; I was just a normal person'[1]. After becoming blind he realized that he had not only read the Bible from the perspective of a sighted person, but that the Bible itself was written by sighted people. This became problematic for him not only because of the Bible's use of sighted images of light and darkness, but also because blindness is frequently used as a metaphor of insensitivity and ignorance[2]. Much of the Bible and its influence on the Christian tradition became a barrier or a 'stumbling block'[3] to him as a blind person. Instead of calling for an abandonment of the Bible, Hull acknowledges that this collection of books has continuing relevance in the Christian tradition and so he enters into what he describes as a 'conversation with the Bible'[4]. In this 'conversation' he reflects on the

---

[1]   Hull, J.M., *In the Beginning there was Darkness* (London, 2001), p.3.

[2]   *Ibid.*, pp.1–4 and pp.67–94.

[3]   Ref. to Leviticus 19.14: 'You shall not revile the deaf or put a stumbling block before the blind'.

[4]   Hull, J.M., *In the Beginning there was Darkness*, p.3.

experiences of blind characters in the Bible, the language of light and sight and their application to the nature of God, the use of blindness as a metaphor, the attitude of Jesus towards blind people, and Jesus' own temporary experience of blindness when he is blindfolded following his arrest.

Hull's sense of alienation from the pages of the Bible is one shared by many Deaf people. This alienation may be felt because the Bible emerges out of hearing people's experiences and makes use of hearing language and images for God, so that God appears to be a very hearing reality. It also does not say very much that is affirming of Deaf people nor does it portray Deaf characters in a very positive way. Alienation may further be felt because many Deaf people struggle with acquiring reading skills (a hearing phenomenon) and so not only the content but also the media through which that content is expressed may cause alienation. Below are three sets of examples of why some Deaf people have said they have felt that the Bible is alienating and exclusive of them, in terms of the theology, language and imagery it contains.

God with No Body or Face

Exodus 3.1–6 tells the beginning of the story of the encounter between Moses and the Lord at the burning bush on Mount Horeb. On hearing that God is talking to Moses, Moses hid his face (v.6). To hide one's face in fear, as Moses does at the burning bush, is to behave like a hearing person who is afraid and would not reflect the actions of the average Deaf person who might find themselves in a similar situation. If Moses had been Deaf, it is likely that he would have continued looking straight at the bush, even if he was afraid, because by covering his face as a Deaf person, he would be cut off from what was happening around him, a prospect that could only add to the fright of the talking bush itself. On the one or two occasions when I have seen this narrative signed by a Deaf person, they have usually been faithful to the text and hide their face, but in the next moment, they lift their face and look up again. Information is received and conversation takes place in visual and spatial realms for Deaf people who need their eyes, face and hands to be free for both. The presence of God may be frightening, but Deaf people must still face God to be able to communicate with him.

Later in Exodus Moses asks to see God's glory. The initial fear experienced at the first encounter with the Lord is perhaps a natural reaction but later Moses seems to grow more confident as he talks with God 'face to face' (Exodus 33.11), although, as we see later, he clearly does not see God's face. Moses' request to see God's glory is only agreed in part because the Lord explains that Moses can only see God's back because no person can see God's face and live. John Hull interprets Exodus 33.21–23 as a passage which has potential significance to partially sighted people. He explains that partially sighted people often cannot see the detail of human faces but they can see a body. He argues that only being allowed to see God's back and not his face suggests that, 'because you cannot see the face, you are not banished from the presence. There is a place for you. It is a place near God'[5]. This 'unseeableness' of God is carried through into the hymns and traditions of the Church as God is

---

[5]   *Ibid.*, p.138.

described in one hymn as, 'Immortal, invisible, God only wise, in light inaccessible hid from our eyes'[6].

Hull's interpretation of the passage from Exodus 33 is a clear reminder of the importance of the multiplicity and cultural particularity of images of God which are needed for theology to be meaningful to all people. This multiplicity may not be complete in the pages of the Bible. The idea that God's face is unseeable does not suggest that there is a place near to God for Deaf people, but that God is an inaccessible being with whom they cannot communicate. Deaf people rely on the face in both BSL and when they are lip-reading. Without face to face contact, Deaf people have a major difficulty in entering into any kind of relationship with God or anyone else. For these reasons Deaf people do not symbolically bow their heads, close their eyes or put their hands together to pray, because such behaviour restricts communication. If God is 'immortal, invisible ... hid from our eyes' he is also irrelevant to Deaf people. For God to be accessible and relevant, he must be a God who can be seen 'face to face' and whose presence can be touched and experienced.

If God cannot be seen, the notion that 'God is spirit' (John 4.24) then makes him almost completely inaccessible to Deaf people. The idea of God as spirit and the notion of experiencing the *Holy Spirit* should be separated here. To say that God *is* spirit is to make an ontological statement about the nature of the whole of God. The Holy Spirit is a revelation of the nature of God which is incomplete without the other two persons of the Trinity. A spirit has no physical presence or body and thus it cannot be seen or touched. Sight and touch are the two primary ways in which Deaf people relate to others and without these, communication and relationship is impossible.

John Parratt argues that, 'the assumption of Christian theology ... is that God by His very nature has a special relationship with human beings and that revelation is part and parcel of that relationship'[7]. God's communication with humanity and humanity's communication with God are the foundation of theological enquiry. Without this element of relationship, the study of God is simply a historical or literary exercise in which faith is irrelevant to human existence. Such hearing images in the Bible such as those described above has often made God a reality with whom it is impossible for Deaf people to be in relationship. If he cannot be seen and he cannot be touched, and even if God is mediated by hearing people, it seems difficult to understand how God can have a special relationship with those who are Deaf. There are Deaf people of faith, however, which suggests that the picture of God which hearing people have spoken and written about and presented as 'Truth', is not the *whole* picture.

God is a Talking Ear

The language of God's speech to humanity is a language which is as prevalent today as at the time of Samuel in the Old Testament. Clergy, in discussing their vocation, often talk about a 'call' from God similar to that of Samuel. They are not necessarily

---

[6]   Smith, W.C., 'Immortal, invisible', in *Mission Praise* (London, 1990), No.327.
[7]   Parratt, J., *A Guide to Doing Theology* (London, 1996), pp.4–5.

referring to a voice which is literally heard, but are generally using the language of speech and hearing as metaphors. To be 'called' in secular terms involves at least two people. One makes an audible gesture such as saying a person's name or making their phone ring and, upon hearing that call, it causes the other person to respond. Likewise, some Christians may talk about a 'word from the Lord' as a way of expressing that they believe God has told them something, for example, through the Bible. Other Christians expound spiritualities which encourage people to listen to the 'still small voice' (1 Kings 19.12) of God which comes after the earthquake. The theology of the Word, discussed in brief at the beginning of this work, further reinforces the alienation of Deaf people. However, despite the inappropriateness of the metaphor of the Word for the Deaf Community, the first glimpse of God's interest in them is present in John's prologue when the Word becomes flesh; the speech of God can be touched, felt and seen as well as heard.

Metaphors, as they are understood by hearing people, rarely have any meaning to Deaf people as they are a linguistic characteristic that is peculiar to hearing people. When Deaf people read them in the Bible or see them signed in church, they often interpret them literally. Occasionally, I have been asked by Deaf people, 'What does God's voice sound like?' They are surprised when they discover that I have no more of an idea than they do of what God's voice is like. The language and culture of hearing people in which so much of the Christian tradition has been transmitted can truly alienate Deaf people from God, because they see God as having a special relationship with hearing people that excludes Deaf people because God communicates with them by speaking to them directly.

Not only does the Bible imply that God relates to human beings primarily through speech, liturgical language often suggests that God prefers to listen to speech as well. 'Hear our prayer' is a common petition made to God during intercessions in the Church of England's liturgy[8] while in some Methodist orders of service, the petition is: 'Lord, hear us. Lord, graciously hear us'[9]. Whilst the language of speech and hearing may be metaphorical, many Christians forget that, and the over-emphasis on this language may lead one to conclude that God is little more than a talking ear. Is that a metaphor we would want exclusively or even predominantly to use for God?

The Lord Gives and the Lord Takes Away

It may be suggested that the way God overcomes the problem of communication with Deaf people, that we have so far seen that the Bible suggests, is to eliminate Deafness. Mark 7.31–37 would appear to be a prime example. There are remarkably few characters in the Bible who have any kind of hearing loss from which to draw examples, particularly in comparison to the numbers of those who were blind or had leprosy. Psalm 58.4–5 features a deaf adder who is particularly cunning in being able to stop its ears so that it does not hear the voice of snake charmers. This is the only time at which deafness in the Bible is at all seen to have any advantages. It is

---

8   Church of England, *Common Worship* (London, 2000), p.214.
9   Methodist Church, *The Methodist Worship Book* (Peterborough, 1999). p.188. This is also used as an alternative in Church of England. *Common Worship*, p.214.

interesting that not hearing only provides advantages to a serpent, an Old Testament symbol of the Devil and the enemy of humanity (see Genesis 3.15).

Isaiah makes reference to 'the deaf' on numerous occasions but generally in the wider context of eschatological prophecies about when the 'ears of the deaf will be opened' (See Isaiah 29.18; 35.5). These prophecies are later picked up in Matthew 11.5 and Luke 7.22. In Matthew 11.3–5 Jesus instructs the disciples of John the Baptist to tell John what they have heard and seen, because these were signs that John would recognize as the actions of the 'one who is to come' (v.3). In verse 5, one of the indications that Jesus is 'the one' is that 'the deaf hear', fulfilling the prophecies of Isaiah. The recovery of hearing for Deaf people is seen in the Bible as an eschatological sign of the Kingdom of God. For many Deaf people, however, Deafness is not seen as a problem which needs to be eliminated. It is the social attitudes towards Deafness which need to be transformed, Deaf people argue. Many (though by no means all) do not want to become hearing people. They believe that their cultural identity, which Deafness gives them, forms a part of who they are and to lose their Deafness would be to become a different person beyond recognition. They would use a different language and view and interpret the world differently. Some Deaf people have also informed me that they would not particularly want to be hearing in heaven either. The Deaf experience and some biblical perspectives on Deafness are sometimes miles apart.

Many critics of the Christian tradition from among disabled people have pointed to how the Bible suggests that impairment is a consequence of human sin[10]. This notion is particularly evident in some of the healing narratives of the Gospels. More careful readings of some of the biblical narratives have shown that the link between sin and impairment is much more ambiguous and was not particularly the position held by Jesus[11]. For example, in John 9.3, Jesus confirms that neither the sin of the man nor that of his parents had caused him to be blind. In neither of the two narratives where a Deaf person is healed (Mark 7.31–37; 9.14–32) is any connection made between sin and the condition of Deafness[12]. Only in Micah 7.16 is the loss of hearing given as a punishment to the nations when they see the 'marvellous things of God' (v.15) and realize what they have done wrong.

Attitudes today about impairment and sin being linked prevail among many groups of people. Some ask of parents of disabled children 'what have they done to deserve a child like that' and some disabled people ask of themselves, 'why me?' particularly if they were once non-disabled and have become disabled. Such questions are rare among the Deaf community as many have been Deaf for as long as they are able to remember. They are proud of their Deafness. Increasingly, as Deaf people begin to understand Deafness as a positive attribute, as a gift not a

---

[10]   My research among Deaf people has shown that this is an attitude many Deaf people have experienced from certain groups of hearing people.

[11]   This connection is disputed by McCloughry, R. and Morris W., *Making a World of Difference* (London, 2002), pp.94–110; and Hull, J.M., *In the Beginning there was Darkness*, p.27.

[12]   This story is about a body possessed by an evil spirit that is deaf and dumb (v.25) and causes the boy to be the same. However, the boy is not 'blamed' for this demon possession.

punishment, the idea that Deafness should be seen by God as a sign of his judgement becomes more and more anathema.

Is There Anything in the Bible for Deaf People?

Lift Up Your Hands

Despite all that seems to alienate Deaf people in the Bible, is there anything within the Bible that Deaf people might be able to engage with and relate to? Deaf people communicate using their hands, face and body and certain passages in the Bible describe the hands as a tool for creativity. Indeed, the creation itself is the work of God's hands – God has hands – (see Hebrews 1.10; Isaiah 45.12) he is not just a 'talking ear' or a 'spirit' but can be described as having at least one other physical quality. Human hands are also an instrument of prayer used in the Psalms to bless the Lord (Psalm 134.2). People spread out their hands to the Lord (Psalm 88.9) and the Lord spreads out his hands to the people (Romans 10.21). Hands are not only a tool of creativity, but they are also used in communication between God and human beings.

Isaiah criticizes those who 'do not regard the deeds of the Lord or see the works of his hands' (Isaiah 5.12). Deaf people are conscious of the potential of the hands for creativity and expression of ideas and self. Perhaps they also see more acutely the way God has used his hands to reveal himself to humanity. For example, in my experience in Birmingham and through interviews I have conducted with Deaf people, one of the most important and special services that Deaf people value attending is Harvest Festival. When I have asked them 'why?', they have responded: 'there are so many things to see' or 'the different colours help me to worship God' or 'All the beautiful things make me think of God's love'. It seems to ignore Deaf culture and their expression of theology when hearing Church leaders ask Deaf people to bring money instead of gifts for Harvest Festival because it is easier to distribute. The beauty of the gifts enable Deaf people to feel closer to God. So, it would seem that the Bible recognizes the hands of humans as important in their relationship with God as well as describing God as someone who uses hands. But what about the rest of the body?

Does God Have a Body?

It has been lamented in recent times by many writers, most notably among feminist writers and scholars examining issues in human sexuality, that the Christian tradition in the West, influenced by other philosophical movements,[13] has set up a dualism between the body and the soul. Stuart explains the dualism thus: 'Human beings were

---

[13]   Stuart, E., *Just Good Friends: Towards a Lesbian and Gay Theology of Relationships* (London, 1995), p.53; Thatcher, A., *Liberating Sex: A Christian Sexual Theology* (London, 1993), p.33; Nelson, J.B., *Body Theology* (Louisville, Kentucky, 1992), p.126f among others agree that key influences have included the philosophies of the body of Plato, Newton and Descartes.

thought to be made up of two parts: the body and the soul/spirit/mind. The former is finite, fallen, prone to sin, whilst the latter is eternal and of God'[14]. Thatcher similarly argues that this dualism does not consider the body to be a part of the 'real self' but inferior to the true self – that is the soul[15]. The *New International Version* (1973) translation of the Bible reinforces the idea that the physical is inferior to the soul by translating 'flesh' as 'sinful nature' in certain contexts in the Pauline letters (e.g. Romans 7.25 and Galatians 5.17) even though it is the exact same Greek word (sarx) used in John 1.14 about Jesus. To these translators, it is our body that constitutes what is sinful in human beings.

This is not the case in all of Christianity. John of Damascus in the Orthodox tradition has written: 'I shall not cease to honour matter, for it was through matter that my salvation came to pass ... Do not despise matter, for it is not despicable; nothing is despicable that God has made'[16]. Thatcher argues that the idea of the inferiority of and sinful nature of the body in opposition to the soul 'is widely held among Protestant and Catholic Christians alike, yet it is unbiblical, and, in a faith which teaches the goodness of the created world, the incarnation of God in flesh and the resurrection of human bodies at the end of the age, its survival is remarkable'[17]. I alluded to this dualism in the Introduction when I referred to Frances Young's analysis of the Christian notion that the *Imago Dei* present in humanity is our rational capabilities. God as spirit 'suggests the unearthly and the disembodied'[18] as does the idea that our ability to reason is the part of human beings that most closely bears the image of God. However, as Thatcher has pointed out above, incarnational theology – and not least within the Bible – affirms the body as God himself chooses to dwell in flesh.

I have suggested that in the prologue of John's Gospel Deaf people begin to glimpse a more accessible picture of God when the abstract conceptual speech or word of God, in the person of Jesus, is understood as a physical reality that can be seen and touched. The miracle in John's Gospel is that the God we think of as Spirit and intellect does not try to escape the body, but chooses to be incarnated in flesh (see also Philippians 2.5–11). This idea of God being seen in human form, present among us, has much more relevance to Deaf people and, as will be explored more fully in the final chapter, it is often the case that Deaf people relate to and understand the person of Jesus Christ much more readily than the other persons of the Trinity. Colossians 1.15–20 reads:

> He [Jesus] is the image of the invisible God, the firstborn of all creation; for in him all things in heaven and on earth were created, things visible and invisible, whether thrones or dominions or rulers or powers – all things have been created through him and for him. He himself is before all things, and in him all things hold together. He is the head of the body, the church; he is the beginning, the firstborn from the dead, so that he might come to have first place in everything. *For in him all the fullness of God was pleased to dwell,*

---

[14] Stuart, E., *Just Good Friends*, p.53.

[15] Thatcher, A., *Liberating Sex*, p.33.

[16] John of Damascus, *In Defence of the Holy Icons* (Crestwood, New York, 1980), pp.23–4.

[17] Thatcher, A., *Liberating Sex*, p.33.

[18] McFague, S., *The Body of God: An Ecological Theology* (London, 1993), p.143.

and through him God was pleased to reconcile to himself all things, whether on earth or in heaven, by making peace through the blood of his cross [my italics].

Here, the epistle writer argues that Jesus is the image of the invisible God and God is pleased to be flesh, again affirming the goodness of the physical body. Many Deaf people relate to the idea of Jesus as God incarnate because the God who was hidden and whose face could not be seen as described in Exodus has been made visible, a presence in our midst. In the incarnation, God is revealed to humanity visibly and can be seen and touched by all. It is interesting to note that in this passage from Colossians the familiar Pauline image of Christ as the head of the body, the church can be found. The incarnate God has a body with many parts which is the continuing recognizable seeable and touchable presence of God in the world today.

Jesus understands Deaf people: Mark 7.31–37

It is arguable that the Christian tradition, as it has been interpreted and applied for many centuries, has colluded in the processes that have tried to 'normalize' Deaf people by making them hearing. In the biblical tradition, there are few references made at all to Deaf people. The most important passage to include a Deaf person as one of the central characters is Mark 7.31–37 and in this passage Jesus removes the man's Deafness and turns him into a hearing speaking person. The man is not named like so many other individuals in the biblical narratives who lived at the margins of society. Elisabeth Schüssler-Fiorenza makes a similar point concerning Mark 14.9 when at the Eucharist 'the name of the betrayer is remembered, but the name of the faithful disciple is forgotten because she is a woman'[19]. The miracle of this story must be seen as going beyond simply removing the man's inability to hear, however, and focus more on the fact that suddenly this man was able to speak. Pinker explains, 'acquisition of a normal language is guaranteed for children up to the age of six, is steadily compromised from then until shortly after puberty and is rare thereafter'[20]. Accepting Pinker's argument which complies with much research on language acquisition among children, as discussed earlier, then when Mark 7.32–37 is read, we can only be astonished that this adult man is able to speak instantaneously. Even for a young infant, the acquisition and mastery of a language takes a number of years, but for an adult it would take even longer. Many hearing people learning sign language usually take seven to ten years of considerable study and practice to master the language, and even then, some do not succeed[21]. It is difficult to imagine what it is like suddenly to be able to speak a second language without any tuition. The miracle of this immediate acquisition of a language must be acknowledged as significant in this story.

---

[19]   Schüssler-Fiorenza, E., *In Memory of Her: A Feminist Theological Reconstruction of Christian Origins* (London, 1983), p.xiii.

[20]   Pinker, S., *The Language Instinct* (London, 1994), p.293.

[21]   Out of twenty hearing people who were fluent BSL users in Birmingham, all had taken in excess of seven years to reach a level of fluency and pass the relevant qualifications in BSL. The only exceptions were hearing children of Deaf parents.

McCloughry and Morris have argued that in light of the marginalized position of disabled people in first century Palestine, 'healing is an act of inclusion'[22]. Jesus touches a haemorrhaging woman[23], responds to a blind man who is shouting to attract Jesus' attention but whom the crowd try to silence and touches a man who is Deaf. To touch certain disabled persons would have meant that Jesus himself would have become ritually impure and outcast (see for example the rules about touching lepers and ritual impurity in Leviticus 13–14) and would remain so until he was 'purified' again. However, each person he comes into contact with becomes part of society once more and by touching them, it is they who become 'pure' rather than Jesus becoming 'impure', they who are included rather than Jesus becoming excluded. The healing of the Deaf man is part of this inclusive tradition of the healing narratives. Not only is he outcast because of ritual impurity, but he is excluded from society because he cannot communicate with others. The ability to communicate, especially in a common language, must surely be seen as crucial to inclusion in society. We only need to look at many asylum seekers and others in the UK today who struggle with the common language of the majority to see how it easily leads to discrimination and marginalization. If Jesus was only concerned with making him hearing and saw this as the main problem, he would not have bothered with his speech as well. By giving him language, and under the ritual purity laws giving him hearing, the man is able to become a part of society once more and participate in it fully.

My initial response to this narrative in Mark was that many Deaf people would not find it to be particularly liberating but that they would understand it as helping to reinforce current social attitudes to Deafness: that it is a physical deficiency that society should seek to eradicate. However, I have found that Deaf people's views of this narrative are much more positive. Vera Hunt, an Anglican Deaf priest, writes 'the healing of the deaf man gives us a picture of Jesus' compassion and love for deaf people. Gives us a picture that he considers us equal. There is no other Gospel story where Jesus actually "spits, touches and looks up to heaven". A physical touch of love and compassion – an acknowledgement that deaf people should be accepted – that deaf people are part of the family of God'[24]. Jesus' actions are very physical and visual which differs from the way Jesus behaves in many of the other healing narratives, where he usually just speaks[25]. His visual response to this man strongly suggests that Jesus has some understanding of how to communicate with Deaf people.

It is extremely interesting to note the word Jesus chooses to use when he speaks to the Deaf man and the fact that it is recorded in the Markan account. 'Ephphatha is

---

[22]   McCloughry, R. and Morris, W., *Making a World of Difference*, p.107. For a Jewish perspective, see Abrams, J.Z., *Judaism and Disability: Portrayals in Ancient Texts from the Tanach to the Bavli* (Washington DC, 1998), pp.54–5.

[23]   This rule can be found in Leviticus 15.19ff. Numbers 5.1–4 also lists skin diseases that lead to exclusion from the camp.

[24]   Hunt, V., 'The Place of Deaf People in the Church', in International Ecumenical Working Group. *The Place of Deaf People in the Church* (Northampton, 1996), p.24.

[25]   NB Jesus writes in the ground in the story of the woman found in adultery (John 8.8).

a gift to the lip-reader'[26] because the main consonant sounds are easily recognizable and distinguishable as lip patterns. Davies rightly notes that 'the Greek equivalent *dianoichtheti* would be difficult'[27] for a Deaf person to be able to lip-read because all of the sounds made come from the back of the mouth making it much more difficult for the Deaf person to read. Jesus' choice of this word and Mark's decision to include it in his narrative suggest that there is significance in its use. It is a word easily recognizable to a Deaf person and suggests further that Jesus has an ability to communicate and relate to Deaf people in a medium they understand. Such Deaf awareness by Jesus and the insight of Mark to include this record is either a remarkable insight or a remarkable coincidence for the social context of first-century Palestine.

Though I have argued that the healing narratives are about inclusion and Mark 7.32–37 is potentially very positive for Deaf people because it shows Jesus' understanding of the communication needs of Deaf people, I do not wish to overlook the problems this narrative raises in terms of the current attitudes towards Deaf people concerning normalization. A person reading this story without a theological background, using a 'reader response'[28] approach to the Bible, may see this passage as deeply problematic, reinforcing the 'normalization' approach to Deafness. The approach I have taken, however, learning from the perspectives of Deaf people, is that this passage reinforces the notion that God in Jesus understood Deaf people, was concerned with their marginalization and knew how to communicate with them.

Theology Without the Bible?

In the first part of this chapter, I have examined and discussed the ways in which various images and language about God within the Bible may work to alienate or include Deaf people. However, it is interesting to consider whether or not we can conceive today of theology without the written text of the Bible or indeed without books at all. It is difficult to imagine for those of us who have been brought up in a highly literate society where so much emphasis is placed on education, that we may not need books at all in order to be creative theologians. In my paper, 'Does the Church need the Bible? Reflecting on the Experiences of Disabled People', I used arguments from the field of linguistics that suggests that the need to communicate through speech and sign language is a natural instinct, while writing is a human invention. In this paper I ask, 'Would God restrict himself to a human invention as a means of communicating with his creation or can we dare to think that God is free of human invention and the restrictions we put on to him to communicate and relate

---

[26]   Davies, J., *Only Say the Word: When Jesus brings healing and salvation* (Norwich, 2002), p.149.

[27]   *Ibid.*, p.148.

[28]   Hull, while highly theologically trained, shows the problems of reading the healing narratives as a disabled person in Hull, J.M., 'Open Letter from a Blind Disciple to a Sighted Saviour: Text and Discussion', in O'Kane, M. (ed.), *Borders, Boundaries and the Bible* (Sheffield, 2001), pp.154–77.

with human beings in whatever way he chooses – irrespective of the Bible?[29]' I do not for one minute deny that God can reveal himself through human creativity, such as music, art or literature and indeed through the Bible, after all it is not unreasonable to assume that God uses whatever a society has at their disposal to make himself known. But I would also like to suggest that it is not unreasonable to think that God is not restricted in his ability to reveal himself by books – especially when so many people in the world do not have access to them.

The Church's history also suggests that the Bible may not be so essential to theology as we might think. Indeed, in the second century, as a Christian scriptural canon was beginning to emerge, some were less than enthusiastic about having the words of Jesus and stories about him written down. Among them were Papias of Hierapolis, who lived in the first half of the second century. Eusebius, concerning something one of the Lord's disciples had said, quotes Papias as saying 'For I did not think that information from books would help me so much as the utterances of a living and surviving voice'[30]. Bruce Metzger further points out that, 'in the oldest Christian communities there was also another authority which had taken its place alongside the Jewish Scriptures, and that was the words of Jesus, as they were handed down in oral tradition'[31]. Jesus spoken words were, Metzger explains, not considered to be inferior to the written words of the Jewish Scriptures[32]. Therefore, in the early Church, the idea of an oral authority which was not enshrined in books was by no means anathema[33].

Further, if doing theology is not the preserve of academics and clerics but an exercise done by the whole *ekklesia* then for most of the history of the Christian Church in the West, theology was done without books. Indeed, as Kwok Pui-Lan points out, 'It is noteworthy that before Johannes Gutenberg introduced printing with movable metal type in 1447, the circulation of costly Bibles in hand-written form was limited to the clergy, theologians, monks, and the aristocracy'[34]. It is also true to say that not until after the Reformation was the Bible translated into the vernacular languages of the people of Europe, and even then a significant majority of people would be unable to read the Bible[35]. Of course people knew many of the stories as they had been interpreted in stained glass or in the paintings on church and cathedral walls,[36] but the Bible as a written text was largely inaccessible. The

---

[29]   Morris, W. (2006), 'Does the Church Need the Bible? Reflecting on the Experiences of Disabled People', in Bates, D.J., Durka, G. and Schweitzer, F.L. (eds), *Education, Religion and Society: Essays in Honour of John M. Hull* (London, 2006) pp.162–72.

[30]   Quoted in Metzger, B., *The Canon of the New Testament: Its Origin, Development and Significance* (New York, 1987), p.52.

[31]   *Ibid.*, p.2.

[32]   *Ibid.*, pp.2–3.

[33]   Kwok Pui-Lan., *Discovering the Bible in the Non-Biblical World* (New York, 1995), p.45, also points to the significance of the oral transmission of sacred texts in other traditions, such as through the verbatim memorization of the *Vedas* in Hinduism and the recitation of the *Qur'an* in Islam.

[34]   Kwok Pui-Lan, *Discovering the Bible in the Non-Biblical World*, p.50.

[35]   See Chadwick, O., *The Reformation* (London, 1964), pp.223–4 on the English Bible.

[36]   See Dowley, T (ed.), *The Bible in Stained Glass* (Swindon, 1990), p.7.

non-literate person's access to biblical narratives was, in such instances, determined by those with access to the Bible and the knowledge and power that gives. Below, I would like to explore some of the ways in which the Bible has been dealt with by a variety of more contemporary groups who have found problems which arise from using the Bible in theology, and to reflect on how their methods might inform or illuminate our understanding of the way Deaf people use the Bible.

Alternative Understandings on How to Use the Bible

One Zimbabwean Approach

The Zimbabwean Methodist theologian, Canaan Banana has called for a 're-writing' of the Bible[37]. Believing that revelation is incomplete and that God is still present and actively revealing himself to the church and world today, he argues that the Bible as we know it should be edited to make it relevant to our times and that the canon should be re-opened in order to include the continued record of God's revelation to the world. It should be noted, that among traditional denominational church groups in Africa and a number of theologians, this point of view is very much in a minority. Rather, many call for methods of 're-interpreting' or re-reading the existing texts from particular cultural perspectives, rather than a complete re-writing of the texts[38]. While the notion that God's revelation is incomplete and still happening in the world, the idea of re-opening the canon of the Bible (a collection of written texts) does little to help Deaf people as by 'recording' God's revelation, Banana is implying writing, which would make little difference to Deaf people. We have already seen that Deaf people struggle with written languages, though it may be possible to include God's revelation among Deaf people in their 'oral' signing culture.

A Malawian Approach

Peter Kalilombe has considered the place of the Bible among non-literate Roman Catholics in Malawi. Emphasizing the importance of the Bible in terms of the Magisterium of the Church tradition, he highlights the problems which people who are illiterate face. He concludes, by asserting, 'It is natural, therefore, that all things being equal, the non-literate will tend to be among the less advantaged, among the powerless and those most likely to be oppressed and exploited. If then they are incapable of taking an active part in the reflecting over the Bible, the project of a

---

[37]   Banana, C.S., 'The Case for a New Bible', in Sugirtharajah, R.S. (ed.), *Voices from the Margin* (London/Maryknoll, New York, 1995), pp.70–82.

[38]   See for example the methods of using the Bible employed by Mosala, Itumeleng J., 'The Implications of the Text of Esther for African Women's Struggle for Liberation in South Africa', in Sugirtharajah, R.S. (ed.), *Voices from the Margin* (London/Maryknoll, New York, 1995), pp.170–1; Kalilombe, P.A., 'A Malawian Example', in Sugirtharajah, R.S. (ed.), *Voices from the Margin* (London/Maryknoll, New York, 1995), pp.421–35 and Oduyoye, M.A., *Introducing African Women's Theology* (Sheffield, 2001), p.12.

liberating theology is largely in vain'[39]. He suggests that non-literate people could benefit from literate people reading the Bible to them, which would presumably mean that their attempts at a liberating theology would no longer be in vain. He says that the Bible could also be transmitted through tape recorders or over loud speakers in the same way in which the Qur'an is transmitted. He suggests singing the Bible, or using the arts to communicate the text. He argues that reading the Bible out loud could be like the story-telling tradition where people gather in public places to hear news and information because speech and hearing have the function that newspapers, reviews and books carry for literate people. He supports his position by quoting Romans 10.17: 'Faith cometh by hearing, and hearing by the word of God'[40].

There is merit in what Kalilombe suggests and Deaf people have traditionally depended on literate hearing or Deaf people to communicate the narratives to them, and I have already discussed how literacy gives power. However, to suggest that a theology that cannot make use of the Bible is in vain and therefore not a liberating theology suggests that truly liberating theology can only by done by the educated and, by implication, powerful. That seems to contradict the very foundations of theologies of liberation, that they emerge out of those on the margins of society and the understanding of theology I argued for in chapter 4.

The Bible and Feminist Approaches

Some feminist theologians in the West and Africa, such as Rosemary Radford Reuther[41], Letty Russell[42], Mercy Amba Oduyoye[43], Isabel Mukonyora[44] and Elisabeth Schüssler-Fiorenza[45], hold the position that the Bible as a source of Christian and theological authority needs to be challenged, arguing that the Bible is only useful in terms of its capacity to affirm the full humanity of women and indeed every human being. Many Asian scholars have agreed with this but have contributed further to the debate by reflecting on the experience of living in a multi-religious and multi-scriptural context and arguing that Christians should be open to God's revelation in other traditions and scriptures[46]. Feminists' selective use of the Bible such as this has never been one that has appealed to Deaf people in the research I have conducted. I have found they prefer to struggle with the difficulties and exclusiveness of the Bible

---

[39]   Kalilombe, P.A., 'A Malawian Example', p.434.

[40]   *Ibid.*, p.427.

[41]   Reuther, R.R., 'Feminist Interpretation', in Russell, L.M. (ed.), *Feminist Interpretation of the Bible* (Philadelphia, 1985), pp.111–23.

[42]   Russell, L.M., 'Introduction: Liberating the Word', in Russell, L.M. (ed.), *Feminist Interpretation of the Bible* (Philadelphia, 1985), pp.11–18.

[43]   Oduyoye, M.A., *Introducing African Women's Theology*, pp.11–15.

[44]   Mukonyora, I., 'Women's Readings of the Bible', in Mukonyora, I., et al. (eds), *'Rewriting the Bible: the real issues* (Gweru, 1993), pp.199–216.

[45]   Schüssler-Fiorenza, E., *Bread Not Stone: The Challenge of Feminist Biblical Interpretation* (Edinburgh, 1984).

[46]   See Kwok Pui-Lan, *Discovering the Bible in the Non-Biblical World* and Sugirtharajah, R.S. *The Bible and the Third World.*

and the theology therein (such as that outlined above) and find ways of living with that rather than arguing that if it does not affirm Deaf people it is not useful.

A Western Disabled Person's Approach

I described in chapter 4 how Hull explains his method of reading the Bible as a 'conversation'[47]. I would suggest that Deaf people also use the Bible in a similar way by viewing a dialogue between the Bible and cultural experience as important, as far as Deaf people are able to make use of the Bible. However, Deaf people rarely leave the text of the Bible as it is. Rather they use the story (not the words of the text) to engage with their experiences. Something needs to be done with it, it needs to be transformed and inculturized in order to be of use in their theology and this is what I will illustrate and discuss below.

Deaf Use of the Bible

The Chinese feminist theologian, Kwok Pui-Lan, has reflected on her experiences of observing and participating in the Bible studies of non-literate Asian women from a variety of contexts. Kwok Pui-Lan argues that Asian women 'dramatize biblical stories, retell gospel messages, and pose critical questions to the Bible from their own experiences ... They treat the Bible as a living resource rather than as an ancient text closed in itself'[48]. She goes on to argue that 'When Asian women gather to discuss and dramatize the stories of women in the Bible, they frequently imagine what the women would have said and acted in the situation'[49]. I would suggest that this largely reflects what Deaf People do with the Bible. Sometimes they are not able to read or hear the text, but they know the stories from other people, or film and art or, if they have English, from their reading abilities. Deaf people are never comfortable just watching a literal translation of the Bible from English into BSL and often struggle reading the text and understanding the meaning of some of the words. If one person is signing the text, they often depart from it and tell the story in a way which is relevant to Deaf People. It would seem to me then that Deaf people are not concerned so much with literal translation as with communication. Often when a Deaf person is faithful to the content and order of the English translation, they end up following the English word order and they fingerspell much of the text. Imagine how uninspiring listening to the Bible being read would be if every single word was spelled out.

Visible Communications is an organization in Britain working to translate stories from the Bible into BSL with the aim of making the Bible accessible to more Deaf people. Most of their work to date has been on the Psalms, stories which Jesus told and Luke's Gospel. These attempts at translating the Bible into sign language onto video on this scale are the first of their kind. The translations made into BSL are based on the Good News Version of the Bible. This is itself problematic because the

---

[47]   Hull, J.M., *In the Beginning there was Darkness*, p.3.
[48]   Kwok Pui-Lan, *Discovering the Bible in the Non-Biblical World*, p.44.
[49]   *Ibid.*, p.52.

Good News Version is one of the least faithful English translations to the original Greek. This means that with the second layer of interpretation into BSL, some of the translations may be far removed from the original texts. Added to this, on occasions, the BSL translations are too faithful to the English cultural influence to the extent that they become meaningless in BSL and to Deaf culture. Despite these problems, they are a valiant attempt at translating the Bible into BSL and are thus a useful resource for beginning to understand how Deaf people interpret the Bible in terms of Deaf culture. Deaf people are involved in every stage of the BSL version's production and Deaf people sign the translations. These are not meant to be fixed translations of the Bible, because the Deaf person always includes their own layer of interpretation using the creative lexicon in any performance in BSL, which will not be copied exactly by another Deaf person. Recently, a more scholarly approach to the translation of biblical texts into BSL has been initiated with more careful attention being paid to both the quality of translation and communication of the text in BSL.[50] The project is still in its early stages and little is available yet for more general public scrutiny.

Dramatizing the Bible and 'Reading the Gaps'

Often drama is used in liturgical contexts and I have seen it used many times. Usually, there is extensive discussion on how to perform a drama and reflection on what the characters would be like as the performers understand it. I have seen a drama on the Christmas story when a whole number of Deaf people were involved in the presentation – indeed the whole congregation[51]. On this occasion, Deaf people were not passively listening and reflecting on the story, as tends to happen in hearing churches, but actively participating in it. One scene involved the announcement of the birth of Jesus to the shepherds by an angel of the Lord. As soon as the angel appeared, the story digressed from the biblical narrative. Firstly, these shepherds saw an angel, they were not so much afraid, as the biblical narrative describes, as confused. What was going on? Were they over-tired? Had they been drinking too much? 'You know what those rough shepherds were like back then' The angel speaks and the confusion is transformed into clarity. The shepherds still are not afraid, but they do rejoice. They are not afraid, because this angel is from God and there is no need to fear God – God is the friend of Deaf people. They rejoice because God has come to earth as a human being. Much of the Deaf interpretation of the narrative adds in ideas and fills in gaps reflecting on the story from the Deaf perspective.

In such a dramatization of the text, we begin to glimpse something of Deaf theology being read into the narrative: there is no need to fear because God is the friend of Deaf people. In using biblical narratives, Deaf people consciously use the way of reading the Bible that Evans describes as 'reading the gaps': This approach recognizes that a reader is 'constructing' the reading of the text, not merely 'discovering' it ready

---

50   Bible Translation Project, URL: http://www.bslbible.org.uk (2007).
51   This story was observed in the Deaf Church meeting in the Diocese of St Asaph (Christmas 2000).

made in all its details'[52]. He goes on to show how art, poetry and literature have read detail into the text that may not necessarily be there. Hull argues that the Bible was written *by* sighted people *for* sighted people. It was also written *by* hearing people *for* hearing people, and Deaf people, by reading themselves into the narratives, find a way of making the Bible more accessible to Deaf people.

Evans' idea of 'reading the gaps' is often applied by Deaf people as they use the Bible. One person told the story from Exodus of Moses leading the Israelites through the Red Sea. The story was told largely from the experience of two imagined Deaf Israelites walking through parted waters. The couple stop walking along the way to chat, which Deaf people often do which can make a short journey made on foot quite slow. In the narrative, there are no Deaf people mentioned in the Exodus text but by this technique of using the Bible and making it their own, Deaf people find it can be meaningful and useful to them and their theology. While this approach to using the Bible would probably be frowned upon by those who employ historical-critical methods to interpret biblical narratives, the Deaf use of the Bible goes no further than the way artists have interpreted images of God (such as images of God wearing a papal tiara[53]), or writers have allegorized biblical stories (e.g. C.S. Lewis[54]). It is a meaningful way of using the Bible and making the stories relevant to Deaf people. Deaf people can learn the stories from those who are literate, but they are empowered in their use of the Bible by applying their experiences and culture to the narratives.

Conclusion: Deaf Theology and the Bible

In concluding this chapter, I would like to draw attention to a number of points in terms of the way in which Deaf People use the Bible to do Theology. 1) For many Deaf people, the Bible is problematic in terms of its language and imagery as well as because it is a written text. 2) Some of the language for God used in the Bible is more inclusive of Deaf people, most notably the theologies that point towards an Incarnational Christology. The incarnation tells of a God who is visible and tangible. Deaf people believe that God understands sign and uses it to express himself as well and his ability to communicate with Deaf people is evident in the person of Jesus in Mark's Gospel. 3) Deaf people often do with the Bible the opposite to that which hearing people have done with it. Rather than beginning with oral traditions and writing them down, Deaf people have familiarized themselves with the narratives in the Bible and in order to make them useful, they are turned back into oral or signing traditions using drama and the 'reading the gaps' method of engaging with biblical narratives. Their theology is informed by using the Bible in this way and their reading

---

[52]   Evans, R. *Using the Bible: Studying the Text* (London, 1999), p.29.

[53]   This image can be found, for example, in the 'Creation Window' in St Florentin Church, Burgundy, France. Such an image implies that God is Roman Catholic and suggests to the viewer that God has a closer relationship with the Pope and Roman Catholicism than with other church traditions. See Dowley, T. (ed.), *The Bible in Stained Glass* (Swindon, 1990), p.12.

[54]   See, for example, Lewis, C.S., *The Lion, the Witch and the Wardrobe* (London, 1980).

of the Bible is informed by their theological perspectives and experiences. The above two chapters have focused on how Deaf people do theology, thinking especially about their tools and methods. In the remaining two chapters, I will examine some of the content of Deaf theology, looking particularly the expression of these theologies in ecclesiology and liturgy and the way that impacts, in the final chapter, on Deaf perspectives on God.

PART III
Theology Without Words

Chapter 6

Theology Without Words:
Ecclesiology and Liturgy

Introduction

In the previous chapter, I described and examined the ways that Deaf people use the Bible as a source of theology. In this and the final chapter, it is my intention to look at some of those things that Deaf people express as theological ideas. Lewis argues that 'Worship is the public expression of the faith of the church; it is theology in action'[1] and so one of the themes I will address in this chapter is the questions surrounding liturgy in the Deaf community, and I can see no other way of getting to grips with the theology of a group of people such as Deaf people than by understanding the community's liturgy and worship. Firstly, however I would like to explore one of the issues connected to liturgy and that is the theme of ecclesiology. These two themes of ecclesiology and liturgy are related to one another because 'all theology has a context'[2], and because liturgical acts usually involve more than one person, it is in the context of community that the liturgy and worship of the Deaf church is expressed. I have already defined in chapter 4 how I understand the church as ekklesia. Here I am concerned with what that means to Deaf people. In the Deaf community, the Deaf church provides a context for the worshipping community. When people meet in the context of worship with fellow Christians who think about God, there is much to be learned about their theology both in terms of methodologies and perspectives on God.

Towards a Deaf Ecclesiology

'Deaf Church' or 'Sign Language Church'

There is currently some debate among certain chaplains in the Church of England who are both Deaf and hearing as to whether the church attended by Deaf people should be called a 'Deaf church' or a 'sign language church'. The term 'sign language church' has emerged because at the periphery of the Deaf community and their churches it is usual to find hearing sign language users and it is thought that so that the churches can include these people in the name that is used, 'sign language church' should be the

---

[1] Lewis, H., *A Critical Examination of the Church and Deaf People* (Birmingham, 2002), p.153.

[2] Green, L., *Urban Ministry and the Kingdom of God* (London, 2003), p.vii.

name of the worshipping Deaf community. While this recognizes something of the reality of the nature of Deaf churches and the Deaf community more widely, I have never heard Deaf people ever use this term, but rather, they use 'Deaf church' as their preferred name. This would be my first defence for retaining the title 'Deaf church'. Secondly, 'Deaf church' is to my mind a more accurate title for the worshipping Deaf community because, while sign language is used in these churches, the liturgies that Deaf people use to help them worship most comfortably are not simply those that are expressed in sign language but also have aspects of Deaf culture interpenetrating every part of them. 'Deaf' embraces the culture and language of Deaf people in a way that 'sign language' does not and further, as I argued in the first chapter, the phrase 'Deaf community' includes those hearing people who are present within the community as workers, family members and friends of Deaf people. The churches where Deaf people worship, therefore, are called 'Deaf churches' for our purposes here reflecting the way that worship should be or is bound up with Deaf culture as Deaf people and not just English translated into sign language.

Deaf People and the Institutions: The Church Among Deaf People

In 1997, the Church of England published the report: *The Church Among Deaf People*, which was presented to and affirmed by General Synod. The report makes a series of recommendations as to how dioceses and the Church of England nationally should approach ministry among the Deaf community. The report encourages dioceses, in a climate of increasing financial difficulties, to ensure that pastoral care and access to worship continue to be provided for Deaf people[3]. It is odd, to say the least, that the chapter on theological reflection comes at the end of the report rather than at the beginning and it shows a certain lack of theological reflection throughout that is usually more present in other Church of England reports[4]. As one reads the report, you cannot help but be aware of the paternalism present within it. Deaf people have clearly been part of the process of writing the report, but throughout, the discussions are about what the Church can do *for* Deaf people. For example, '… it is the responsibility of the Church to provide Ministry among Deaf People'[5] and 'Deaf people see themselves, and are recognized to be, full members of the community. They expect to take full command of their own lives and to be offered and to accept appropriate leadership opportunities. Chaplains should seek to encourage these attitudes of independence and self-determination among Deaf Christians'[6]. Within a whole chapter on ministry, only one paragraph is dedicated to the ordained ministry of Deaf people, although a shorter chapter on Deaf lay ministry follows. Throughout, the tone set by the report is 'What can the Church do for Deaf people?' and 'How can the Church help Deaf people?' While it is true that Deaf people remain on the margins of ecclesiastical structures in the Church of England, based on my earlier definition of the church as ekklesia, it should be

---

3   Church of England, *The Church Among Deaf People* (London, 1997), pp.51–7.
4   *Ibid.*, pp.58–62.
5   *Ibid.*, p.13.
6   *Ibid.*, p.24.

at once recognized that Deaf people are the church wherever they meet together for worship. To use language of what the Church can do for Deaf people shows a church that does not recognize that Deaf people are the church already, but prefers to see Deaf people as objects of their paternalistic benevolence. Dominant majorities liberate minorities, not by providing an improved service, but by giving up their power to enable the Deaf churches truly to be empowered.

Hitching: Deaf Ecclesiology and the Theology of Moltmann

Roger Hitching has written on the subject of Deaf churches. In his book, he discusses the ecclesiology of Moltmann and applies it, somewhat uncritically, as a model by which Deaf people could be church. Hitching is rightly negative about the role of the institutional churches and their work with Deaf people. He argues, 'Deaf people have suffered oppressive practices in many of these institutional churches' and blames 'their organisational structures' that leave them 'unable to respond to changes taking place in society. As a result they fail to continue to provide adequate practical safeguards against the misuse of power and can unintentionally transmit discriminating attitudes and practices from one generation to the next'[7]. He also criticizes the Church of England report published in 1997 on the future of their ministry among Deaf people, because 'the view of Deaf people in the report is that of a group of people for whom things should be provided'[8]. It is somewhat ironic, however, that Hitching should make this comment about the Church of England report when his own book attempts to impose Moltmann's ecclesiology, useful as it may be, onto Deaf churches and he thereby becomes a part of the same paternalistic tradition that looks at the Deaf community, tells them what they need, and how they should achieve it without much reference to Deaf people themselves. Remarkably, the alternative type of church that Hitching suggests has greater potential for the inclusion of Deaf people is 'Charismatic and Pentecostal Churches ... churches ... whose theology has been influenced by Calvin'[9]. I find such a proposition quite extraordinary, not least because of the suggestion that Charismatic and Pentecostal churches are virtually identical, but because, while such churches may have more flexible structures, it is often their theology that has excluded Deaf people based on the biblical hermeneutic that perceives Deafness to be the result of sin. Chapter 5 describes the way Deaf people have been perceived to be sinful and in need of 'healing' in many such churches[10].

Hannah Lewis

Hannah Lewis, who completed her doctoral studies at Birmingham University, submitted a thesis on the Church and Deaf people. Lewis' basic approach is to offer a

---

[7]   Hitching, R., *The Church and Deaf People* (Carlisle, 2003), p.2.

[8]   *Ibid.*, p.35.

[9]   *Ibid.*, p.3.

[10]   See also McCloughry, R. and Morris, W., *Making a World of Difference* (London, 2002), pp.94–110.

deconstruction of Deaf churches historically and to propose a way of reconstructing a model of what the Deaf churches should look like. Her methodological premise is that of liberation theology. Lewis rightly asserts, as far as I am aware, that she is 'writing down for the first time a history of the DEAF-CHURCH by a Deaf person'[11]. There is no need to repeat that history here, but Lewis summarizes her analysis of Deaf church history thus: 'I have briefly sketched the history of the DEAF-CHURCH, its origins among the STRONG-DEAF of the nineteenth century, inspired by the evangelical revival, its evolution into a hearing controlled welfare organisation over the first 70 years of the twentieth century and the rise of the modern day institutionally focussed church among deaf people'[12]. She goes on to examine the ways in which Deaf people have been constructed in theology and in the Church as an organization in ways that have led to the suppression and marginalization of Deaf people by the Church and theology. These include a discussion of traditional theological perspectives in churches on Deaf people as 'morally impure'[13], as a 'travesty of divine image'[14], as 'virtuous sufferers'[15], and the perspective that 'faith comes by hearing'[16].

While recognizing some of the difficulties that Deaf people have with accessing the Bible, which I have discussed earlier, Lewis begins her reconstruction of a Deaf ecclesiology by arguing for a 'Deaf Liberation Hermeneutics'[17]. I have already discussed why I think such an approach is questionable and have argued that the role of the Bible is not and does not need to play a central role in the theology of the Deaf community. Lewis and I clearly place different emphases on the role of Bible in theology and Lewis openly acknowledges her own biases with reference to the biblical scholar, Phyllis Trible: 'Trible is "clear about her commitment to the biblical tradition" ... I would firmly identify myself with Trible ... in the purpose of my work in relation to the biblical text'[18]. Lewis goes on to address Christological questions about Jesus and places 'Deaf Liberation Christology firmly in the field of other liberation Christologies which use indigenous culture to dramatically revise western views of Jesus and which are about transforming the world of today into a more just society'[19]. The climax of her argument focuses on worship in Deaf churches, as this chapter also does, and she argues for a reconstruction of liturgy in the Deaf churches. She argues, 'This reconstructing must be done by Deaf people themselves. No hearing person, no matter how sympathetic or experienced in sign can do that for us. The reconstruction of the liturgy as transformative is a process not an end product. If we, as a group, are not involved in the creation of liturgy then we will not be transformed by it and it will not contribute to the ultimate aim of the liberation of Deaf people, body, mind and soul'[20].

---

[11]   Lewis, H., *A Critical Examination of the Church and Deaf People*, p.50.
[12]   *Ibid.*, p.68.
[13]   *Ibid.*, pp.72–77.
[14]   *Ibid.*, pp.77–82.
[15]   *Ibid.*, pp.82–85.
[16]   *Ibid.*, pp.85–90.
[17]   *Ibid.*, pp.111–34.
[18]   *Ibid.*, p.112.
[19]   *Ibid.*, p.152.
[20]   *Ibid.*, p.171.

Much of what Lewis has to offer is informative, challenging and engaging in her perspectives on Deaf people, the history of the Deaf church and her arguments for a church that is Deaf centred. However, it is evident that the methodological background of Lewis' and my thesis are in many ways fundamentally different. For example, in her chapter on Deaf worship, we have already seen that Lewis argues for a liturgy that emerges out of Deaf experience, but much of her own research into how liturgy could become Deaf is informed by Deaf people who are either highly educated and literate and are often those working as chaplains in the Church of England or Roman Catholic Church. In hearing as well as Deaf churches, there is a danger that liturgies are constructed by educated elites, who may be Deaf or hearing, but those liturgies may ignore the ways in which Deaf culture and experience is already present in the praxis of Deaf worship by ordinary Deaf people. If worship is to engage with and be relevant to communities, it must come from the grassroots of those communities and not from the educated elites who may offer help and guidance. My analysis of Deaf ecclesiology and liturgy is based on research done at the grassroots and, while translated into English, I hope will inform any reconstructions of Deaf liturgical practices, or more precisely, encourage hearing and/or educated readers not to take over Deaf people's space to create their own liturgies that express their unique theological perspectives.

The Deaf Church: An Ecclesiology

Thus far, I have argued that 'Deaf church' is the appropriate title to use for the place where Deaf people worship and that is one of the contexts from which Deaf theology emerges. I have further argued, in agreement with Hitching, that the institutional churches have been oppressive of Deaf people not least because of the paternalism that continues to be present in the churches illustrated by the publication of the report from the Church of England and in disagreement with Hitching, that the Charismatic and Pentecostal churches and churches in the Calvinist tradition have equally played their own part in oppressing Deaf people. Hitching uses Moltmann's ecclesiology as a paradigm by which Deaf churches could be liberating for Deaf People, while Lewis uses a liberation theology perspective. All of these, in their own way, may help Deaf churches to move forward, but they all seem more concerned with how the Deaf church should be rather than how it is; what a Deaf ecclesiology could be, rather than how Deaf people already view and meaningfully interpret their church. That is not to say that current practices are perfect or that Deaf churches may not need vision for the future. That is not my intention at all. From here, by looking at Deaf ecclesiology and liturgy, I aim to communicate some 'grassroots' Deaf perspectives on their worship.

Deaf Church: A Place of Inclusion

Deaf people welcome people from various backgrounds into their church community. I have found in all the Deaf churches I have attended that hearing people who can use sign language and are prepared to worship in the context of Deaf culture are welcomed and included equally with Deaf people – something far from true in many hearing churches – though Deaf people, rightly, try to retain their roles of leadership in the worship for Deaf people. For those hearing people who struggle with BSL and the different cultural approach to Deaf worship, Deaf people tend to be patient and willing to be alongside hearing people to help them to feel as included as possible. Members of the Deaf community who attend the Deaf churches range from all kinds of socio-economic backgrounds, although the socio-economic status of Deaf people is generally lower than that of hearing people[21].

In a Eucharistic Service when the peace is exchanged, it is usual for everybody to exchange the peace with everyone else, often by hugging or kissing one another. This type of fellowship illustrates an important part of the ecclesiology of Deaf people. I do not want to be over-sentimental about Deaf churches in the way that sometimes Jean Vanier tends to be about the worshipping communities at L'Arche[22]. It would be wrong to suggest that everyone is friendly and loving towards everyone else all of the time. Deaf people are human beings with the capacity to like or dislike others just like hearing people. However, the sense of inclusion and welcome, from my interviews with Deaf people and from my observations as a part of Deaf churches, is one of the most important aspects of Deaf ecclesiology. Significant in informing ecclesiology among both Deaf and disabled people has been St Paul's image of the Church as the Body of Christ. This is discussed more fully in McCloughry and Morris (2002)[23]. This image is taken seriously by many Deaf people who also relate to a perspective on the Church in which each member should be fully valued, hardly surprising noting the history of Deaf people and their general exclusion from the Church. Remarkably, however, they have not become the persecutors, which often happens among cultures that have traditionally been oppressed, that once they have power of any sort, they use it to suppress others[24].

The Deaf Church in the Deaf Community: An Ecclesiology of Suspicion

Centres for Deaf people, now the focus of meeting for the Deaf community, were usually established and run by churches under the oversight of a 'missioner'. At the beginning of the twentieth century, Ladd argues most organizations and welfare

---

[21]   RNID, *Facts and Figures on Deafness and Tinnitus* (London, 2003), argues that 68.1% of people who are d/Deaf or Hard of Hearing who are of employable age are in employment compared to 81.2% of the general population. In addition, 33% of d/Deaf and Hard of Hearing People in employment earn less that £10,000 per annum compared to only 11.8% of the general population.

[22]   Vanier, J., *The Scandal of Service: Jesus Washes Our Feet* (London, 1997), is a powerful exploration of the experience of the liturgy of the foot-washing used at the L'Arche community. However, the discussion Vanier presents, while moving and challenging, recognizes few of the problems or harsh realities of living and working with people with severe learning disabilities. I worked in such an environment myself, and while there were moments of great joy, there were also moments of intense frustration. Vanier rarely spends time in his writing acknowledging this.

[23]   McCloughry, R. and Morris, W., *Making a World of Difference*, pp.74–82.

[24]   See Girard, R., *The Scapegoat* (London, 1986).

societies that had been Deaf led had been taken over by the Anglican Church in England and Wales[25]. Ladd explains, 'New waves of missioners to the Deaf were trained to administer the newly created Deaf colony; finding by then a low standard of Deaf achievement around the country, it was easy for them to create a discourse based on the (supposed) Deaf inability to support themselves or manage their own affairs'[26]. He continues, 'Ironically, in light of the lessening of the power of Christian discourses throughout majority British Society, the twentieth century saw the Deaf community come increasingly under its thrall'[27]. *The Church among Deaf People* (1997) offers a different perspective of the role of the missioner: 'The Church in England, especially the Church of England ... can take credit for the foundation of many organisations which care for the profoundly deaf in their midst ... The Church can also take credit that through these organisations, and the church services they offered, sign language was kept alive and at a high level through many years when much educational theory tried to deny it'[28].

While the histories of modern day sign languages can be traced back to educational institutions founded by churchmen[29], the Church of England's role in Deaf history combines both positive and negative aspects. Deaf centres founded by the churches have become important centres as the focus of the community for Deaf people, as I outlined in chapter 1, and the oral tradition of Deaf people confirms that sign languages have always been used in churches for Deaf people. Conversely, however, many Deaf people have stories of attending churches with school or parents in which no effort was made to include Deaf people. Many Deaf centres and organizations are no longer in the hands of the churches, which, as Ladd argues, were undoubtedly paternalistic[30], but they continue to perpetuate the charitable attitudes towards Deaf people[31] and continue to be managed and controlled by hearing people. Deaf churches themselves are largely under the oversight of a hearing chaplain with only three stipendiary Deaf clergy working in the Church of England and a handful of non-stipendiaries[32]. The Church of England continues to appoint hearing clerics as chaplains among Deaf people with little or no knowledge of Deaf culture and BSL, thus imposing hearing liturgies and traditions onto the Deaf community. In that context, Deaf churches are viewed very negatively by many Deaf people. Most Anglican Deaf churches consist of very few people under the age of sixty

---

[25] Ladd, P., *Understanding Deaf Culture* (Clevedon, 2003), p.139.

[26] *Ibid.*, p.139.

[27] *Ibid.*, p.139.

[28] Church of England, *The Church Among Deaf People*, pp.12–13.

[29] See, for example, the account of Abbé Charles-Michel de l'Epée in Lane, H., *When the Mind Hears* (New York, 1989), pp.42–66.

[30] See the Ladd, P., *Understanding Deaf Culture* (Clevedon, 2003), pp.46–7.

[31] Alker, D., *Really Not Interested in the Deaf* (Darwen, 2000), discusses a classic example of one charity's paternalism towards Deaf People and the oppressive ways that can be expressed.

[32] In 2004, the Secretary to the Committee for Ministry Among Deaf and Disabled People in the Church of England confirmed that there are 3 stipendiary Deaf clergy and one stipendiary Deaf lay minister currently exercising a ministry in the Church of England, either in hearing parishes and/or as chaplains among Deaf people.

with younger Deaf people being very negative about the role of the Church in their midst. It is often seen as a continuing symbol of an oppressive past and Deaf people increasingly distance themselves from it. In this sense, Deaf ecclesiology outside of the Church reflects an understanding of the church that is deeply negative and oppressive of the language and culture of Deaf people. Within the Church many Deaf people feel the same, struggling to bring about change in a church that still does not understand their needs. Paradoxically, however, in this ecclesiology of suspicion, they often stick with the Church because it is the only context of meeting with fellow Christians and of corporate Deaf worship for most Deaf people.

The Deaf Church and the Wider Church

Deaf people's relationship with the wider church can be equally negative. The Church of England, as with most other institutional Church structures has little place for Deaf people. A national network of Deaf churches, Deaf Anglicans Together (DAT), exists to represent Deaf people in the Church of England, but that body has no formal representation in any of the national Church structures. In the Church of England, Deaf people are outside of the parish system which, while exempting them from some of the bureaucracy that brings, leaves Deaf people on the margins of Church structures. Deaf people therefore can have no representation on Deanery Synods and therefore are excluded from Diocesan and General Synod unless ordained Deaf people are elected on. Since 2005, three members of Deaf Anglicans Together have been able to sit on General Synod and contribute to debates, but without voting rights. The parish system also creates problems for Deaf people offering themselves for ministry, as I discovered when a Deaf person wanted to put herself forward for ordination in one diocese. In another diocese, when a new chaplain was appointed, the members of the Deaf church were told by a senior cleric in that diocese that they would have no say in the new appointment because they did not make a financial contribution to the diocese in the form of a parish share. While Deaf people are disempowered in the Church, they continue to have imposed onto them hearing clergy and ways of worship, alienating many Deaf people from much sense of common ground with the wider church context. In this sense, Deaf ecclesiology tends to be much more locally centred.

The Deaf Church and Ecumenism

Deaf churches are the primary focus of the worship of many Deaf people. Some Deaf people will worship amid hearing congregations as their choice and will use an interpreter in order to do so. A very small number of Deaf people have said that, in the Anglo-Catholic or Roman Catholic traditions, they have not made use of an interpreter because the visual nature of the liturgical ritual has enabled them to follow the service and feel a part of what is going on. Green describes how in the Anglo-Catholic churches of the East End of London, 'The worship was colourful and not book-dependent since the mass was learnt by heart'[33].However,

---

[33]   Green, L., *Urban Ministry*, pp.31–2.

the majority of Deaf people who choose to worship do so in Deaf churches because they provide a space in which Deaf people can participate in a service that is led in BSL and feel fully a part of the worshipping community. It has been stressed over and over by Deaf people I have encountered, that for worship to be meaningful for them, they must not only be able to take an active part in it, it must also be in their own language and culture. This point is also further illustrated by the video, *The Invisible Church*, from Visible Communications, where one Deaf woman says: 'Deaf people need their own church with sign language. Their own church is easier for them. In the Deaf church we worship God through sign language'.[34]

There are three main traditions of Deaf churches in England. Both the Roman Catholic Church and the Church of England usually have some provision for Deaf people in the form of a diocesan chaplain and the churches the chaplains serve in generally follow the tradition of the denomination. The third tradition comes under the umbrella of the Hands Together Network which is a network of Christian churches that tend to be in the Free Church and/or the Evangelical Traditions. Deaf Christians are united by their need to worship in a language and culture that is meaningful to them. Many older Deaf people have experiences of going to church as children either with parents or their school and feeling total exclusion from the act of worship because they could not understand anything that was happening around them in the liturgies that consisted mostly of words. United by their common linguistic and cultural needs, Deaf people generally pay little attention to the liturgical or denominational tradition of the community in which they are worshipping. It is not uncommon to find in an Anglican Church members who would call themselves Baptist, Methodist, Roman Catholic, or some other tradition you could name. In fact, Deaf people are sometimes members of more than one church and may even go to all three of the main church traditions. It was interesting to observe at one Anglican service a number of Roman Catholic Deaf people were present and were about to receive communion from the Anglican priest but were stopped by the hearing person who was with them. A discussion of the International Catholic Deaf Religious in 1996 asserted, 'it is vitally important that we continue to keep the spirit of openness and welcome all Christians. We agree that the one key factor that concerns us all is our deafness'[35]. Deaf people show very little concern for the historical issues that have divided churches into varying denominations but are usually comfortable to worship with Deaf people who are from a variety of traditions, as long as the language and culture of the liturgy is one that Deaf people feel they can own. Ecclesiastical divisions are more significant between Deaf and hearing churches rather than between differing denominations.

---

[34] Visible Communications, *The Invisible Church* (Northampton, 1996), section of this video.

[35] International Catholic Deaf Religious, 'The Debate', in McDonough, P. (ed.), *Ephphatha: proceedings from the International Catholic Deaf Religious Conference 1996* (Monmouth, 1996), p.48.

Ecclesiology and Ministry

Ministry in many of the mainstream denominations in England works on a much more collaborative model between leader and people rather than traditional models of church clericalism. Clark argues that clericalism exists in all denominations whereby secular ideas of professionalism are imported into the churches. He argues, 'This in effect relegates the laity to the ranks of the religiously unlettered and unqualified'[36]. Such a structure leads to divisions of power and, as Green argues, 'power can be dominating, even demonic'[37] whereby the unlettered and unqualified can be suppressed and marginalized. Historically, as in most aspects of their lives, Deaf people have been marginalized and suppressed by the powerful who think they know best for them and hence, few Deaf people have gone forward to offer themselves for ministry in the churches. It suits the powerful to keep the powerless in their place and only in more recent times have Deaf people been more able to enter recognized church ministries. Churches are increasingly working towards a more collaborative approach between those in positions of leadership (especially if they are ordained) and the laity at large. In many Free Churches, I acknowledge that this has been in place for much longer than in the Church of England which is adopting collaborative models of ministry as much for financial as theological expediency.

Increasingly, more and more Deaf people are involved in ministry and are receiving some theological training through sign language, though this is usually led by hearing people. Thus, in the Church of England, there are a number of Deaf people now licensed as Pastoral Assistants and Readers. A handful of Deaf people have been ordained in the Church of England, mostly into non-stipendiary ministry with only three actually receiving a stipend with one church army officer. There are two Deaf priests in the UK in the Roman Catholic Church. The lack of Deaf people in stipendiary ministry, and indeed, in senior clerical positions in the Church of England, demonstrates a move towards more collaborative ministerial models that include Deaf people, though without relinquishing too much hearing power.

Many chaplains among Deaf people work alone to offer pastoral care to all Deaf people across a whole diocese. In many instances Anglican and Roman Catholic dioceses are either geographically extremely large or have large populations. The extent to which a chaplain, whether they are Deaf or hearing, is able to offer effective pastoral care and minister to all Deaf people in that area is questionable, though many chaplains do work extremely hard, working far beyond the hours that would normally make up a working week. Consequently, at an unofficial level, there are strong models of collaborative approaches to ministry among the Deaf community. In Birmingham, for example, it was common for Deaf and hearing members of the Deaf churches to regularly be involved in visiting ill or housebound Deaf people, who can be very isolated, in going with each other to hospital appointments, as well as in the preparation and leading of worship. Strong support networks for all Deaf people, whether Christian or not, were clearly evident from the Deaf churches.

---

[36] Clark, D., *The Liberation of the Church: The Role of Basic Christian Groups in a New Re-Formation*, Birmingham, 1984), p.29.

[37] Green, L., *Urban Ministry*, p.126.

Of course, some were more involved in such a collaborative ministry than others, and some Deaf people who attended the church chose not to be involved at all, but generally, ministry was much more collaborative in the area of pastoral care than in hearing churches. Deaf people, while still searching for and struggling to attain their own identity and still relying on hearing people to some degrees, were much more liberated to work in a collaborative model of ministry. It is arguable that the practical issues of one person having to serve a group of people spread over a large geographical area have forced a more collaborative approach to ministry in Deaf churches.

Deaf Liturgy and Worship

The worship and liturgy of the Deaf community is key to understanding many of the ways that Deaf people think about God. 'It is tempting, but dangerous to identify worship with books'[38] argues James White, who also argues that liturgy 'is a work performed by the people for the benefit of others'[39]. Many Anglican liturgies are dictated by the use of books and it is not unusual to be handed two or three books and the odd sheet of paper on entering into church. In many Church traditions, whether they have a written liturgical tradition or not, there is a heavy reliance on the use of words. However, White here suggests that worship is something that is 'done'; it is an active work of a community. In Deaf churches, 'Every service is different. Sign language cannot be written in a book and so there is no fixed text. The Bible readings are told afresh at every service. The prayers are recreated'[40]. Because of the productive lexicon in BSL and as has been emphasized so many times, BSL cannot be written down, the worship and liturgy of Deaf people could never be studied by looking simply at liturgical texts. Rather, Deaf people's worship involves significant elements of spontaneity and freedom. The rest of this chapter will focus on the worship and liturgies of Deaf people, because it is in the context of worship that Deaf people seemed to feel most free to express their ideas and thoughts about God.

Theology without Words: Aspects of Deaf Liturgy

The Use of Texts

I have already written extensively on the use of texts in Deaf culture and specifically in the area of theology and the use of the Bible, and I have argued above that liturgy should not only be understood as a written text. In Birmingham, however, and in many other Deaf churches, liturgical texts are used as the basis of Deaf liturgies; arguably this is because of the ways that Deaf churches continue to be controlled

---

[38]   White, J.F., *Introduction to Christian Worship*. Revised Edition (Nashville, 1990), p.44.

[39]   *Ibid.*, p.32.

[40]   Church of England, *The Church Among Deaf People*, p.15.

by hearing people. The English words of liturgies, therefore, tend to be projected on to a white screen and in Birmingham, a part of the church itself is specifically designed and included for this purpose. From my observations, Deaf people still tend to struggle with following these words and are most at home when the liturgy departs from the words.

Sacred Space

White describes a sacred space as '... a holy place, because it is occupied by and associated with a community of Christian people who are known, publicly known, for their acts of charity and peacemaking and who have drawn their building into the struggle for a radical openness to the will of God'[41]. White laments the way that theologians have traditionally ignored the significance of the theology of space[42]. However, as in any liturgical context, how space is used to facilitate liturgical activity and reflect the theology of the community using that space is extremely important. Deaf people need to be able to see, so worship tends to take place in environments that are well lit. The front wall is usually a good colour against which a signer can stand (in Birmingham this is blue). The seats at Birmingham are arranged in rows, with a space down the middle, and the seats are movable allowing Deaf people to adjust them in order for them to see properly. Other churches use different models, such as sitting in a circle, but visibility is crucial and determines the arrangement of furniture. In Birmingham, increasing amounts of artwork have been used to aid worship, usually reflecting the liturgical season. Posters, a picture of the last supper, crucifix, candles all add to the colour of the worship. Worship is usually led by a minister from the front reflecting hearing practices. This is not always necessary and, as I discuss the interactive nature of Deaf liturgy below, a more circular approach to setting out liturgical space would facilitate introducing more aspects of Deaf culture. The type of sacred space described above that Deaf people use suggests that Deaf people want to be involved in liturgy and that they are active participants who need to see what is happening. It also suggests that Deaf people feel free, not to follow convention too much, but can arrange their space in a way that meets their needs, pointing to a more positive perspective of Deaf people in the liturgical context.

Sermons: Informal and Interactive

Deaf liturgy is invariably both informal and interactive. It is usual for Deaf people to feel free to interrupt the leader, to ask questions and engage in whatever discussion is appropriate at any time. Deaf people also often feel free to walk in and out of worship and chat to each other during worship, which is probably because, as described earlier, the church in Birmingham is located within a Deaf club which is also the social environment of Deaf people. That is not to suggest that Deaf worship is chaotic. However, there is space for learning, for reverence, and awe, and the

---

[41]   White, S., 'The Theology of Sacred Space', Brown, D. and Loades, A., *The Sense of the Sacramental* (London, 1995), pp.42–3.

[42]   *Ibid.*, pp.33–6.

service is also generally structured in some way even though it allows flexibility. The sermon is one point in particular where interaction is especially encouraged. Sermons are rarely if ever monologues in Deaf churches. There is always freedom to ask questions and engage with issues as Deaf people would in any other context. For example, I once led a sermon on 'what it means to be holy'. It would have been difficult for me to convey my thoughts about this abstract concept by expressing my thoughts in a ten-minute monologue. By using discussion and interaction, we were able to think together about the idea. Deaf people asked me questions, and they did the thinking about the implications of 'what it means to be holy' as Deaf people today. By Deaf people making connections in this way with their own experiences, a concept of holiness was discussed and developed with meaning to Deaf people. This reflects many teaching and learning techniques used in adult education. For example, Meg Orr discusses a model of teaching and learning that involves teachers and students sharing ideas and skills together so that all learn together[43].

Conversation

Conversations and interaction are a significant part of Deaf culture and are important in discovering further dimensions to the ways in which Deaf people's theology is expressed. Conversations take place both inside and outside of worship on a variety of subjects and the following example, which considers the use of intercessory prayer in worship, should help to demonstrate how theology is developed in conversation. One chaplain among Deaf people in the Church of England noted how Deaf people often begin and end prayers in a very formal way: 'Almighty God ... through Jesus Christ our Lord, Amen'[44]. In the middle of the prayers, however, the use of this formal style disappears and a more informal dialogue among Deaf people takes place. In this process of communication, questions may be asked about how to sign something and a short discussion may ensue on that subject. As the discussion progresses signs may be decided upon for that particular context and as a result ideas are formulated and thought through.

Often members of the Deaf community who are unwell are also prayed for and a discussion as to the condition of that person proceeds. The result is that often many more people are prayed for than just the person who is unwell, such as their family and friends. They may end by saying, 'we hope they'll be back here soon, we miss them'. Thus they recognize that when one person is ill, a wider community is affected by it. Such a notion can be found to be resonating with 1 Corinthians 12.14ff, where the Body of Christ, as the community of the baptized, is described. The argument explains that every part of the body is needed to make up the whole and if one part is missing, the whole body is affected: 'If one member suffers, all suffer together with it' (v.26a). Thus Deaf people's conversations here reflect the strong sense of identity,

---

[43] Orr, M., 'The Role of the Teacher in the Theological Education of the Laity', Astley, J. (ed.), *Learning in the Way: Research and Reflection on Adult Christian Education* (Leominster, 2000), p.74.

[44] For example, the prayer used at the beginning of the Eucharistic Prayers in the Church of England. See Church of England, *Common Worship* (London, 2002), p.168.

which being a member of a Deaf community and/or a Deaf church brings and that all members of that community are important and valued. Other discussions in prayer have included comments on the election of a new president in the United States, or the earthquake in El Salvador, or the peace process in Northern Ireland, or the war in Iraq. As these issues are discussed, thought about and prayed for, the reality of situations and the interaction of God in the world become significant issues. The role of conversation as a context in which to develop theology is therefore important for Deaf people in worship.

Love of Neighbour: Sharing the Peace

It is generally the case, at the sharing of the peace that Deaf people usually like to share the peace with everyone, hugging and kissing one another as opposed to the typically uncomfortable handshakes of many hearing congregations. Touch is an important aspect of Deaf culture, it is a way of getting attention and it is often used in communication. The peace demonstrates the importance of the practice of love of the neighbour within the Deaf community. This physical affirmation and demonstration of love to each other perhaps goes against the way Deaf people have so often been excluded and marginalized from society and so enables them to affirm each other's humanity through touch and a kiss.

Hymns and Music: Creating a Sense of Communion?

Crichton argues, 'Of all the great figures used of the Church, body, mystery, sacrament, the people of God, the last is the most useful ...' He argues that 'Liturgy is celebrated with others and the relationships between the members of the worshipping community are of the highest importance ... At the practical level, all liturgical rites are arranged for the participation of the community'[45]. Similarly, the Methodist Service Book and the Church of England's Common Worship both assert that the Church is the people of God[46] and that when the Church is gathered for worship, its liturgies should involve participation[47]. Gelineau argues, 'No other sign brings out this communal dimension [to worship] so well as singing'[48]. He explains 'Many individual voices ... can actually be fused together, so that when they blend and follow the same rhythm, only one voice is heard, that of the group'[49]. Music has an additional function in worship in that it is not only the sounds that are created that help people to worship but because, as Lancelot argues, it has a sacramental dimension

---

[45]   Crichton, J.D., 'A Theology of Worship', Jones, C. et al. (eds), *The Study of Liturgy* (London, 1992), p.20.

[46]   Methodist Church, *Methodist Worship Book* (Peterborough, 1999), p.vi, and Church of England, *Common Worship*, p.x.

[47]   Methodist Church, *Methodist Worship Book*, p.vi, and Church of England, *Common Worship*, p.x.

[48]   Gelineau, J., 'Music and Singing in the Liturgy', in Jones, C. et al. (eds), *The Study of Liturgy* (London, 1992), p.495.

[49]   *Ibid.*, p.495.

to it in that it can be understood as being 'an outward sign or an inward grace'[50]. It must be in some way 'iconic' involving 'transcendence and transfiguration'[51]. Clearly one way of symbolizing the unity of a group of people is through the use of music. Begbie articulates this brilliantly in his paper, 'Through Music: Sound Mix' (2000). Two or more separate noises brought together by time, rhythm and harmony create one united sound and this reinforces in liturgical contexts the nature of the worshipping community as diverse members with a common purpose as one body. Prayers that are all said together are also used to a similar end. How, then, do such findings relate to the Deaf community?

It is hard to create a sense of unity in exactly the same way using a language that is communicated visually because two actions, done by two people, cannot seemingly occupy the same space at the same time in the way that two sounds can be heard together at one and the same time. Conversely, a group of people who are dancing keeping to the same time, rhythm and movement can create something that is both beautiful and that looks unified. One attempt at creating the sense of communion in worship that music offers to hearing people has been to use hymns and songs in Deaf liturgies. This works by using music, and in Birmingham involves a hearing person leading a Deaf choir who all sign the words of the hymn keeping together in time. Many Deaf churches use a similar approach to incorporating music and many hearing people comment on how beautiful they find this corporate and visual expression of praise. However, far from expressing great beauty and having a sacramental or iconic dimension to it, signed hymns usually involves Deaf people looking uncomfortable, unable to understand the rhythm of the music while following the unexpected hand movements of the hearing leader. Rarely do hymns use all the many facets that Deaf people communicate with normally, like facial expressions. It should also be acknowledged, however, that some Deaf people have explained that they enjoy watching signing to music and that it does help them to worship. Deaf people have stressed the importance of worship as a place of unity and I have illustrated how this importance is expressed through the care shown to one another in prayer and the way in which the peace is exchanged, for example. Many younger Deaf people resist signing to music and are beginning to explore more obviously Deaf ways of expressing themselves in a way that can be beautiful and artistic. The role of music is one which I predict will gradually disappear from Deaf worship along with so many other impositions from the hearing world, making way for worship that is more authentically Deaf.

---

[50] Lancelot, J., 'Music as Sacrament', Brown, D. and Loades, A. (eds), *The Sense of the Sacramental: Movement and Measure in Art and Music, Place and Time* (London, 1995), p.182.

[51] Tavener, J., 'Towards a Sacred Art', Brown, D. and Loades, A. (eds), *The Sense of the Sacramental: Movement and Measure in Art and Music, Place and Time* (London, 1995), p.174.

Towards a Deaf Liturgy

Since the beginnings of the Protestant Reformation in Europe, there has been a move across the churches of the West for the liturgy of worshipping communities to be made available in the vernacular languages of people. It was one of the principles of the Reformation in Europe that the Bible and the liturgies were translated and adapted to varying degrees to provide access to them for the people. A similar trend was followed in Britain with, for example, the translation of the Bible into Welsh and English and the production of *The Book of Common Prayer*. Article XXIV of the thirty-nine articles states: 'It is a thing plainly repugnant to the Word of God, and the custom of the Primitive Church, to have publick Prayer in the Church, or to minister the Sacraments in a tongue not understanded of the people'[52]. As a result of Vatican II, the Constitution on the Sacred Liturgy 'preserved the normative status of Latin in the liturgy for use in modern vernaculars ... and local Episcopal conferences have widely exploited their authority in this matter'[53]. While the principle of liturgies being made available in a language the people understand is widespread in the Western churches, this seems to have had little impact on the way liturgy and worship has been led by hearing people working among the Deaf community. At the present time, there is an increased interest among Deaf people in the institutional churches to look at how Deaf people can most appropriately express their worship in a culturally relevant way.

Lewis argues: 'In the Deaf church, the predominance of hearing chaplains leading worship has meant that what is seen as the normative language of the preacher or priest often is sign with voice and a high proportion of English'[54]. My experience of the various Deaf churches I have visited is that Lewis is accurate in her summary of the current practice. There is usually the problem that either a hearing chaplain does not have competent signing skills or s/he feels it is appropriate to use some sort of signed English in worship rather than BSL. *The Church Among Deaf People* report claims that 'many older deaf people have been taught that if sign language is to be used, especially in a formal setting, it should be SSE[55] ... Older deaf people continue to insist that it is the only proper language for a formal service'[56]. Despite these claims, I have never once seen a Deaf person express this idea and I suggest that such arguments are put forward simply to justify past practices. Even though many older Deaf people do use a form of SSE to communicate because of their oral education, at a meeting with Deaf people, many said that while they often understand another Deaf person's SSE, they often do not follow SSE used by hearing people. I would suggest this is because even though Deaf people may use some English word order, they also include grammatical features from BSL, such as placement and facial expression to great effect in a way that hearing people rarely do when using SSE. Hence worship and liturgy in Deaf churches, because of some of its hearing leadership has been no

---

[52]   *Book of Common Prayer* (Cambridge, 1662), p.621.

[53]   Wainwright, G., 'The Language of Worship', in Jones, C. et al. (eds), *The Study of Liturgy* (London, 1992), pp.524–5.

[54]   Lewis, H., *A Critical Examination of the Church and Deaf People*, p.165.

[55]   SSE is an acronym for Sign Supported English.

[56]   Church of England, *The Church Among Deaf People*, p.19.

more accessible than in hearing churches. The main difference is that Deaf churches have become places in which Deaf people have been able to meet together. There is pressure from among the Deaf community to take liturgy forward to be more fully accessible to Deaf people and below I will discuss three approaches.

Three Approaches to Creating a Deaf Liturgy

Translating or Interpreting the Hearing Texts

One way that is used to make liturgies more accessible to Deaf people is through a process of literal translation or interpretation of liturgical texts. Needless to say, this process is usually led by hearing people but may involve Deaf people. Interpretation of a liturgy can be done by an individual hearing interpreter who, as in any hearing situation where a Deaf person is present, would translate the spoken words to the Deaf person. In some instances this approach to Deaf worship still occurs in many Deaf church contexts whether Deaf people have chosen to worship alongside hearing people or in a church specifically assigned to Deaf people. Many people with an authorized lay ministry among Deaf people do not have good signing skills and so the worship is interpreted for Deaf people, even when the Church is supposed to be there specifically for the Deaf community. This way of worshipping has its place. It is a way of including Deaf people in a hearing service in an adequate way, but few Deaf people in the interviews I conducted thought that this would be acceptable on a frequent basis. Deaf people, like hearing people, feel most comfortable expressing themselves in their first language and frequently getting information second hand, is ultimately accepting second best. In Zimbabwe, I attended a service that was led in Shona with an interpreter next to me. I felt very much on the margins of that service as my interpreter, as hard as he was working, had to leave information out because there was not always enough time to explain the cultural nuances I would not understand. This must also be true for Deaf people who use an interpreter to participate in hearing worship.

Rather, than simply interpreting liturgies as they are spoken, some chaplains among Deaf people and some lay Deaf people have developed an interest in translating liturgies into BSL, creating BSL liturgies, and even suggesting that they should be authorized by the Church of England[57]. This would be done by a process of discussion and debate, using leading scholars formally trained in theology who fully understand BSL to translate the written texts into BSL. This is the kind of approach used in mainstream churches when liturgies are translated into vernacular languages. In practice, how this would work in the Deaf community is nearly impossible to conceive of at the present moment. Firstly, where would scholars with a sound knowledge of BSL and formal theological training come from? Secondly, approaches to formal academic and ecclesiastical theology, as I have already argued, have traditionally excluded Deaf participation. Thirdly, should a translation be possible, once it is complete, how would it be recorded and disseminated? The charity Visible

---

[57] Shrine, R., 'Towards a BSL Liturgy', in *Signs* (London, 2002), pp.16–17.

Communications, whose work is described in chapter 5, have spent nearly a decade translating about half of Luke's Gospel and a few other random biblical narratives. The process is highly expensive and incredibly time-consuming and it is hard to see how such a translation of the liturgy could be set down in any other way. To my mind, there is no good reason to put resources into such a project in liturgy. Fourthly, should the first three stages be overcome, how would these translations be used in liturgy? Would the president watch a video and copy the signs he saw or would the video itself celebrate the Eucharist? If everything is available on video, there would also be no need for any lay involvement in the worship and they would become passive recipients rather than active participants in the worship. For too long, Deaf people have been passive recipients of worship and, as they begin to become more involved as lay leaders and ordained ministers, I have found many Deaf people enjoy and would not want to give up their involvement in worship. Thus whether a liturgy is interpreted or translated, I fail to see how it can be of much use to Deaf people.

Translating with Cultural Sensitivity

The second approach would be again to interpret/translate, but this time to try to make the liturgy sensitive to Deaf culture. One common example in many Deaf churches is 'Receive our Prayer' replacing 'Hear our Prayer' as the response during the intercessions. In hymns or in Bible readings phrases like 'sing to the Lord' are replaced with 'sign to the Lord'. These minor changes to the liturgy of Deaf people are not recognized formally, but are changes made by local custom. 'Receive' and 'hear' do not mean exactly the same thing as the metaphor for 'hearing' someone in English also implies some sort of response that receiving does not imply. However, it is impossible to always get a direct translation as was seen in the problems of translating English concepts of God into Shona outlined earlier. Shrine has highlighted further problems in communicating many of the central concepts of the Christian faith to Deaf people. He argues that there is no one-to-one equivalent between BSL signs and English for such words as 'grace', 'glory' or 'messiah'[58]. His concern is that there needs to be signs that can convey the meaning of these words accurately. However, exactly what one means by 'glory' or 'grace', for example in English, is extremely ambiguous. Indeed, the word 'God' can evoke images in people's minds as diverse as a kind bearded old man to a cruel God who can allow atrocities like the Holocaust. As I argued much earlier in this work, language is arbitrary to the reality about which it speaks and many of the signs, inadequate as they are, currently in use, will do in BSL as long as it has meaning to the Deaf community among whom it is used. Schweitzer writes, 'Jesus does not require of men to-day that they be able to grasp in either speech or in thought Who He is'[59]. Language is a limited and inadequate tool for expression of the Divine, be it in English or BSL.

However, merely changing the odd word to include Deaf experience cannot be equated with translating a liturgy using cultural sensitivity and awareness which

---

[58]   Shrine, R., 'Towards a BSL Liturgy: Reflections on the Way Ahead'. Unpublished Paper (London, 2002).

[59]   Schweitzer, A., *My Life and Thought: An Autobiography* (London, 1933), p.56.

may otherwise be described as 'Inculturation'. Chupungco describes inculturation as having three elements: 'The first is interaction or dialogue between the church's liturgical worship and the local culture with its components of values, rites, symbols, patterns and institutions. The second is the integration into the liturgy of such cultural elements as are pertinent and suitable. The third is the dynamic whereby the Christian form of worship is enriched by culture without prejudice to its nature as a divine-human institution'[60]. In Deaf churches, there is clearly interaction and dialogue between Deaf culture and the Church's liturgy as can be seen in the minor examples of changes given above. The second of the three elements also takes place to varying degrees. I described above how during the intercessions, the prayers would take the form of an informal conversation reminiscent of what happens among Deaf people outside of the context of worship. This has proved to be a highly pertinent and appropriate way of using Deaf culture in worship. The way in which Deaf people share the peace also shows a way that Deaf cultural ways are present in Deaf worship. Lewis has similarly identified these two aspects of current liturgical practice in Deaf churches as demonstrating Deaf culture. I would also add a third which comes at the point in the sermon. Invariably, sermons in Deaf churches are interactive rather than a monologue as in many hearing churches. Thirdly, worship is clearly enriched by Deaf culture but I would suggest that it is not done so without prejudice to Deaf culture. Indeed, it is often the case that hearing styles of liturgy are imposed onto Deaf people. For example, many churches have Deaf people all signing things together in unison as prayers are said corporately in hearing churches.

Deaf People Creating Deaf Liturgies

Attempts have been made within the Roman Catholic Church and the Church of England to provide liturgies designed specifically for Deaf people to respond to their needs. The Roman Catholic Church have a 'Eucharistic Prayer for the Deaf' written in English to be used only with Deaf people. However, the rubric at the beginning states 'This prayer may never be used without it being signed. The celebrant must always pronounce all the words'[61]. By including a rule by which the celebrant must say every word written in the prayer, immediately turns this into a prayer for the hearing rather than 'the Deaf'. In the Church of England, the 'Preface' to *The Book of Common Prayer* begins with a statement on liturgical authority explaining, 'It hath been the wisdom of the Church of England, ever since the compiling of her Publick Liturgy, to keep the mean between the two extremes, of too much stiffness in refusing, and of too much easiness in admitting any variation from it'[62]. The Church of England it would seem has always had space for liturgical flexibility. This tradition has been built upon by the resolution of General Synod that allows chaplains, with

---

[60]   Chupungco, A.J., *Liturgical Inculturation: sacramentals, religiosity and catechesis* (Collegeville, Minnesota, 1992), pp.244–5.

[61]   This Prayer is not published, but can be obtained from the Catholic Deaf Association. While this introductory phrase is often removed, it does form part of the prayer in its authorized form. McDonough, P., *Personal Communication*, 2004.

[62]   *Book of Common Prayer*, p.v.

the written permission of diocesan bishops, to use 'an authorized form of service performed in British Sign Language'[63]. While I accept that an Anglican diocesan bishop is responsible for what his ministers preach, teach and practise liturgically, I am not aware of any diocesan bishop currently in the Church of England with the ability to judge whether a BSL liturgy is consistent with Christian tradition, and thereby be in a position to give chaplains permission to use it.

Lewis, in deconstructing Deaf liturgies, argues that the liturgical practice in the Deaf churches needs to be reconstructed. In that process of reconstruction, she argues that some of the key features will be greater attention to the layout of buildings, practices that reflect Deaf culture such as those already present in Deaf churches during the sermon, intercessions and peace, and by liturgies being led by Deaf people[64]. I wholly subscribe to what Lewis suggests. In addition, a Deaf liturgy, which in my view would fully reflect Deaf culture, would be something quite unrecognizable to most current practices. If Deaf liturgy made no use of any part of hearing culture, there would be no signed songs or any other corporate signing together, no set liturgy other than that developed by custom, and no reading from the Bible, only the recitation of Biblical stories transmitted through oral or more accurately, signing traditions. Many hearing metaphors would disappear altogether like 'hear our prayer' or 'all your works echo the silent music of your praise'[65]. A truly Deaf liturgy will only ever be achieved by Deaf people having the freedom to create and express worship in ways that emerge from Deaf culture and experience. Similarly, it is among some of the African Independent Churches spreading throughout the African continent that liturgies and theologies are developing, which claim to be authentically Christian and 'exemplify appropriations of the gospel in keeping with African cultural thought forms and practices'[66].

The Question of Authority

I cannot help but feel that churches must get away from any notion of *authorized* Deaf liturgies. I can only assume that the concept of an authorized liturgy must be significantly influenced by hearing culture. The notion of the authorization of texts is a Western tradition emerging initially out of ancient Greek culture and societies that place a strong emphasis on the role of literature and the formation of the biblical canon and the Church's Creeds emerged out of that tradition. Different cultures, far from using literature all in the same way, offer many diverse approaches to the role of literature in society[67]. By authorizing texts, the language of the texts is fixed and, even though it is open to varying individual and corporate interpretations, the theology within it in the liturgical context ceases to have the freedom to engage in

    63   Shrine, R., 'Towards a BSL Liturgy', in *Signs* (London, 2002), pp.16–17.
    64   Lewis, H., *A Critical Examination of the Church and Deaf People*, pp.153–76.
    65   Church of England, *Common Worship*, p.201.
    66   Stinton, D., 'Africa, East and West', in Parratt, J. (ed.), *An Introduction to Third World Theologies* (Cambridge, 2004), p.119.
    67   See, for example, many of the papers in Street, B. (ed.), *Cross Cultural Approaches to Literacy* (Cambridge, 1993).

creative dialogue with the culture and context and respond adequately to the needs of varying communities. Deaf culture has much more in common with oral, non-literary cultures where liturgies are not fixed but dynamically emerge out of the experience of the community. Among the Deaf community, I have already argued above that recording liturgies for authorized use is impractical and I would suggest instead that Deaf liturgies ought to emerge out of Deaf culture and be relevant to it, retain the freedom that Deaf culture enjoys from texts that are fixed and develop ways of worshipping that can be passed on from one generation to another through local custom in Deaf signing traditions. If only the institutional churches could feel able to liberate Deaf people from the confines of the liturgical text and the need to give liturgies ecclesiastical authority, so that Deaf people can express themselves in worship in culturally relevant ways.

Conclusion

In this chapter, I have engaged with issues concerning ecclesiology and liturgy. I have described the ecclesiological and liturgical practices of the Deaf community in Birmingham with reference to other contexts in Britain, and I have drawn from that some of the ways in which Deaf people have developed theologies relating to the Church and worship. I have further attempted to engage with some of the developments in Deaf churches and liturgies that are currently being discussed by Deaf people in connection with some of the ecclesiastical hierarchies in Britain, who have been willing to engage with some of the issues. I have then offered my own reflections on the subject in the hope that it may be able to make a useful contribution to the debate – mainly that Deaf liturgy should be left to Deaf communities to create and only involve hearing people when Deaf people invite them to make a contribution. In the final chapter, building on all that has been discussed so far in this book, I would like to move on to engage with some Deaf perspectives on God.

Chapter 7

Deaf in the Image of the Deaf God

Introduction: 'Be Perfect ... as your Heavenly Father is Perfect'

Being in some way like God has always been a part of the Christian theological understanding of what it means to be human. This theme can be found as early as in the first chapter of Genesis: 'So God created humankind in his image' (Genesis 1.27). Matthew suggests that Jesus sees this likeness of God in human beings (or at least the potential for it) when he tells the disciples to 'be perfect ... as your heavenly Father is perfect' (Matthew 5.48). Numerous theologies have since developed along a similar theme, not least, for example, in the medieval period in the writing of Thomas Á Kempis' *The Imitation of Christ*[1] and in more recent times in the writings of Leonardo Boff[2] and Jürgen Moltmann[3] in their respective works on the Trinity. These later works contrast the Genesis narrative, in that they are about the human striving to be like God whereas Genesis states that humans are already made in the image of God. The Greek word for image is 'ikōn'[4] from which we derive the word 'icon'. In the Orthodox tradition, the icon is a creation designed to point the viewer beyond themselves and the creation towards the Divine: icons fulfil a 'sacramental function, constituting a channel of divine grace ... the icon acts as a point of meeting, a place of encounter'[5]. Whether humans are already made as ikōns of God or they are striving to be ikōns of God (perhaps a mixture of the two), I suggest that these two strands are part of the same tradition of connecting the Divine with human being and recognizing that in some way the human form points beyond itself towards God. But what does such a notion mean for a person who is Deaf, especially that of being ikōns which are striving to be perfect like their heavenly Father?

Deafness, Perfection and Sin

In the English language, perfection is understood as, 'complete, faultless; not deficient; exact, precise; entire'[6]. The Christian doctrine of original sin suggests that no

---

[1] Á Kempis, T., *The Imitation of Christ* (London, 1963).

[2] Boff, L., *Trinity and Society* (Tunbridge Wells, 1988).

[3] Moltmann J., *History and the Triune God* (London, 1991).

[4] 'Image' or 'likeness'. See Abbott-Smith, G., *A Manual Greek Lexicon of the New Testament* (Edinburgh, 1994), p.131.

[5] Ware, K., 'The Spirituality of the Icon', in Jones, C. et al. (eds), *The Study of Spirituality* (London, 2000), p.197.

[6] Swannell, J., (ed.), *The Little Oxford Dictionary of Current English*. Sixth Edition (Oxford, 1986), p.397.

human being is perfect or faultless but is in their very nature sinful. In Genesis, humans are described as already being ikōns of God whereas in later writings such as Paul's letter, humans must strive to become more like God, presumably in light of the fall. Paul writes in Romans, 'all have sinned and fall short of the glory of God' (Romans 3.23) and 'one man's (Adam's) trespass led to condemnation for all' (Romans 5.18), and so imperfection in this sense is something all humanity shares because perfection is interpreted as being in a state without sin, a condition theology asserts humans have never had since the beginnings of creation.

In chapter 5, I discussed the way that some passages in the Bible suggest that Deafness and disability is a result of human sin, not the sinful state of humanity so much as it being a punishment for individual sins. This attitude is still present in the mindset of many revealed in the adage: 'What has so-and-so done to deserve that?' This common phrase implies that Deaf and disabled people are in some way more sinful than hearing or non-disabled people because God has specifically chosen to punish them. If Deafness is thought about in this way, it can be argued that Deaf and disabled people are lesser ikōns of God than non-disabled people because Deafness and disability are perceived 'imperfections' that are signs of God's punishment.

The notion that God punishes those who are sinful finds no evidence to support it in human experience. Relatively good people suffer while those who are engaged in evil acts seem to receive no punishment at all – a theme echoed in some of the Psalms[7]. Jesus also rejects the idea in John 9.3, when he says 'neither this man nor his parents sinned; he was born blind so that God's works might be revealed in him'. At first, such a notion appears to be highly disturbing. However, the Greek 'hina' here translated as 'so that' could equally be translated as 'with the result that'. Read in light of the social model of disability and the increasing awareness among Deaf people that their Deaf condition is something to be affirmed and celebrated, can a person be born Deaf or disabled and the result still be that God's glory is revealed in that person? It is arguable that if Deafness itself can in any way be viewed as having the potential to be positive and creative, then the experiences of many Deaf people suggests that Deafness is not some awful punishment but a part of the creative intentions of a loving God[8].

Deafness and Physical Perfection

In the contemporary Western situation, perfection is frequently interpreted not only as being without sin, but also in terms of physical beauty and strength. The media portrays the perfect human not as one who is without sin, but as one who is 'young, white, able-bodied, slim, fit, intelligent, ambitious and financially successful'[9]. Those who do not fit such criteria are considered to be 'incomplete, faulty, deficient and unwhole'. If the Father is the prototype for perfection and if perfection is interpreted

---

[7]   See, for example, Psalm 73.1–14 and Psalm 74.1–8.

[8]   Weir, M.K., 'Made Deaf in God's Image', in *International Ecumenical Working Group, The Place of Deaf People in the Church* (Northampton, 1996), pp.7–9.

[9]   Morris, W., 'Disability Included! A Model for Church Communities', *Viewpoints*, 8 (2001): 8.

as physical beauty in our current social context, then it would seem that Deaf people have more to do to be perfect and be ikōns of God, because Deafness is a condition often viewed in society as ugly and undesirable, hence the vast amounts of money invested in so far unsuccessful medical research to try and eliminate Deafness. Thus when a Deaf person inevitably does not meet the criteria for perfection she is marginalized and excluded from society along with old people, black people, those who are not fit or are overweight, and those who are poor.

Theology naturally begins with human experience and employs human languages and images in its quest to understand and make sense of God. This creates, however, the very serious danger that God is manipulated and defined by social criteria and becomes nothing more than a puppet to justify certain human enterprises. Confronted with the evil of the First World War, Karl Barth became acutely aware of these dangers and argued that the starting point for theology should not be experience but Christ: 'Instead of analyzing human existence, in order then to inquire after Christ's contribution to its religious aspect, he (Barth) analyzes Christ's existence, in order then to inquire after our religion's place therein'[10]. Mosala also argues from the South African perspective that 'No other political or ideological system in the modern world that I know of derives itself so directly from the Bible as the ideology of Apartheid'[11]. Western civilizations have often described God as though he were made in their image and have turned him into an instrument of oppression towards Deaf people among many others. The feminist writer Mary Daly makes this point brilliantly when she says 'If God is male then the male is God'[12]. Not only must Deaf people not be understood as being punished for sin and therefore lesser ikōns of God, but in addition, the concept of perfection, in the light of the Gospel itself, needs to be re-interpreted in contra-distinction to Western cultural notions of perfection being about physical prowess, intellectual abilities or social success.

Being Perfect: Deaf People as Ikōns of God

The Greek verb in Matthew 5.48 translated as 'perfect' is 'teleiow', which may also be translated as 'to bring to maturity' or 'to complete'. It may also mean 'to fulfil'[13]. Such translations immediately take us away from the idea that perfection is about being completely without sin or physically superior. To be complete, fulfilled or to be brought to maturity, about which Jesus is speaking in Matthew 5.48, offers a radically different perspective on what it means to be perfect, because perfection in the sense it is used in the Gospels is not related to physical and mental prowess or socio-economic success, but to an inner state of being attainable by all. Those forces

---

[10]   Jenson, R.W., 'Karl Barth', in Ford, D. (ed.), *The Modern Theologians: An Introduction to Christian Theology in the Twentieth Century.* Second Edition (Oxford, 1997), p.23.

[11]   Mosala, I.J., 'The Implications of the Text of Esther for African Women's Struggle for Liberation in South Africa', in Sugirtharajah, R.S. (ed.), *Voices from the Margin* (London/ Maryknoll, 1995), p.168.

[12]   Daly, M., *Beyond God the Father: Towards a Philosophy of Women's Liberation* (London, 1986), p.19.

[13]   Abbott-Smith, G., *A Manual Greek Lexicon of the New Testament*, p.442.

which stop people being fulfilled or complete are the forces of evil taking humanity away from being ikōns of the Father, because they oppress and marginalize people and are thus contrary to the will of God who desires that his people are 'teleios' just like himself. In this way Deaf people along with everyone else can aspire to be perfect as their heavenly Father is perfect, and Deaf people can do so in their condition of Deafness and many Deaf people do feel complete and fulfilled as Deaf people. To be Deaf does not mean that one is more sinful and it does not mean you are deficient or faulty or incomplete. Using this principle of perfection, there is reason to argue that Deaf people can strive to be perfect as their heavenly Father is and aspire to more fully be in his image: 'ikōns' of their Father in their Deaf condition.

Is God Deaf?

If Deaf people can be described as being in God's image, aspiring to fulfilment in their Deaf condition, dare I suggest also that God might in some way be described as Deaf and if so what is meant by this? Christian faith argues, a priori, that God is mystery and so even for those who claim that Christ is 'the way the truth and the life', it can never be grasped as to what exactly that means. Theology is restricted in what it can say about God to metaphor and analogy based only on human experience. Human experience is a valid basis for discussion about God (despite its dangers) as 'humankind is created in his (God's) image' (Genesis 1.27). To avoid the dangers of this approach to theology, experience should be measured alongside God's revelation to humanity throughout history. While human beings and their experiences are so extremely diverse, to say that human experience helps us to understand God arguably does not bring us much closer to comprehending the reality of God.

Is it then appropriate to speak about God using abstract, neutral language? In other words, can theology say that God is neither white nor black, male nor female, Deaf nor hearing, but that God is Spirit and no human category should be used to describe any quality of God? John Hull argues, 'There is a God of blind people and there is a God of sighted people, but beyond and above there is the God above the gods, who transcends both blindness and sight and is the God of everyone'[14]. This may be the underlying principle of theology and belief in God, but for human beings to talk about God in this way is meaningless for most of the time. Humans cannot possibly conceive of and relate to a God who is neither one thing nor the other and yet both at the same time. In contrast James Cone argues, 'There is no place in black theology for a colourless God in a society where human beings suffer precisely because of their colour'[15]. He goes on to say, 'Because God has made the goal of blacks God's own goal, black theology believes that it is not only appropriate but necessary to begin the doctrine of God with an insistence on God's blackness.'[16] Likewise, in human suffering it would make God irrelevant to say that he was neutral about it. For example, if God is a white, Western, affluent God as portrayed in Western art *and* a poor, oppressed, Latin American God at the same time, the poor of Latin America

---

[14]   Hull, J.M., *In the Beginning there was Darkness* (London, 2001), p.134.

[15]   Cone, J.H., *A Black Theology of Liberation* (New York, 1990), p.63.

[16]   Cone, J.H., *A Black Theology of Liberation*, p.63.

would have no grounds on which to argue that God is on their side against the evil powers of oppression. From the Exodus onwards the history of God's revelation has shown God to be on the side of the oppressed. If God is the God of everyone, a diversity of expressions of the Divine are needed for God to be meaningful to everyone, but this needs to be consistent with the God of liberation[17].

The mystery of God provides countless possibilities for Christians around the world to talk creatively about God in terms of their own history, language, culture and social conditioning, as they reflect on what it means to be made in God's image. God is not neutral to the human condition but involved and concerned with it. In the African context Mercy Amba Oduyoye reflects on Nasimiyu who says, 'God the Christ is the one who takes on the conditions of African women: conditions of weakness, misery, injustice and oppression'[18]. Across the world different cultures and traditions are talking about God in their own terms. God is described as black[19], female[20], African[21], as a Dalit[22], a Minjung[23], as Ancestor[24], Healer[25], Liberator[26], as one who suffers with the oppressed[27]. Such talk has become almost common parlance in some circles of theological debate. For nearly forty years and more, feminist theologians and theologians of liberation and culture have been talking about God in culturally relevant ways, although their writings have often remained on the margins of theology in the Church and academy as the experience from which they write remains on the margins of society. But there is still undoubtedly even greater discomfort when anyone talks about God as Deaf, disabled, limited, vulnerable, and broken. Nevertheless, this is the starting point at which Deaf and disabled people are remythologizing the Christian tradition in terms of their own context. So can we talk

---

[17] Oduyoye, M.A., *Introducing African Women's Theology* (Sheffield, 2001), p.12 for example employs a similar method for talking about God. Theology's potential to lead to liberation is the criterion by which theology can be judged as authentic.

[18] Oduyoye, M.A., *Introducing African Women's Theology*, p.61.

[19] Cone, J.H., 'Black Theology in the United States', in Fabella, V. and Sugirtharajah, R.S. (eds), *The SCM Dictionary of Third World Theologies* (London, 2003), p.211.

[20] See Grant, J., *White Woman's Christ, Black Woman's Jesus* (Atlanta, 1989).

[21] In many parts of Africa, names for God and images of God are distinctively African drawing on African Traditional Religions and Contemporary Experience. In this sense, God is very much African. See, Oduyoye M.A., *Introducing African Women's Theology*, pp. 44–6 and Nyamiti, C., 'The Doctrine of God', in Parratt, J. (ed.), *A Reader in African Christian Theology* (London, 1997), pp.57–64.

[22] Kim, K., 'India', in Parratt, J. (ed.), *An Introduction to Third World Theologies* (Cambridge, 2004), p.63.

[23] Byung Mu Ahn, 'Jesus and People (Minjung)', in Sugirtharajah, R.S., *Asian Faces of Jesus* (New York, 1993), p.169.

[24] Stinton, D., 'Africa, East and West', in Parratt, J. (ed.), *An Introduction to Third World Theologies* (Cambridge, 2004), p.127

[25] Bonino, José Míguez, 'Latin American', in Fabella, V. and Sugirtharajah, R.S. (eds), *The SCM Dictionary of Third World Theologies* (London, 2003), p.55.

[26] Phiri, I.A., 'Southern Africa', in Parratt, J. (ed.), *An Introduction to Third World Theologies* (Cambridge, 2004), p.147.

[27] *Ibid.*, p.147.

about God as being Deaf? Before addressing this question, I will look at some of those theologies that suggest God can be described as disabled.

Perspectives on the Disabled God

Burton Cooper: The Disabled God as One Who Suffers

One of the earliest writers to propose that God is disabled is Burton Cooper[28] in a journal article published in *Theology Today* in 1992. Cooper appears cautious in putting forward this idea, and in talking about God as disabled, he immediately qualifies the statement with the phrase, 'metaphorically of course'[29], as if the whole of theological discourse were not metaphorical in nature anyway. God is disabled, according to Cooper, because of Christ's participation in the world's suffering and more specifically, his identification with the suffering of disabled people. He explains, 'God feels the world in the way the disabled person feels the world. To call God disabled reminds us of the concreteness of God's loving presence in the world'[30]. Cooper may have been one of the first to explicitly describe God as disabled, but by focusing on suffering, he probably alienated more disabled people by his thesis than non-disabled people. Of course disabled people suffer because of either physical pain, socio-economic deprivation or, if they become disabled later in life, because of the grief caused by loss. But increasingly disabled people do not like the language of suffering as it is usually accompanied by attitudes of pity for their supposed 'tragedy'. If Christ did identify with disabled people, for that to be meaningful it would need to go beyond the issue of suffering. Deaf people in particular reject the language of suffering – especially physical suffering – in relation to their impairment. Their identity is much more tied up with a common history, language and culture than with suffering. They rarely suffer physically because being Deaf is not physically painful, even if they do suffer socially, economically, politically and theologically.

Nancy Eiesland: The Disabled God

Nancy Eiesland's, *The Disabled God: Toward a Liberatory Theology of Disability* (1994) has been the most significant and influential thesis on the nature of God as disabled. Her arguments, as with most of those that talk about God as disabled, are Christocentric. Eiesland's theology emerges out of her experience as a disabled person and presents an entirely different perspective from Cooper by focusing not on God's participation in human suffering, but on Christ's physically impaired body. Eiesland is concerned with the use of symbols and the way they are used theologically, arguing that her contextual approach enables her to unmask 'the ways in which theological inquiry has frequently instituted able-bodied experience as the

---

28   Cooper, B., 'The Disabled God' *Theology Today*, xlix (2), (1992): 173–82.
29   *Ibid.*, p.173.
30   *Ibid.*, p.179.

theological norm'[31]. Eiesland's thesis is that 'in the resurrected Jesus Christ, they (the disciples) saw not the suffering servant for whom the last and most important word was tragedy and sin, but the disabled God who embodied both impaired hands and feet and pierced side and the imago Dei'[32]. The significance of focusing on the wounds of the resurrected Christ is that as the disabled God he is also 'the image of Jesus Christ the stigmatized Jew, person of colour, and representative of the poor and hungry – those who have struggled to maintain the integrity and dignity of their bodies in the face of the physical mutilation of injustice and rituals of bodily degradation'[33]. The disabled God shows how impairment ought not to be perceived as the result of personal sin, but that Christ suffers and those who are impaired suffer because of social injustice. She continues, 'This is the God who indicts not only deliberate injustice, but unintended rituals of degradation that deny the full personhood of marginalized people'[34].

Eiesland's argument concludes with a focus on the Eucharist. This central sacrament of the church as Christ's body (which should be a body of inclusion according to 1 Corinthians 12.12ff) often becomes for disabled people a 'ritual of exclusion and degradation'[35]. Hull has said: 'I have occasionally been in situations when a helpful member of the congregation wants to guide me to the communion rail. They have stood behind me holding both my elbows, and walked me forward as if I was a cart. I find that very awkward and humiliating'[36]. However, in the Eucharist when disabled people are included in the body, 'we encounter the disabled God, who displayed the signs of disability, not as a demonstration of failure and defect, but in affirmation of connection and strength'[37]. For Eiesland it is Christ's body that is impaired and she finds this liberating and concludes that in the Eucharist that the disabled God is present today.

Amanda Shao Tan and Randall Otto: The Disabled Christ

Amanda Shao Tan chooses to use the language of the 'disabled Christ' rather than Eiesland's disabled God, making her perspective even more Christocentric. Tan begins her arguments by defining disability as 'functional limitation'[38] and links that to the incarnation of Christ: 'The disability of Christ stems from the wide gap between who he is, what he has and what he can do in contrast to who he became, what he forfeited, and the limitations and confinements to which he subjected

---

[31]   Eiesland, N., *The Disabled God* (Nashville, 1994), p.99. Eiesland's comments here are resonated in Hull, J.M., *In the Beginning there was Darkness*, in which Hull speaks from his experience becoming blind and feeling alienated from the Bible because he realized that it was written by sighted people using sighted language and imagery (p.3).

[32]   Eiesland, N., *The Disabled God*, p.99.

[33]   *Ibid.*, p.102.

[34]   *Ibid.*, p.103.

[35]   *Ibid.*, p.113.

[36]   Morris, W., 'Interview: Professor John Hull', *All People*, 85 (2000): 7.

[37]   Eiesland, N., *The Disabled God*, p.116.

[38]   Tan, A.S., 'The Disabled Christ', *Transformation: An International Evangelical Dialogue on Mission and Ethics*, 15/4 (1998): 9.

himself'[39]. She goes on to argue that whilst Christ was not marginalized because of any sickness or impairment he had, he was degraded and humiliated by the ways in which the religious leaders ostracized him. This 'blemished reputation' of Jesus can be likened, she argues, 'to those who were the sick and disabled of his time'[40]. She continues, 'pinned to the cross, he knew how it felt to be physically incapacitated'[41] that made him experience pains and difficulties that many disabled people also feel. She sums up by saying, 'Thus, in the willing forfeiture of everything that he could have and everything that was his, and in the suffering that came as a result of his voluntary deprivation, Jesus became disabled'[42].

Tan's thesis has been criticized in an article by Randall Otto[43] and he identifies two ways in which he suggests her argument is problematic. Firstly, he points out that the incarnation of Christ was a voluntary act. The difficulty of relating this to disabled people, he argues, is that, 'it (disability) is imposed upon them *involuntarily*, whether by the genetic make-up passed on to them or by environmental factors adversely affecting them'[44]. It is true that people become impaired involuntarily. However, the extent to which the incarnation was a voluntary act could be said to be ambiguous. When Jesus is in the garden of Gethsemane, there is, from the perspective of the Gospel writer, a sense in which Christ feels compelled to face the incapacitation of the cross. He is compelled by his knowledge of the Father's will (Matthew 26.39) and arguably by his love for humanity. The incarnation is a part of God's plan for humanity – and of salvation history – and his love for them compels him to act in certain ways. Anselm also insists on the *necessity* of the incarnation as Galvin sums up Anselm's view: 'The debt (for sin) must be repaid, and a human being must repay it; yet apart from the incarnation no human being can do so'[45]. While I do not particularly subscribe to Anselm's view on the purpose of the incarnation, it does show how some aspects of the Christian tradition have argued for the necessity of Christ's incarnation and his subsequent death on the cross.

Secondly, Otto criticizes Tan's discussion of the way in which in first-century Palestine, there was a general assumption that sickness or impairment were the result of sin. He argues that suffering was also 'brought about or allowed for the refining of faith'[46]. Like Cooper, Otto uses suffering and disability synonymously. Reflecting on John 9.3, Otto explains, 'God allows some to have disabilities so that they may more clearly demonstrate the sufficiency of God's grace and the perfection of his power amidst their weaknesses'[47]. To use suffering and disability as interchangeable descriptions of the same thing shows Otto's lack of understanding of disability. Otto

---

[39]   *Ibid.*, p.10.

[40]   *Ibid.*, p.12.

[41]   *Ibid.*, p.12.

[42]   *Ibid.*, p.12.

[43]   Otto, R., 'Incarnated or Incapacitated? Another Look at "The Disabled Christ"' *Phronesis*, 4/1 (1997): 65–75.

[44]   *Ibid.* p.66.

[45]   Galvin, J.P., 'Jesus Christ', in Schüssler-Fiorenza, F. and Galvin, J.P. (eds), *Systematic Theology: Roman Catholic Perspectives* (Dublin, 1992), p.278.

[46]   Otto, R., 'Incarnated or Incapacitated?', p.67.

[47]   *Ibid.*, p.67.

has also misunderstood Tan. Tan's arguments concerning the link of sin and disability are a reflection only of first-century Palestinian attitudes. When the disciples ask Jesus in John 9.2, 'who sinned, this man or his parents that he was born blind?' it strongly indicates that it was a first-century Palestinian view that sin and disability were related. Like Jesus in John 9.3, Tan clearly refutes the idea that disability is a punishment from God. For those disabled people who suffer either because of social injustice or physical pain, far from helping to refine their faith, it often results in a rejection of any idea of a God of love and justice.

Otto's paper is most disturbing of all because of the alternative model of the disabled Christ which he puts forward. It is difficult to know what the appearance of Christ was like, he argues, but some ideas can be gleaned from the suffering servant passages. He suggests that early Church Fathers interpreted sections of Isaiah 52–53 as references to Christ's physical appearance. He quotes, for example, Ireneaus: 'He [Jesus] was a man without comeliness, and liable to suffering', and Tertullian: 'His [Jesus'] body did not reach even to human beauty'. Isaiah 53.2 says, 'He had no beauty or majesty to attract us to him ...'[48] Through these references to the appearance of Christ, he argues that, 'Jesus might have been deformed'[49]. Whilst, the passages from Isaiah may suggest that the suffering servant was not be beautiful, they do not suggest that he would be disfigured or deformed, they simply said he would not be beautiful or 'comely'. To suggest that Jesus was 'ugly' and that this links him to disabled people is, to my mind, deeply offensive for it can work only to perpetuate those deep-rooted social stereotypes that a person cannot be both disabled and at the same time display beauty.

Taylor and McCloughry and McCloughry and Morris

Commenting on Amy Shao Tan's argument on the incarnation and disability, Taylor and McCloughry say, 'Jesus does not need to go through every experience that we do in order to have significance for us. He lived his own unique life just as we do. We do not have to manipulate its details to create a life more obviously in solidarity with disabled people. The solidarity is there in the events of the incarnation, the Crucifixion and the Resurrection'[50]. Concerned about compromising the idea of God's omnipotent power[51], McCloughry and Taylor opt for talking about a disabled God who is impaired in the person and acts of the historical Jesus, and so like Tan, they prefer the title 'The Disabled Christ' rather than 'The Disabled God'. As disabled people experience limitation in a world dominated by non-disabled people, so the historical Jesus experiences limitation by emptying himself of his 'Godly capabilities'. The historical Jesus is a useful figure for demonstrating God's solidarity with disabled people, but this was an historical event now finished. In many ways, the historical Jesus is chronologically distant to disabled people today. Both Tan, and Taylor and McCloughry speak about the disabled Christ in the past

---

[48]   *Ibid.*, p.67.

[49]   *Ibid.*, p.68.

[50]   Taylor, M. and McCloughry, R., 'A Disabled God?', *Third Way* (October 1998): 14.

[51]   *Ibid.*, p.14.

tense. God must continue to be relevant to disabled people today as a God who is still in some way experiencing the oppression and limitation of disabled people. This is why the resurrected Christ as the 'disabled God' about which Eiesland talks is so compelling.

McCloughry and Morris have attempted to address this question of searching for language that has meaning for disabled people today. They quote Nancy Eiesland who says, 'I saw God in a sip-puff wheelchair, that is the chair used by quadriplegics enabling them to manoeuvre by blowing and sucking on a straw-like device. Not an omnipotent self-sufficient God, but neither a pitiable suffering servant. In this moment, I beheld God as survivor, unpitying and forthright. I recognized the incarnate Christ in the image of those judged "not feasible", "unemployable", with "questionable quality of life". Here was God for me'[52]. The metaphor of a disabled God is a powerful recognition that God's solidarity with disabled people is continuing because it takes the emphasis away from the historical Jesus to the eternal God. In a further sense, McCloughry and Morris refer back to Eiesland's idea of Christ's woundedness. They argue, 'Christ has taken his experience up into God. This Christ ascends into his glory but even in his glory he bears the marks as well as the experience of his physical body'[53]. In heaven, they argue, Christ is not 'normalized' to be like 'perfect' human beings, but that the wounds and marks of earth are somehow transformed in heaven[54].

John Hull: God is Blind

In John Hull's, *In the Beginning There was Darkness* (2001), he seeks for a way of understanding God and being able to be in relationship with him as a blind person rather than more generally as a disabled person. In using sight as a metaphor for God's knowledge, Hull argues, the image in the Bible has limitations because 'human sight is defective, whereas God's knowledge is perfect'[55] and so in the Bible God is sometimes described as being beyond sight or even that he does not need sight. In Psalm 97, Hull explains, it describes God as being surrounded by clouds and thick darkness so that 'human sight cannot penetrate it' suggesting that God, like blind people, is indifferent to darkness. To this extent, Hull explains that it is possible to argue that God is blind, because neither light nor darkness make any difference to him, as they do not to blind people either. The key here in being able to describe God as blind, as with the arguments about God as disabled, stem from searching for a way of finding God being able to identify with the experience of the disabled person today.

---

[52]   Eiesland, N., *The Disabled God*, p.89.

[53]   McCloughry, R. and Morris, W., *Making a World of Difference*, p.69.

[54]   *Ibid.*, pp.72–3.

[55]   Hull, J.M., *In the Beginning there was Darkness*, p.133.

Mary Weir: God Made Visible

Mary Weir, as far as I am aware, is the only one person to suggest in a written publication that God is Deaf. This view is not uncommon among many Deaf people – as will be seen later – but most images of God as disabled have not focused on what is distinctively Deaf. Like Tan, Mary Weir focuses her attention on Christ's incarnation. However, rather than interpreting the incarnation in terms of incapacitation, Weir sees in the incarnate God the Christ who 'is made concrete, real, see-able, comprehensible, and yes, touchable to my Deaf sensibilities'[56]. Weir suggests that the incarnate Word, the Logos is 'Deaf like me'[57] because he is concerned to be visible and tangible. Weir does not discuss this idea in much detail, but she has highlighted what is one of the key concepts at the heart of Deaf theology. In what follows later, I will explore more fully what that means for Deaf people in Britain today.

The Disabled God: A Summary

For Cooper, God can be spoken about as disabled because of his suffering. Eiesland and Tan both focus on Jesus Christ as the disabled God. For Eiesland, God is disabled because he is wounded and his wounds remain with him even in his resurrected condition. For Tan, Christ is disabled because of the limitation experienced through the incarnation. Otto suggests that Christ is disabled because of his physical appearance as it is described in the suffering servant passages and certain texts from the Church Fathers. McCloughry and Taylor argue that Jesus did not need to experience every kind of disability to be relevant to all disabled people, but is in solidarity with them through his life, death and resurrection. Like Eiesland, McCloughry and Morris argue that God has taken his wounds with him beyond the crucifixion through the resurrection and into heaven, suggesting that the marks of human experience do not disappear in heaven. Hull talks about a blind God for whom darkness and light make no difference – he is perfectly at home in both. None of these texts focusing on the disabled God address the experience of Deafness. Only Mary Weir does that in her short article. Cooper, Eiesland, Tan and Otto, all express their theology as though the God they are describing is relevant to all disabled people. Hull is explicit that he is writing about the experience of total blindness and he does not try to say that his argument is relevant to all disabled people or even all visually impaired people. This illustrates a trend emerging in the area of theology and disability; a recognition that the experiences of those with different types of impairment are not the same and should not be homogenized. In the preface to *Making a World of Difference* (2002), McCloughry and Morris acknowledge 'the difficulty of talking about disability when the experience of people with impairments is so diverse'[58]. This is particularly so for the Deaf community whose experiences and life concerns are often different to many disabled people. Like McCloughry and Morris, Deaf people are concerned not just

---

[56] Weir, M.K., 'Made Deaf in God's Image', p.9.
[57] *Ibid.*, p.9.
[58] McCloughry, R. and Morris W., *Making a World of Difference*, p.vii.

with the figure of the historical Jesus, but also how God – primarily through the Christ of faith – is relevant to Deaf people living in the twenty-first century. Below, I will address the perspectives of Deaf people concerning whether they think of God as in any way Deaf.

The Deaf God

Deaf communities throughout the world are different from one another and similarly, Deaf individuals who live in the same town, city or country also represent a diverse set of experiences. Inevitably, the variety of experience in the Deaf community leads to multiple theological perspectives. It would thus be inappropriate and inaccurate to present just one theological idea about God from the Deaf community when more than one exists even in Birmingham. While this variety exists, for the purposes of discussion here, I would like to suggest that the God of Deaf theology can be divided into two general categories, although these comprise of multiple levels of interpretation. Firstly, there is a focus on God as one who is Deaf in a physical sense. This is almost like referring to God as black, female or African, for example. Secondly, as has been discussed earlier, many Deaf people understand their Deafness as much more than simply being biologically unable to hear. It also includes being part of a culture. Consequently, in the Deaf community there is a strong sense (sometimes consciously and sometimes subconsciously) that God is culturally Deaf and I would suggest that for Deaf people, this is far more important in their thinking than the idea of God as being unable to hear in a physical sense. This is demonstrated primarily through the way Deaf people sign about their experience of God, their understanding of Jesus from the Gospel narratives and other stories about God in the Bible, and how God is presented when those stories are told about him in BSL. These two categories will be discussed in detail below with greater emphasis placed on the second category.

God is Physically Deaf

Above, I have argued that many theologies of disability are Christocentric, focusing on the incarnation and trying to articulate from the Bible and its interpretation a way of being able to recognize that Christ experienced disability or, at least, limitation. In this sense, they are concerned with the physical body of Jesus and how Jesus in his body was disabled. Whenever I have asked Deaf people if they think God was or is in any way 'physically Deaf', they invariably respond by saying 'No, I don't think so', or 'I think that God is neither Deaf nor hearing. He is like a spirit so he is both and neither'. Such responses are similar to what John Hull argues about God being beyond light and darkness. Some Deaf people, however, do have a theology that would go as far as describing God as physically Deaf. Nancy Eiesland's 'Disabled God', in which she identifies in the person of Jesus Christ an impairment that are his wounds, may have general significance to Deaf people as to other disabled people, but is it to argue that Jesus was in any way physically Deaf?

Did Jesus experience Deafness?

Following the arrest of Jesus, Hull refers to the passage in Mark 14.65 as being of special significance to blind people: 'Some began to spit on him, to blindfold him, and strike him, saying to him "Prophesy"'. Hull explains that 'during this period of humiliation and mockery, Jesus understood what it was like as a blind person ... It is in this sadistic game of blind man's buff that blind people can most readily identify with the sufferings of Jesus Christ'[59]. Is there any point in the Bible at which the historical Jesus experiences something of what it is like to be Deaf? In terms of physical Deafness there is no account in the Gospels that describes Jesus as being unable to hear. It is also impossible (certainly without modern technology) that Jesus would have been able to completely block out sound to experience Deafness like one can blindfold one's self to block out all light.

Perhaps, however, Jesus did read lips and body language. For example, in Mark 2.8, Jesus knows what the scribes are saying about him without being able to hear them. He may have been watching their lip patterns and demeanour in order to get this information. In Mark 7.1–37, When Jesus heals the Deaf man, he speaks in words that are easy to lip-read. However, to suggest that Jesus could lip-read from these accounts is conjecture and neither of these stories suggest that Jesus was actually Deaf. In order to move on to a specific understanding of God as Deaf as some Deaf people interpret it, it is necessary to return to the idea of Deaf people as being made in the image or as ikōns of God – one of the ideas with which this chapter started.

Imago Dei

Rather than focusing on the traditional ecclesiological implications of the image of the body of Christ in 1 Corinthians 12, Weir discusses the cosmological significance of this image for Deaf people as an affirmation of 'the essential goodness of the vast diversity of humankind'[60]. For Weir, to be made in the image of God is to live as the body of God in all its diversity: 'not just males, certainly not just able-bodied people, but all human beings reflect God'[61]. She proposes that, 'We are made in God's image in the sense that we are made to live in relationship, in loving diversity. When one part of God's image, God's body claims to be it all, a kind of violence occurs which is very close to idolatry'[62].

Weir is not alone in suggesting that God's image is reflected through the relationships of diverse people. Beginning with the central doctrine of God, reference has already been made to Leonardo Boff and Jürgen Moltmann. Boff reflects on the Trinity as a model for society: 'In the Trinity there is no domination by one side, but convergence of the Three in mutual acceptance and giving. They are different but none is greater or lesser, before or after. Therefore a society that takes its inspiration from Trinitarian communion cannot tolerate class differences, dominations based on

---

[59]   Hull, J.M., *In the Beginning there was Darkness*, p.165.
[60]   Weir, M.K., 'Made Deaf in God's Image', p.6.
[61]   *Ibid.*, p.6.
[62]   *Ibid.*, 1996, p.6.

power (economic, sexual or ideological) that subjects those who are different to those who exercise that power and marginalizes the former from the latter'[63]. Moltmann has followed a similar theme in *History and the Triune God* (1991) where he argues, 'They (the persons of the Trinity) interpenetrate each other mutually to such a degree that they exist in one another and indwell one another mutually ... The fellowship of the triune God is thus the matrix and the sphere of life for the free community of men and women, without domination and without subjection, in mutual respect and mutual recognition'[64]. Boff and Moltmann both begin with God as a model for society while Weir starts with the concept of an ideal society as a reflection of the image of God. Wherever we start with this, the result is the same: God is a community of loving relationships, and this is also how society should be. It is only by society becoming a community of loving relationships that humans are able to more fully understand what it means to be made in the image of God. Therefore, we learn about humanity from God and about God from human experience.

For many Deaf people, the notion of community as an image of God is particularly relevant in at least two ways. Firstly, the Deaf community is an important focus for many Deaf people. Being with other Deaf people and communicating in their common language is important to Deaf people and Deaf identity is one which is very much tied up with being a part of that community as was argued in the first chapter. Because most Deaf people argue that their identity is formed so much by being in relationship with other Deaf people who are a part of the Deaf community, it is difficult to see how their perspective of God could be of one who does not take community life seriously. On this level therefore some members of the Deaf community appropriately see that community as a reflection of the image of God.

Secondly, community is important because of the place of Deaf people in communities which are dominated by hearing people. Deaf people do not live in isolation or in ghettos but live in the midst of hearing societies. In the wider communities in which Deaf people find themselves, Deaf people invariably take second place. Because of the barriers of language there are often poor levels of access to medical care and legal help, and to the wider life of churches. It is rare in any community other than the Deaf community itself – and that is not always so – that Deaf people have any decision making powers and control over their own lives, thus the devastating consequences of their educational experiences, for example.

Similarly, a project in Birmingham which was set up to address the needs of Deaf people in prisons showed that when a Deaf person was in prison, it was likely that there would not be another Deaf person there. If staff were unable to use sign language and the Deaf person could not make much use of English, that Deaf person would be isolated and alone – unable to ask for simple requests. A report by the project co-ordinator records how Deaf people have told stories about some officers interpreting even their efforts to communicate as aggression. One prisoner explained,

A course in managing behaviour was organized with a BSL interpreter. I attended only one session that I really enjoyed. I was cleaning an area one day and asked an officer to

---

63   Boff, L., *Trinity and Society*, p.151.
64   Moltmann, J., *History and the Triune God* (London, 1991), pp.xv–xvi.

move as they were in the way. He did not see my gestures so I tapped him on the shoulder to indicate that I was going to clean the area. Unfortunately he did not know I was Deaf and he interpreted this as an act of violence and this resulted in me being put on block and transferred. I subsequently lost my place on the course.[65]

It is often the case more generally in society that Deaf people's lives and actions are not understood and thus the Deaf community itself becomes the only place of comfort and security for Deaf people. Society and churches do not reflect the image of the Trinitarian God when they exclude or marginalize Deaf people by ignoring their language needs or even punish them because their communication method is different. The image of God the Trinity as a model for community, as a way for the body of God to live, is a strong indictment against those hearing people who exclude Deaf people, whilst at the same time affirming that Deaf people should be equal participants in the community and society as a whole. If it is the case that when all people are in community together that they can then claim to be made in the image of God, there must be some aspect of God which is Deaf as well as hearing, sighted, blind, old, young, black, white, male and female. It is not only that God is Trinity and in community that is important from the Deaf perspective, but that God somehow contains within the Godhead all the *good* diversity – and more – that is contained on earth. For this to be meaningful to the Deaf community, some appropriately describe God as Deaf. Deaf theology is a theology that is rooted in Deaf experience. If Deaf people believe that Deafness can be good and that in their Deaf condition, they are made in God's image, then it is fair to say that somehow, God must be physically Deaf. As a consequence, to talk about God as Deaf also works to affirm Deafness as good and necessary parts of God's image on earth.

God and Cultural Deafness

Some Deaf people think about God as Deaf in a very physical way. Some other Deaf people are convinced categorically that to say that God is Deaf in any sense is nonsense. I would suggest that these two extreme perspectives of God invariably correspond to the Deaf person's own understanding of Deafness. In Zimbabwe, for example, it was rare to meet a Deaf person who would believe that God was Deaf. Likewise, their understanding of Deafness was consistently more negative than that of Deaf people in Britain. More Deaf people in Britain felt that it was possible to say that God was Deaf. Among people in Britain, a greater number of younger than older people were content to talk about God as being physically Deaf. Again, I suggest that this is linked to the individual's perception of Deafness. If Deafness can be perceived of as something positive that can be celebrated, there is no reason why God cannot be discussed in these terms.

However, the majority of Deaf people in Britain and Zimbabwe when asked about God's Deafness gave a response similar to the following given by one Deaf person:

---

[65]   Gerrard, H., *A Double Sentence: Deaf Prisoners in the UK* (Birmingham, 2000), p.17.

> I don't know if God is Deaf, I'm not really sure. He can definitely hear. I think God understands sign language though, and he knows how to relate to Deaf people. He understands Deaf culture.

It is such responses as these which led me to explore further the possibility that God is considered to be culturally Deaf because he knows how to use sign language and how to engage with Deaf people. If this is what many Deaf people think, it would be far more important to the Deaf community than the question of whether God can hear or not in a physical way. This is where Deaf perspectives of God begin to diverge from those of disabled people, as their concern, as it is more generally in society, is with culture rather than biology.

Being in relationship with and understanding an invisible God is more difficult for Deaf people than for hearing people on some levels. I am not referring here to any notion that it is harder for Deaf people to obtain and develop faith in God but that much of the language used about God is culturally hearing. One Deaf person explained that if two hearing people are in separate rooms, they can easily communicate with one another without needing to see each other. In some ways, this may work as an analogy for the hearing person's relationship with God. Communication and relationship can take place without the need to see each other. For Deaf people, there is a need to be able to see someone in order to communicate with them. In the previous chapter, I discussed how the incarnation is undoubtedly significant for Deaf people, but not so much because Deaf people are able to identify with a God who is limited, as Tan argues. The Word or speech of God, for Mary Weir and many Deaf people, is transformed in the incarnation into a person with whom she can relate as a Deaf person[66]. She describes Christ as a sign that Deaf people can at last communicate with God. Touch is important in relationships with Deaf people. Jesus could be touched in his bodily form, and was not afraid to be touched. When Thomas does not believe that Jesus had risen from the dead, Jesus invites Thomas to touch him. God knows how to relate to Deaf people and he understands their culture.

I suggest that Deaf people do not think of the incarnation of Jesus Christ as simply an historical event, but that the Christ of faith is present and active in the world today. Such a position is not unique. For Forrester, the significance of the incarnation is the way that God in Jesus Christ made himself 'equal with humankind' and identified 'particularly with the lowest, the poorest and the most oppressed'[67]. Liberation theologians have argued that today, God can still be found among those with whom Christ made himself equal and with whom he identified. Rebecca Chopp in her survey of Latin American liberation theology argues that it 'arises out of the poor's experience of God, an experience that is dependent … upon God's choosing to reveal God's self in the poor'[68]. Deaf people's understanding of God in many ways is not so obviously political as that of liberation theology, but nevertheless the

---

[66]   Weir, M.K., 'Made Deaf in God's Image', p.9.

[67]   Forrester, D.B., *On Human Worth: A Christian Vindication of Equality* (London, 2001), p.94.

[68]   Chopp, R.S., 'Latin American Liberation Theology', in Ford, D. (ed.), *The Modern Theologians: An Introduction to Christian Theology in the Twentieth Century.* Second Edition (Oxford, 1997), p.409.

incarnate God is still present and discovered in the world by Deaf people. Some of these ways are outlined below.

'God Touches Me'

When I have asked Deaf people about prayer and how they feel they are able to be in relationship with God, some have explained about an extraordinary sense of the presence of God with them as they pray. However, not only have they described a sense of God's presence, but also that he has touched them in a physical way. They have felt as though God was with them and that God made this known by making use of the human sense of touch. This sense of touch is one which is rare in many religious traditions. In the Judaeo-Christian tradition, God cannot be seen or touched because he is holy[69]. That which is holy has become untouchable just as those who, at the opposite extreme, have become untouchable; those who were excluded from society because of religious impurity or as those living on the streets of Latin America, as the Dalits in India, and the homeless and even some disabled people in Britain. Standing in opposition to such notions, is the incarnate Christ, the image of the untouchable God who stands in solidarity with the untouchables of society. Scientists and psychologists would no doubt be interested in Deaf people's experiences and I have gathered no objective proof (if that were possible) to support what they have said about God touching them. Such experiences may indeed be interesting psychological phenomena, but also they point again to a view of God who understands Deaf culture and makes use of that to reveal himself to Deaf people.

God Uses Sign Language

As was described in chapter 4, stories are an important part of Deaf culture. Stories about Jesus from the Gospels, therefore, are particularly significant in the Deaf community and many know the stories about Jesus much better than any other part of the Bible. In telling stories from the Gospel narratives, Deaf people have no inhibitions about all the characters in the narrative using sign language. In chapter 5, I described the work of an organization called Visible Communications. Using some of their videos, I would like to provide some examples below to demonstrate how Deaf people suggest in their translations of stories that God and most other biblical characters use sign language, and therefore again showing that God understands Deaf culture.

1. Luke 1.26–36: The Visit of Gabriel to Mary[70]
   In this story, some of the characters are located using placement at the beginning of the narration, even though they will not come into the story until later – such as Elizabeth, to whom Mary later goes to relate the story of Gabriel's visit. Gabriel comes down from heaven (which is placed higher up at eye level) to

---

[69]   See the biblical references in chapter 5.

[70]   Taken from Visible Communications, *The Birth of Jesus Christ: The Gospel of Luke in Sign Language* (Northampton, 1997).

Mary (who is placed by the chest). In this version, Mary does not notice Gabriel at first, so Gabriel has to tap Mary on the shoulder to get her attention. This is one way in which Deaf people get someone's attention instead of speaking and God's messenger uses this technique. The Deaf narrator never has to say which character is signing, they simply change the way they are facing to indicate that the role they have taken on has changed. Mary looks up at Gabriel and Gabriel looks down at Mary demonstrating the place of heaven, and possibly the difference in status between Mary and the angel at this point. The narrative then happens in front of you. When Mary learns that she will give birth to Jesus, she pauses and her face expresses confusion, shock and bewilderment (this is an addition to the written narrative) and she signs 'Me, Virgin' as though the angel was being utterly ridiculous. In the Bible stories, the characters behave as Deaf people do. They use facial expression, signs, placement and role-shift and so the story is never a direct translation, but an interpretation infused with Deaf culture. Thus there is freedom to engage Christian faith and experience with culture.

2. Some other examples from Luke

Most significantly, when the historical person of Jesus appears in a scene, he behaves as a Deaf person as well. In Luke 5.27[71], when Jesus calls Levi to follow him, in the written text, Jesus speaks to him from what appears to be some distance and says, 'follow me'. In the BSL version, Jesus walks over to Levi (he cannot call to him as he would not hear), taps him on the shoulder and signs, 'come on, follow me'. In Luke 6.18, the written text says, the crowd came to hear Jesus. In the BSL version[72], they come to *see* him, perhaps because in communicating with Deaf people, Jesus has little use for speech, only sign language. Jesus also uses facial expression. In Luke 5.30ff the Pharisees and scribes challenge Jesus because he has gone to a banquet at Levi's house. They say, 'why do you eat and drink with sinners?' In the BSL translation, Jesus is exasperated by this question and shows his feelings in his face[73]. His eyes close so that he is almost squinting and he signs to them in an aggressive way, 'those who are well have no need of a physician ...' (v.31). Jesus, therefore, uses BSL as his mode of communication with Deaf people.

Further illustrating the Christocentricity of Deaf people's understanding of God, however, is the translation of the baptism of Jesus in Luke 3.21–22[74]. In verse 22, a voice comes from heaven which we must assume is the voice of the Father. In the BSL version, this is signed as someone speaking – it is a voice from heaven and not a sign. It is common for the physical person of Jesus in the

---

[71]   Taken from Visible Communications, *Jesus and His Disciples: The Gospel of Luke in Sign Language* (Northampton, 2000).

[72]   Taken from Visible Communications, *Jesus and His Disciples: The Gospel of Luke in Sign Language* (Northampton, 2000).

[73]   Taken from Visible Communications, *Jesus and His Disciples: The Gospel of Luke in Sign Language* (Northampton, 2000).

[74]   Taken from Visible Communications, *Jesus Begins His Ministry: The Gospel of Luke in Sign Language* (Northampton, 1999).

stories to behave as a Deaf person, but the Father (when this distinction is made in the Godhead) behaves as a hearing person. Deaf people on the whole have a very high Christology and Christ is undoubtedly prayed to and worshipped in liturgical settings. The fact that the Father speaks and the Son signs, still indicates the belief that in the incarnation, God is accessible to and relevant to Deaf people.

3. When Deaf People Pray

When Deaf people pray, they also use sign language. I described earlier how in Deaf churches, prayer becomes a conversation among the community of those gathered. Because Deaf people use BSL and Deaf culture in prayer, this further suggests that they believe that God understands BSL. No Deaf person has ever suggested, among those with whom I have signed, that God uses some kind of celestial interpreter nearby to tell him what they are signing. Prayer in BSL is direct and God understands it. And so, if God can understand BSL, it is logical to argue that he must also be able to use it as a way of communicating. When Deaf people are talking about Jesus they unashamedly turn him into a Deaf person. To my mind, on a cultural level there is no difference here to the way in which in Victorian culture, Jesus was painted as a slim, very white male which was the ideal image of that time, or how in African culture, Jesus is painted as an African. It is true that the African Jesus and a Deaf Jesus are different to the Victorian Jesus because in Africa and the Deaf community he is a figure who liberates and affirms the African and Deaf humanity, rather than him being misused as a figure of domination and oppression. It is appropriate, therefore, to use Deaf culture as a category for theological debate.

God is Deaf: Conclusion

This chapter has explored what it means when Deaf people have said that they believe God is Deaf and has done this in dialogue with other writers who argue that God is disabled. Theories about the Deaf God have focused on two main categories reflecting on God as physically Deaf and/or culturally Deaf. Far more Deaf people subscribe to the notion that God is culturally Deaf, because being unable to hear is not the primary criteria by which one is a member of the Deaf community. The discussion about God's Deafness demonstrates a significant movement away from the arguments of many theologies of disability because Deaf theology is concerned not with Jesus' personal experience of disability, but with the historical Jesus' and the Christ of faith's ability to relate to and be involved with the Deaf community. What Deaf people's perspectives of God do have in common with other theologies of disability is their Christocentrism, and in particular the notion of the incarnation as both an historical and continuing reality with relevance to human experience. This suggests that the person of the Trinity with which most Deaf people identify and relate to is Jesus Christ. The Father and the Spirit usually figure less prominently in Deaf people's understanding of God when the distinction between those three persons is necessary, as opposed to discussions about the Godhead using the generic term 'God'. The translation of the baptism of Jesus points to a perception that the Father still speaks as a hearing person would, even if the Son knows how to relate to Deaf people. In being able to discuss an idea of God as Deaf, it also leads one to a position of being able to affirm Deaf humanity, recognizing that Deaf people can be 'ikōns of God'.

Conclusion

'So Many Other Things'

I began this work by quoting the first verse from the Prologue of St John's Gospel as a means of introducing what has been a recurring theme throughout: the way that words, either spoken or written, have been the reason for the exclusion of Deaf people, not only in theology but also in society more generally. At the very end of the Gospel, John himself acknowledges the limitations of, at least, the written word: 'But there are also so many other things that Jesus did; if every one of them were written down, I suppose that the world itself could not contain the books that would be written' (John 21.25). John recognizes in this final verse that even he, a gifted writer, cannot articulate even the beginnings of the significance of Jesus Christ and his relationship with humanity in a single book, or indeed any book. It is my view that Deaf theology is a theology that does not need or use words, but is a theology of vision, space, touch and relationship. It is a theology that emerges out of life and experience, and seeks LIFE and life in all its abundance (cf. John 10.10). Words themselves are an inadequate means of seeking to express the reality of God and their meanings have been given significance by the Church and theology beyond what any language could possibly contain. I have drawn on theologians who argue that theology can be expressed through music, time, art, space, silence, buildings, creation, human beings and likewise, I have argued that sign language, the language of the Deaf community, can express theological ideas and concepts without the need for the written or spoken word (chapters 4 and 5).

But more than this, not only can sign language adequately express theology, but its ability to do so is as great as any spoken or written language. Sign languages are full and complete languages, they can express abstract as well as concrete ideas. Deaf theology is not dependent on the written text, because I have argued, neither is God dependent on this human invention either[1]. As well as arguing this point, it has also been my intention to demonstrate it by drawing on the experiences and theological perspectives of Deaf people. They are a community who have experienced the suppression of their language and in no place more so than as children in schools as well as in society more generally (chapters 1 and 2). Their campaigns to have their language recognized have now finally succeeded. Out of this experience has emerged a theology expressed in sign language that, while not formally laid out in doctrines, creeds or theological books, is complex, varied and the result of the development of a shared tradition of the Deaf community. Deaf people have developed theological perspectives that can be found in the way they use language, through their worship

---

[1]   See also Morris, W., 'Does the Church Need the Bible? Reflecting on the Experiences of Disabled People', in Bates, D.J., Durka, G and Schweitzer, F.L. (eds), *Education, Religion and Society: Essays in Honour of John M. Hull* (London, 2006), pp.162–72.

and liturgical practices, by the way they meet together as a church and live out what it means to them to be church (chapter 6). And finally, I have argued for a complex perspective from the Deaf community about the nature of a God who is Deaf and the extent to which it can be said that he understands the Deaf condition (chapter 7).

Rather than being theologies that are expressed in texts, Deaf theology is lived out and in this sense it is a highly 'practical' theology. Their perspectives on ecclesiology are the result of working out how to be an ecclesiastical community, how to exercise ministry to one another and how to find a role in society and the wider church. Their liturgical traditions are developing slowly but, while some distinctively Deaf liturgy is practised locally, it is struggling to flourish as part of a wider church whose liturgies are often based on the written text. Their perspectives on God also emerge out of lived experience. Though hearing people in the West have largely expressed an image of God that resembles cultural ideals of what it means to be perfect, not least physically, Deaf people see in God a friend who knows how to communicate with Deaf people, is bothered about sign language and Deaf culture, who can be spoken about as Deaf.

I can also echo the sentiments of St John who finds that writing a text presents physical limitations concerning how much can be contained within a confined space. That has also been a problem here. Deaf theology, because it is non-written, is ever changing and responding to new situations and circumstances. While this obviously makes Deaf theology extremely diverse, it also means that Deaf theological perspectives are rich and varied and are constantly being created and then re-created. I have thus had to be selective in what I have used in this book, including only what seems to be of greatest significance in the Deaf community and church at the present moment (discussed in chapter 3).

In a study of theology from outside of the academy and Church, Brian Castle uses the analogy of a city and the activities that take place inside and outside its walls as a way of understanding the way theology is often perceived. He argues that it is often the activities that take place within the city that are focused on and given most importance in ancient and more contemporary times[2]. In the biblical era, outside of the city is where the ritually impure could be found, where animals were killed and where the sinful were punished[3]. Outside of the walls is the place of impurity and disgrace and those who lived there were treated accordingly. No doubt Deaf people would have been among them. He argues, however, that 'in the New Testament, the death, resurrection and ascension of Jesus Christ challenged this as all the pivotal events of the Christian faith happened beyond the city walls'[4]. Likewise, it is outside of the camp, rather than within it, that 'Moses pitches the tent of meeting, to which the Lord comes to speak with Moses'[5]. Thus there is a great irony in that the 'place of impurity and disgrace becomes the place of heavenly blessing'[6].

---

[2]   Castle, B., *Unofficial God?: Voices from Beyond the Walls* (London, 2004), pp.2–12.
[3]   *Ibid.*, p.7.
[4]   *Ibid.*, p.7.
[5]   *Ibid.*, p.7.
[6]   *Ibid.*, p.8.

Deaf theology is a theology that has emerged from outside of the city walls, the place to which they have traditionally and continue to be marginalized by society, the academy and the Church. As someone within the academy, I have taken the decision to go out through the gate of the city, to see what it is like outside and while there, I recognized the activity and presence of God manifest that is often quite different to the way God is spoken about from within. We see in such texts as Sugirtharajah's *Asian Faces of Jesus* (1993), *Voices from the Margins* (1995); Ursula King's *Feminist Theology from the Third World* (1994) and Brian Castle's *Unofficial God?* (2004), to name but a few, an increasing chorus of voices representing the theology that has always been taking place outside the city walls. I do not add a voice to this chorus, but offer the contributions of Deaf people who express their theology in their unique way. This book is an attempt to report back to the city some of what I have found, in the hope that it will contribute to breaking down the walls that have put Deaf people on the margins and kept them out of the academy and the Church, so that they can take their rightful place, along with all other marginalized groups, as part of the one complete 'body of Christ' (1 Corinthians 12.12ff).

Bibliography

Biblical Quotations taken from: *Holy Bible. New Revised Standard Version* (New York: Oxford University Press, 1989), unless otherwise stated.

Á Kempis, Thomas, *The Imitation of Christ* (London: Fount Paperbacks, 1963).

Abbott-Smith, G., *A Manual Greek Lexicon of the New Testament* (Edinburgh: T&T Clark, 1994).

Abrams, Judith Z., *Judaism and Disability: Portrayals in Ancient Texts from the Tanach through the Bavli* (Washington DC: Gallaudet University Press, 1998).

Advisory Board for Ministry, *The Church Among Deaf People* (London: Church House Publishing, 1997).

Ahlgren, I., 'Sign Language as the First Language', in Ahlgren, I. and Hyltenstam, K. (eds), *Bilingualism in Deaf Education: International Studies on Sign Language and Communication of the Deaf* (Hamburg: Signum, 1994), pp.55–60.

Ahlgren, I. and Hyltenstam, K. (eds), *Bilingualism in Deaf Education: International Studies on Sign Language and Communication of the Deaf* (Hamburg: Signum, 1994).

Alker, D., 'The Changing Deaf Communities', in International Ecumenical Working Group, *The Place of Deaf People in the Church* (Northampton: Visible Communications, 1996), pp.178–82.

Alker, Doug, *Really Not Interested in the Deaf?* (Darwen, Lancashire: Doug Alker, 2000).

Andrews, Isolde, *Deconstructing Barth. A Study in the Complementary Methods in Karl Barth and Jacques Derrida* (Frankfurt: Peter Lang, 1996).

Baker, Rob and Knight, Pamela, '"Total Communication" – current policy and practice', in Gregory, S., Knight, P., McCracken, W., Powers, S. and Watson, L. (eds), *Issues in Deaf Education* (London: David Fulton Publishers, 1998), pp.77–87.

Ballard, Paul and Pritchard, John, *Practical Theology in Action: Christian Thinking in the Service of Church and Society* (London: SPCK, 1996).

Banana, C.S., 'The Case for a New Bible', in Sugirtharajah, R.S. (ed.), *Voices from the Margin* (London/Maryknoll, New York: SPCK/Orbis Books, 1995), pp.69–82.

Banana, C.S., *The Church and the Struggle for Zimbabwe* (Gweru: Mambo Press, 1996).

Banham, D. (ed.), *Monesteriales Indicia: The Anglo-Saxon Monastic Sign Language* (Hockwold-cum-Wilton: Anglo Saxon Books, 1991).

Barter, J.A., 'A Theology of Liberation in Barth's Church Dogmatics IV/3', *Scottish Journal of Theology*, 53(2) (2000): 154–76.

Barth, Karl, *Church Dogmatics: The Doctrine of the Word of God.* vol. I.i (Edinburgh: T&T Clark, 1975).

Barth, Karl, *Church Dogmatics: The Doctrine of the Word of God.* vol I.ii (Edinburgh: T&T Clark, 1956).

Bayer, Oswald, 'Theology in the Conflict of interpretations – before the text', *Modern Theology*, 16(4) (2000): 495–502.

Bebko, J.M., 'Learning, Language, Memory and Reading: The Role of Language Automatization and its Impact on Complex Cognitive Activities', *Journal of Deaf Studies and Deaf Education*, 3(1) (1998): 4–14.

Begbie, Jeremy, 'Through Music: Sound Mix', in Begbie, Jeremy (ed.), *Beholding the Glory: Incarnation Through the Arts* (London: Darton, Longman & Todd, 2000), pp.138–54.

Begbie, Jeremy (ed.), *Beholding the Glory: Incarnation Through the Arts* (London: Darton, Longman & Todd, 2000).

Betenbaugh, H.R., 'Disability: A Lived Theology', *Theology Today*, 57(2) (2000): 203–10.

Bible Translation Project (URL: http://www.bslbible.org.uk, 2007) [online. Last accessed: 30/01/2007].

Birmingham City Council, *Scrutiny Report to the City Council: Review of Signing Services* (Birmingham: Birmingham City Council, 2003).

Birmingham Institute for Deaf People (BID), *Did You Know?* (Birmingham: BID, 2004).

Black, Kathy, *A Healing Homiletic: Preaching and Disability* (Nashville: Abingdon Press, 1996).

Boff, Leonardo, *Trinity and Society* (Tunbridge Wells: Burns & Oates, 1988).

Boff, Leonardo and Boff, Clodovis, *Introducing Liberation Theology* (Tunbridge Wells: Burns & Oates, 1987).

Bonino, José Míguez, 'Latin American', in Fabella, V. and Sugirtharajah, R.S. (eds), *The SCM Dictionary of Third World Theologies* (London: SCM Press, 2003), pp.54–6.

Book of Common Prayer (Cambridge: Cambridge University Press, 1662).

Bragg, L. (ed.), *Deaf World: A Historical Reader and Primary Source Book* (New York: New York University Press, 2001).

Brannen, Julia (ed.), *Mixing Methods: Qualitative and Quantitative Research* (Aldershot: Avebury, 1992).

Brennan, M., 'The Visual World of British Sign Language: An Introduction', in Brien, D. (ed.), *Dictionary of British Sign Language/English* (London: Faber and Faber, 1992), pp.1–133.

Brien, D. (ed.), *Dictionary of British Sign Language/English* (London: Faber and Faber, 1992).

British Deaf Association, *British Deaf News* (London: British Deaf Association, April 2003).

British Deaf Association, *What is BSL?* (URL: www.britishdeafassociation.org.uk/bsl/page.php?page=what%20is%20bsl?, 2004) [online. Last accessed: 24/08/2004].

British Deaf Association, *BSL Recognition* (London: British Deaf Association, 2003).

Brock, Rita Nakashima, 'Dusting the Bible of the Floor: A Hermeneutics of Wisdom', in Schüssler-Fiorenza, Elisabeth, *Searching the Scriptures: A Feminist Introduction* (London: SCM Press, 1993), pp.64–75.

Bromiley, G.W., *Introduction to the Theology of Karl Barth* (Edinburgh: T&T Clark, 1979).

Byung Mu Ahn, 'Jesus and People (Minjung)', in Sugirtharajah, R.S. (ed.), *Asian Faces of Jesus* (New York: Orbis Books, 1993), pp.163–72.

Castle, Brian, *Unofficial God?: Voices from Beyond the Walls* (London: SPCK, 2004).

Chadwick, Owen, *The Reformation* (London: Penguin Books, 1964).

Charry, E.T., 'On Things We Can't Fix', *Theology Today*, 57(2) (2000): 157–60.

Chitambo, Ezra, 'What's in a Name? Naming Practices among African Christians in Zimbabwe', in Fiedler, K., Gundani, P and Mijoga, H. (eds), *Theology Cooked in an African Pot* (Zomba, Malawi: Association of Theological Institutions in Southern and Central Africa, 1998), pp.106–19.

Chitambo, Ezra, 'Fact and Fiction: Images of Missionaries in Zimbabwean Literature', *Studies in World Christianity*, 7(1) (2001): 80–94.

Chopp, Rebecca S., 'Latin American Liberation Theology', in Ford, David (ed.), *The Modern Theologians: An Introduction to Christian Theology in the Twentieth Century: Second Edition* (Oxford: Blackwell Publishing, 1997), pp.409–25.

Chubb, R., *Lifting Holy Hands: ABM Paper 7* (London: Central Board of Finance of the Church of England, 1994).

Chupungco, Anscar J., *Liturgical Inculturation: sacramentals, religiosity and catechesis* (Collegeville, Minnesota: Liturgical Press, 1992).

Church of England, *The Church Among Deaf People* (London: Church House Publishing, 1997).

Church of England, *Common Worship: Services and Prayers of the Church of England* (London: Church House Publishing, 2000).

Clark, David, *The Liberation of the Church: The Role of Basic Christian Groups in a New Re-formation* (Birmingham: National Centre for Christian Communities, 1984).

Clarke, Sathianathan, *Dalits and Christianity: Subaltern Religion and Liberation Theology in India* (New Delhi: Oxford University Press, 1999).

Cone, James H., *A Black Theology of Liberation: Twentieth Anniversary Edition* (Maryknoll, New York: Orbis Books, 1990).

Cone, J.H. and Williams, G.S. (eds), *Black Theology: A Documentary History Volume One: 1966–1979* (New York: Orbis Books, 1993).

Cone, James, H., 'Black Theology in the United States', in Fabella, V. and Sugirtharajah, R.S. (eds), *The SCM Dictionary of Third World Theologies* (London: SCM Press, 2003), pp.210–12.

Cooper, Burton, 'The Disabled God', *Theology Today*, xlix (2) (1992): 173–82.

Corker, Mairian, *Deaf Transitions: Images and Origins of Deaf Families, Deaf Communities and Deaf Identities* (London: Jessica Kingsley, 1996).

Corker, Mairian, 'Disability Politics, Language Planning and Inclusive Social Policy', *Disability and Society*, 15(3) (2000): 445–62.

Crichton, J.D., 'A Theology of Worship', in Jones, Cheslyn, Wainwright, Geoffrey, Yarnold, Edward and Bradshaw, Paul (eds), *The Study of Liturgy* (London: SPCK, 1992), pp.3–31.

Daly, M., *Beyond God the Father: Towards a Philosophy of Women's Liberation* (London: The Women's Press, 1986).

Davies, John, *Only Say the Word: When Jesus brings healing and salvation* (Norwich: Canterbury Press, 2002).

Davis, E., *Zimbabwe Struggles Against Aids Onslaught* (URL: www.news.bbc. co.uk/i/hi/health/background_briefings_/aids/338874.stm, 1999) [online. Last accessed: 24/08/2004].

Derrida, Jacques, *Speech and Phenomena: And Other Essays on Husserl's Theory of Signs* (Evanston: Northwestern University Press, 1973).

Dimmock, A.F., *Cruel Legacy: An Introduction to the Record of Deaf People in History* (Edinburgh: Scottish Workshop Publications, 1993).

Dimmock, A.F., 'Deaf History', in British Deaf Association, *British Deaf News* (London: British Deaf Association, December 1998), p.7.

Disability Rights Commission, *Code of Practice: Rights of Access Goods, Facilities, Services and Premises* (London: The Stationary Office, 2002).

Disabled People's Direct Action Network, *Who Represents Disabled People?* (URL: www.johnnypops.demon.co.uk/poetry/articles/dan/pr-oct-2003.htm, 2003) [online. Last accessed: 02/02/2007].

Dowley, Tim (ed.), *The Bible in Stained Glass* (Swindon: Bible Society, 1990).

Dulles, Avery, *Models of the Church: A Critical Assessment of the Church in all its Aspects*, Second Edition (Dublin: Gill & Macmillan, 1987).

Eiesland, N.L. and Saliers, D.E. (eds), *Human Disability and the Service of God: Reassessing Religious Practice* (Nashville: Abingdon Press, 1998).

Eiesland, N.L., *The Disabled God: Toward a Liberatory Theology of Disability* (Nashville: Abingdon Press, 1994).

Evans, Robert, *Using the Bible: Studying the Text* (London: Darton, Longman & Todd, 1999).

Fabella, V. and Torres, S. (eds), *Doing Theology in a Divided World* (Maryknoll: Orbis Books, 1985).

Fiedler, K., Gundani, P and Mijoga, H. (eds), *Theology Cooked in an African Pot* (Zomba, Malawi: Association of Theological Institutions in Southern and Central Africa, 1998).

Fischer, R. and Lane, H. (eds), *Looking Back: A Reader on the History of Deaf Communities and their Sign Languages* (Hamburg: Signum, 1993).

Forrester, Duncan B., *On Human Worth: A Christian Vindication of Equality* (London: SCM Press, 2001).

Freire, Paulo, *Pedagogy of the Oppressed* (London: Penguin Books, 1972).

French, S., 'Disability, impairment or something in between?', in Swain, J., Oliver, M., French, S. and Finkelstein, V., *Disabling Barriers – Enabling Environments* (London: Sage Publications, 1993), pp.17–25.

Fromkin, Victoria and Rodman, Robert, *An Introduction to Language*, Fifth Edition (Orlando: Harcourt Brace College Publishers, 1993).

Gallaway, Clare, 'Early Interaction', in Gregory, S., Knight, P., McCracken, W., Powers, S. and Watson, L. (eds), *Issues in Deaf Education* (London: David Fulton Publishers, 1998), pp.49–57.

Galvin, J.P., 'Jesus Christ', in Schüssler-Fiorenza, Francis and Galvin, John P. (eds), *Systematic Theology: Roman Catholic Perspectives* (Dublin: Gill & Macmillan, 1992), pp.249–324.

Gardner, H., *The Shattered Mind* (New York: Vintage, 1974).

Garver, Newton, 'Preface', in Derrida, Jacques, *Speech and Phenomena: And Other Essays on Husserl's Theory of Signs* (Evanston: Northwestern University Press, 1973), pp.ix–xxix.

Gelineau, J., 'Music and Singing in the Liturgy', in Jones, Cheslyn, Wainwright, Geoffrey, Yarnold, Edward and Bradshaw, Paul (eds), *The Study of Liturgy* (London: SPCK, 1992), pp.493–507.

Gerrard, Heather, *A Double Sentence: Deaf Prisoners in the UK* (Birmingham: Deaf Prison Project, December 2000).

Girard, René, *The Scapegoat* (London: Athlone Press, 1986).

Graham, E., Walton, H. and Ward, F., *Theological Reflection: Methods* (London: SCM Press, 2005).

Graham, E., Walton, H. and Ward, F., *Theological Reflection: Sources* (London: SCM Press, 2007).

Grant, Jacquelyn, *White Woman's Christ, Black Woman's Jesus* (Atlanta: Scholars Press, 1989).

Gray, Colin D. and Hosie, Judith A., 'Deafness, Story Understanding, and Theory of Mind', *Journal of Deaf Studies and Deaf Education*, 1(4) (1996): 217–33.

Great Britain, Foreign & Commonwealth Office. *Country Profiles: Zimbabwe* (URL: www.fco.gov.uk/servlet/Front?pagename=OpenMarket/xcelerate/ShowPage&=Page&cid=1007029394365&a=kcountryProfile&aid=1019745115464, 2004) [online. Last accessed: 24/08/2004].

Green, Laurie, *Let's Do Theology: A Pastoral Cycle Resource Book* (London: Mowbray, 1990).

Green, Laurie, 'Oral Culture and the World of Words', *Theology*, CII(809) (1999): 328–35.

Green, Laurie, *Urban Ministry and the Kingdom of God* (London: SPCK, 2003).

Gregory, S., Knight, P., McCracken, W., Powers, S. and Watson, L. (eds), *Issues in Deaf Education* (London: David Fulton Publishers, 1998).

Gregory, Susan and Knight, Pamela, 'Social Development and Family Life', in Gregory, S., Knight, P., McCracken, W., Powers, S. and Watson, L. (eds), *Issues in Deaf Education* (London: David Fulton Publishers, 1998), pp.3–11.

Grewel, Ini, Joy, Sarah, Lewis, Jane, Swales, Kirby and Woodfield, Kandy, *'Disabled for Life?' Attitudes Towards, and Experiences of Disability in Britain.* Research Report No. 173 (London: Department of Work and Pensions, 2002).

Groce, Nora Ellen, *Everyone Here Spoke Sign Language: Hereditary Deafness on Martha's Vineyard* (Cambridge, Massachusetts: Harvard University Press, 1988).

Gutierrez, Gustavo, *A Theology of Liberation* (London: SCM Press, 1988).

Gutierrez, Gustavo, *The God of Life* (London, SCM Press, 1991).

Hammersley, M. and Atkinson, P., *Ethnography: Principles in Practice*, Second Edition (London: Routledge, 1995).

Hannaford, R. and Jobling, J. (eds), *Theology and the Body. Gender, text and Ideology* (Leominster: Gracewing, 1999).

Harris, H.A., 'Protestant Fundamentalism', in Partridge, C.H., *Fundamentalisms* (Carlisle: Paternoster Press, 2001), pp.33–51.

Hart, K., 'Jacques Derrida (b1930): Introduction', in Ward, Graham (ed.), *The Postmodern God: A Theological Reader* (Oxford: Blackwell, 1997), pp.159–67.

Hart, T., *Regarding Karl Barth* (Carlisle: Paternoster Press, 1999).

Healey, J. and Sybertz, D., *Towards an African Narrative Theology* (Nairobi: Pauline Publications Africa, 1996).

Hennelly, A.T. (ed.), *Liberation Theology: A Documentary History* (Maryknoll: Orbis Books, 1990).

Hitching, Roger, *The Church and Deaf People: A Study of Identity, Communication and Relationships with Special Reference to the Ecclesiology of Jörgen Moltmann* (Carlisle: Paternoster, 2003).

Hollins, S. and Grimer, M., *Going Somewhere: People with Mental Handicaps and their Pastoral Care* (London: SPCK, 1988).

Hull, John M., *On Sight and Insight: A Journey into the World of Blindness* (Oxford: Oneworld Publications, 1997).

Hull, John M., 'Could a blind person have been a disciple of Jesus?', *Viewpoints* 7 (1999/2000): 4–5.

Hull, John M., *In the Beginning there was Darkness* (London: SCM Press, 2001).

Hull, J.M., 'Open Letter from a Blind Disciple to a Sighted Saviour: Text and Discussion', in O'Kane, Martin (ed.), *Borders, Boundaries and the Bible* (Sheffield: Sheffield Academic Press, 2001), pp.154–77.

Hull, John M., 'From Experimental Educator to Nationalist Theologian: The Hymns of Isaac Watts', *Panorama*, 14(1) (2002): 91–105.

Hull, John M., '"Sight to the Inly Blind?" Attitudes to Blindness in the Hymnbooks', *Theology*, CV(827) (2002): 333–41.

Humphries, Beth and Truman, Carole (eds), *Re-thinking Social Research: Anti-discriminatory approaches in research methodology* (Aldershot: Avebury, 1994).

Hunt, Vera, 'The Place of Deaf People in the Church: My Story', in International Ecumenical Working Group, *The Place of Deaf People in the Church* (Northampton: Visible Communications, 1996), pp.20–33.

Hurding, Roger, 'Healing Today: A forward gain?', *Contact: The Interdisciplinary Journal of Pastoral Studies*, 133 (2000): 20–6.

International Catholic Deaf Religious, 'The Debate', in McDonough, Peter (ed.), *Ephphatha: Proceedings from the International Catholic Deaf Religious Conference 1996* (Monmouth: A&K Publications, 1996), pp.46–8.

International Ecumenical Working Group, *The Place of Deaf People in the Church* (Northampton: Visible Communications, 1996).

Jenson, Robert W., 'Karl Barth', in Ford, David (ed.), *The Modern Theologians: An Introduction to Christian Theology in the Twentieth Century*, Second Edition (Oxford: Blackwell Publishing, 1997), pp.21–36.

John of Damascus, *In Defence of the Holy Icons* [English Translation: D Anderson], (Crestwood, New York: St Vladimir's Seminary Press, 1980).

Johnson, Luke T., *The Writings of the New Testament: An Interpretation* (London: SCM Press, 1986).

Johnstone, David, *An Introduction to Disability Studies*, Second Edition (London: David Fulton Publishers, 2001).

Jones, Gareth, *Critical Theology* (London: Polity Press, 1995).

Kalilombe, Patrick A., 'A Malawian Example: The Bible and Non-literate Communities', in Sugirtharajah, R.S. (ed.), *Voices from the Margin* (London/ Maryknoll, New York: SPCK/Orbis Books, 1995), pp.421–35.

Kim, Kirsteen, 'India', in Parratt, J. (ed.), *An Introduction to Third World Theologies* (Cambridge: Cambridge University Press, 2004), pp.44–73.

King, U. (ed.), *Feminist Theology from the Third World* (London: SPCK, 1994).

Knight, P., 'Deafness and Disability', in Gregory, S., Knight, P., McCracken, W., Powers, S. and Watson, L. (eds), *Issues in Deaf Education* (London: David Fulton Publishers, 1998), pp.215–24.

Kwok Pui-Lan, *Discovering the Bible in the Non-Biblical World* (New York: Orbis Books, 1995).

Kyle, J.G. and Woll, B., *Sign Language: The Study of Deaf People and their Language* (Cambridge: Cambridge University Press, 1985).

Ladd, Paddy, *Understanding Deaf Culture: In Search of Deafhood* (Clevedon: Multilingual Matters, 2003).

Lancelot, James, 'Music as Sacrament', in Brown, David and Loades, Ann (eds), *The Sense of the Sacramental: Movement and Measure in Art and Music, Place and Time* (London: SPCK, 1995), pp.179–85.

Lane, H., *When the Mind Hears: A History of the Deaf* (New York: Vintage Books, 1989).

Lane, H., 'The Medicalization of Cultural Deafness in Historical Perspective', in Fischer, R. and Lane, H. (eds), *Looking Back: A Reader on the History of Deaf Communities and their Sign Languages* (Hamburg: Signum, 1993).

Lane, H., Hoffmeister, R. and Bahan, B., *A Journey into the Deaf World* (San Diego: DawnSignPress, 1996).

Lane, H., *The Mask of Benevolence: disabling the Deaf Community*, New Edition (San Diego: DawnSignPress, 1999).

Lartey, E.Y., *In Living Colour: An Intercultural Approach to Pastoral Care and Counselling* (London: Cassell, 1997).

Lartey, E., 'Practical Theology as Theological Form', in Woodward, J. and Pattison, S. (eds), *The Blackwell Reader in Pastoral and Practical Theology* (Oxford: Blackwell, 2000), pp.128–34.

Lartey, E., *Pastoral Theology in an Intercultural World* (Peterborough: Epworth, 2006).

Lewis, C.S., *The Lion, the Witch and the Wardrobe* (London: Fontana, 1980).

Lewis, Hannah M., *A Critical Examination of the Church and Deaf People: Toward a Deaf Liberation Theology* (Unpublished PhD Thesis: University of Birmingham, 2002).

Lewis, H., *Deaf Liberation Theology* (Aldershot: Ashgate, 2007)

Lowe, Alan, *Evangelism and Learning Disability: Learning from the Faith and Light Communities* (Grove Evangelism Series No. 42. Cambridge: Grove Books Ltd., 1998).

Lyall, David, *Integrity of Pastoral Care* (London: SPCK, 2001).

Matambirofa, Francis, *How Language Affects Attitudes* (Unpublished Paper presented at the National Media Workshop, Kwekwe, Zimbabwe, 1994a).

Matambirofa, Francis, *Language, Disability & Attitudes, and Cultural Beliefs and Practices Associated with Disability* (Unpublished Paper presented at Victoria Falls, Zimbabwe, 1994b).

Matambirofa, Francis, *Language and the Role of the Mass Media in Improving Attitudes about Disabled Persons in Zimbabwe* (Unpublished Paper presented at the National Disability Awareness Seminar, Harare, Zimbabwe, 1995).

Maxwell, Madeline, 'Some Functions and Uses of Literacy in the Deaf Community', *Language in Society*, 14 (1985): 205–21.

Mbiti, J., 'An African Views American Black Theology', in Cone, J.H. and Williams, G.S. (eds), *Black Theology: A Documentary History Volume One: 1966–1979* (New York: Orbis Books, 1993), pp.379–84.

McCloughry, Roy and Morris, Wayne, *Making a World of Difference: Christian Reflections on Disability* (London: SPCK, 2002).

McDonough, P., 'The Place of Deaf People in the Church – A Deaf Priest's View', in International Ecumenical Working Group, *The Place of Deaf People in the Church* (Northampton: Visible Communications, 1996), pp.35–54.

McFague, Sallie, *Models of God: Theology for an Ecological, Nuclear Age* (London: SCM Press, 1987).

McFague, Sallie, *The Body of God: An Ecological Theology* (London: SCM Press, 1993).

Methodist Church, *The Methodist Worship Book* (Peterborough: Methodist Publishing House, 1999).

Metzger, Bruce M., *The Canon of the New Testament: Its Origin, Development and Significance* (New York: Oxford University Press, 1987).

Miller, A., Imrie, H., Bradford, W. and Cox, K., *Student Assessment in Higher Education: A Handbook for Assessing Performance* (London: Routledge, 1998).

Miller, Nancy B. and Sammons, Catherine C. (eds), *Everybody's Different: Understanding and Changing Our Reactions to Disabilities* (Baltimore: Paul H Brookes, 1999).

Moltmann, Jürgen, 'An Open Letter to José Míguez Bonino', in Hennelly, A.T. (ed.), *Liberation Theology: A Documentary History* (Maryknoll: Orbis Books, 1990), pp.195–204.

Moltmann, Jürgen, *History and the Triune God* (London: SCM Press, 1991).

Monteith, W.G., *Pastoral Care and Ethical Issues: Disability: Faith and Acceptance* (Edinburgh: St Andrew Press, 1987).

Moore, Basil, 'What is Black Theology?', in Moore, Basil (ed.), *Black Theology: The South African Voice* (London: C. Hurst & Co., 1973), pp.1–10.

Moore, Stephen, D., *Poststructuralism and the New Testament: Derrida and Foucault at the Foot of the Cross* (Minneapolis: Fortress Press, 1994).

Morrey, W., *Seeing is Hearing: Reflections on being deafened* (Bangor: University of Wales, 1994).

Morris, Wayne, 'A Question of Language: The Problem of Deafness or Theology?' *British Journal of Theological Education*, 10(2) (1999): 70–9.

Morris, Wayne, 'Interview: Professor John Hull', in Church Action on Disability, *All People*, 85 (2000): 6–8.

Morris, Wayne, 'Disability included! A model for church communities', *Viewpoints*, 8 (2001): 7–8

Morris, Wayne, 'Does the Church Need the Bible? Reflections on the Experiences of Disabled People', in Bates, D.J., Durka, G. and Schweitzer, F.L. (eds), *Education, Religion and Society: Essays in Honour of John M. Hull* (London: Routledge, 2006), pp.162–72.

Morris, Wayne, 'Learning, Teaching and Assessment with Deaf Students', *Discourse: Learning and Teaching in Philosophical and Religious Studies*, 6/1 (2006): 145–73.

Mosala, Itumeleng J., 'The Implications of the Text of Esther for African Women's Struggle for Liberation in South Africa', in Sugirtharajah, R.S. (ed.), *Voices from the Margin* (London/Maryknoll, New York: SPCK/Orbis Books, 1995), pp.168–78.

Moser, C.A. and Kalton, G., *Survey Methods in Social Investigation*, Second Edition (Aldershot: Gower Publishing Company Ltd., 1971).

Mukonyora, Isabel, 'Women's Readings of the Bible', in Mukonyora, I., Cox, J.L. and Verstraelen (eds), *'Rewriting' the Bible: the real issues* (Gweru, Zimbabwe: Mambo Press, 1993), pp.199–216.

Mukonyora, Isabel, 'The Dramatization of Life and Death by Johane Masowe', *The Journal of Humanities of the University of Zimbabwe*, XXV(ii) (1998): 191–207.

Muller-Fahrenholz, Geiko, *Partners in Life: The Handicapped and the Church* (Geneva: World Council of Churches, 1979).

Musopole, Augustine, 'Needed: A Theology Cooked in an African Pot', in Fiedler, K., Gundani, P and Mijoga, H. (eds), *Theology Cooked in an African Pot* (Zomba, Malawi: Association of Theological Institutions in Southern and Central Africa, 1998), pp.7–47.

Musselman, Carol, Mootilal, Anju and MacKay, Sherri, 'The Social Adjustment of Deaf Adolescents in Segregated, Partially Integrated, and Mainstreamed Settings', *Journal of Deaf Studies and Deaf Education*, 1(1) (1996): 52–63.

National Health Service, *Newborn Hearing Screening Programme: Information for parents to be and parents of new born babies* (London: National Deaf Children's Society, 2002).

Naudé, John, 'Wonderfully Made', in Church Action on Disability, *All People*, 90 (2002): 9–10.

Nelson, James B., *Body Theology* (Louisville, Kentucky: Westminster/John Knox Press, 1992).

Neuman, W. Lawrence, *Social Research Methods: Qualitative and Quantitative Approaches*, Second Edition (Massachusetts: Allyn and Bacon, 1994).

Nouwen, Henri, J. M., *The Wounded Healer: Ministry in Contemporary Society* (London: Darton, Longman & Todd, 1994).

Nyamiti, Charles, 'The Doctrine of God', in Parratt, John (ed.), *A Reader in African Christian Theology* (London: SPCK, 1997), pp.57–64.

O'Collins, G., 'Dogmatic Theology', in Richardson, A. and Bowden, J. (eds), *A New Dictionary of Christian Theology* (London: SCM Press Ltd., 1983), pp.163–4.

Oduyoye, Mercy Amba, *Introducing African Women's Theology* (Sheffield: Sheffield Academic Press, 2001).

Oliver, M., *Disabled People and Social Policy: from exclusion to inclusion* (London: Longman, 1998).

Orr, Meg, 'The Role of the Teacher in the Theological Education of the Laity', in Astley, Jeff (ed.), *Learning in the Way: Research and Reflection on Adult Christian Education* (Leominster: Gracewing, 2000), pp.72–89.

Otto, Randall, 'Incarnated or Incapacitated? Another Look at "The Disabled Christ"', *Phronésis*, 4(1) (1997): 65–75.

Pailin, David A., *A Gentle Touch: From a Theology of Handicap to a Theology of Human Being* (London: SPCK, 1992).

Parattai (J. Theophilus Appavoo), 'Dalit Way of Theological Expression', in Devasahayam, V. (ed.), *Frontiers of Dalit Theology* (Madras: ISPCK/GURUKUL, 1997), pp.283–9.

Parratt, J., *A Guide to Doing Theology* (London: SPCK, 1996).

Parratt, J. (ed.), *A Reader in African Christian Theology* (London: SPCK, 1997).

Parratt, J., 'The Globalisation of Christian Theology', An Inaugural Lecture given by John Parratt as Professor Historical Studies at the University of Birmingham, February 26th, 2002.

Pattison, Stephen, *Alive and Kicking: Towards a Practical Theology of Illness and Healing* (London: SCM Press, 1989).

Pattison, Stephen, *Pastoral Care and Liberation Theology* (London: SPCK, 1997).

Pearson, Brian, 'Interactive Methods of Preaching', in Hunter, Geoffrey, Thomas, Gethin and Wright, Stephen, *A Preacher's Companion: Essays from the College of Preachers* (Oxford: Bible Reading Fellowship, 2004), pp.107–10.

Petitto, Laura A. and Seidenberg, Mark S., 'On the Evidence for Linguistic Abilities in Signing Apes', *Brain and Language*, 8 (1979): 162–83.

Phiri, Isabel Apawo, 'Doing Theology as African Women', in Parratt, J. (ed.), *A Reader in African Christian Theology* (London: SPCK, 1997), pp.45–56.

Phiri, Isabel Apawo, 'Southern Africa', in Parratt, J. (ed.), *An Introduction to Third World Theologies* (Cambridge: Cambridge University Press, 2004), pp.137–62.

Pickersgill, Miranda, 'Bilingualism – current policy and practice', in Gregory, S., Knight, P., McCracken, W., Powers, S. and Watson, L. (eds), *Issues in Deaf Education* (London: David Fulton Publishers, 1998), pp.88–97.

Pierson, Jim, *No Disabled Souls: How to welcome people with disabilities into your life and your church* (Cincinnati: The Standard Publishing Company, 1998).

Pilch, John J., 'Improving Bible Translations: The Example of Sickness and Healing', *Biblical Theology Bulletin*, 30(4) (2000): 129–34.

Pinker, Steven, *The Language Instinct* (London: Penguin Books Ltd., 1994).

Pitcairn, K., 'Exploring Ways of Giving a Voice to People with Learning Difficulties', in Humphries, Beth and Truman, Carole (eds), *Re-thinking Social Research: Anti-discriminatory approaches in research methodology* (Aldershot: Avebury, 1994), pp.62–9.

Poizner, H., Klima, E.S. and Bellugi, U., *What the Hands Reveal About the Brain* (Cambridge, Massachusetts: MIT Press, 1990).

Pole, Christopher and Lampard, Richard, *Practical Social Investigation: Qualitative and Quantitative Methods in Social Research* (Harlow: Pearson Education Ltd., 2002).

Power, D. and Leigh, G. (ed.), *Educating Deaf Students: Global Perspectives* (Washington DC: Gallaudet University Press, 2004).

Raja, A. Maria Arul, 'Reading the Bible From a Dalit Location: Some Points For Interpretation', *Voices From the Third World* XXIII(1) (2000): 77–91.

Ramsey, I.T., *Religious Language* (London, SCM Press Ltd., 1957).

Rée, Jonathan, *I See a Voice: A Philosophical History* (London: Flamingo, 2000).

Reserve Bank of Zimbabwe. *Foreign Exchange Auction Exchange* (URL: www.rbz.co.zw/currencyexc/forex_12082004.asp, 12/08/2004) [online. Last accessed: 08/02/2007].

Reuther, Rosemary Radford, 'Feminist Interpretation: A Method of Correlation', in Russell, Letty M. (ed.), *Feminist Interpretation of the Bible* (Philadelphia: Westminster Press, 1985), pp.111–24.

Robinson, K., 'Cochlear Implants: Some Challenges', in Gregory, S., Knight, P., McCracken, W., Powers, S. and Watson, L. (eds), *Issues in Deaf Education* (London: David Fulton Publishers, 1998), pp.196–202, pp.58–68.

Royal National Institute for Deaf People, *Facts and Figures on Deafness and Tinnitus* (London: RNID, 2003).

Royal National Institute for Deaf People, *Working with a Communication Support Worker in Education* (London: RNID, 2004).

Russell, Letty M., 'Introduction: Liberating the Word', in Russell, Letty M. (ed.), *Feminist Interpretation of the Bible* (Philadelphia: Westminster Press, 1985), pp.11–18.

Sacks, Jonathan, *Faith in the Future* (London: Darton, Longman & Todd, 1995).

Sacks, O., *Seeing Voices* (London: Picador, 1991).

Samartha, Stanley J., 'Scripture and Scriptures', in Sugirtharajah, R.S. (ed.), *Voices from the Margin* (London/Maryknoll, New York: SPCK/Orbis Books, 1995), pp.9–36.

Sapir, Edward, 'Sound Patterns in Language', *Language: Journal of the Linguistic Society of America*, 1 (1925): 37–51.

Schüssler-Fiorenza, Elisabeth, *In Memory of Her: A Feminist Theological Reconstruction of Christian Origins* (London: SCM Press, 1983).

Schüssler-Fiorenza, Elisabeth, *Bread Not Stone: The Challenge of Feminist Biblical Interpretation* (Edinburgh: T&T Clark, 1984).

Schüssler-Fiorenza, Elisabeth, 'Transforming the Legacy of *The Woman's Bible*', in Schüssler-Fiorenza, Elisabeth, *Searching the Scriptures: A Feminist Introduction* (London: SCM Press, 1993), pp.1–24.

Schüssler-Fiorenza, F., 'Systematic Theology: Tasks and Methods', in Schüssler-Fiorenza, F. and Galvin, J.P., *Systematic Theology: Roman Catholic Perspectives* (Dublin: Gill & Macmillan, 1992), pp.1–87.

Schweitzer, A., *My Life and Thought: An Autobiography* (London: George Allen & Unwin Ltd., 1933).

Shakespeare, Tom (ed.), *The Disability Reader: Social Science Perspectives* (London: Cassell, 1998).

Shrine, R., *The Language and Culture of Deaf People* (Unpublished MA Thesis: St John's College, Nottingham, 1997).

Shrine, R., 'Towards a BSL Liturgy: Reflections on the Way Ahead'. Unpublished paper given at a meeting of members of the Church of England's Liturgical Commission, Praxis, and the Chaplains Among Deaf People (London: Notre Dame University Centre, 1 February, 2002).

Shrine R., 'Towards a BSL Liturgy', in *Signs* (London: National Deaf Church Conference, Autumn 2002), pp.16–17.

Sluga, Hans and Stern, David G. (eds), *The Cambridge Companion to Wittgenstein* (Cambridge: Cambridge University Press, 1996).

Smith, Walter Chalmers, 'Immortal, Invisible', in *Mission Praise* (London: Marshall Pickering, 1990), No.327.

Sobrino, J. and Hernandez-Pico, Juan, *Theology of Christian Solidarity* (New York: Orbis Books, 1985).

Sobrino, J., *Jesus as Liberator: A Historical Theological Reading of Jesus of Nazareth* (Tunbridge Wells: Burns & Oates, 1993).

Sölle, Dorothee, *Thinking About God* (London: SCM Press, 1990).

Steele, Richard B., 'The Moral Psychology of Parenting Children with Genetic Disorders', *Theology Today*, 57(2) (2000): 161–74.

Stinton, Diane, 'Africa, East and West', in Parratt, J. (ed.), *An Introduction to Third World Theologies* (Cambridge: Cambridge University Press, 2004), pp.105–36.

Stokoe, W.C., *Sign Language Structure: An Outline of the Visual Communication System of the American Deaf* (University of Buffalo – Studies in Linguistics, Occasional Paper 8, 1960).

Street, Brian V. (ed.), *Cross-cultural Approaches to Literacy* (Cambridge: Cambridge University Press, 1993).

Stuart, Elizabeth, *Just Good Friends: Towards a Lesbian and Gay Theology of Relationships* (London: Mowbray, 1995).

Sugirtharajah, R.S. (ed.), *Asian Faces of Jesus* (Maryknoll, New York: Orbis Books, 1993).

Sugirtharajah, R.S. (ed.), *Voices from the Margin*, New Edition (London/Maryknoll, New York: SPCK/Orbis Books, 1995).

Sugirtharajah, R.S., *The Bible and the Third World: Precolonial, Colonial and Postcolonial Encounters* (Cambridge: Cambridge University Press, 2001).

Sutton-Spence, Rachel and Woll, Bencie, *The Linguistics of British Sign Language: An Introduction* (Cambridge: Cambridge University Press, 1999).

Svartholm, Kristina, 'Second Language Learning in the Deaf', in Ahlgren, I. and Hyltenstam, K. (eds), *Bilingualism in Deaf Education: International Studies on Sign Language and Communication of the Deaf* (Hamburg: Signum, 1994), pp.61–70.

Swain, John, French, Sally and Cameron, Colin, *Controversial Issues in a Disabling Society* (Buckingham: Open University Press, 2003).

Swannell, J. (ed.), *The Little Oxford Dictionary of Current English*, Sixth Edition (Oxford: Oxford University Press, 1986).

Swinton, J. and McIntosh, E., 'Persons in Relation. The Care of Persons with Learning Disabilities', *Theology Today*, 57(2) (2000): 175–84.

Swinton, J., *Spirituality and Mental Health Care: Rediscovering a 'Forgotten' Dimension* (London: Jessica Kingsley Publishers Ltd., 2001).

Swinton, John, *A Space to Listen: Meeting the Spiritual Needs of People with Learning Disabilities* (London: Foundation for People with Learning Disabilities, 2001).

Swinton, John, *Why Are We Here?: Meeting the Spiritual Needs of People with Learning Disabilities* (London: Foundation for People with Learning Disabilities, 2004).

Tan, A.S., 'The Disabled Christ', *Transformation: An International Evangelical Dialogue on Mission and Ethics* 15(4) (1998): 8–14.

Tavener, John, 'Towards a Sacred Art', in Brown, David and Loades, Ann (eds), *The Sense of the Sacramental: Movement and Measure in Art and Music, Place and Time* (London: SPCK, 1995), pp.172–8.

Taylor, George and Darby, Anne, *Deaf Identities* (Coleford, Gloucestershire: Douglas McLean, 2003).

Taylor, M. and McCloughry, R., 'A Disabled God?', *Third Way* (October 1998): 12–15.

Thatcher, Adrian, *Liberating Sex: A Christian Sexual Theology* (London: SPCK, 1993).

Tillich, Paul, *Theology of Culture* (London: OUP, 1964).

Truman, C., 'Feminist Challenges to Traditional Research: Have They Gone Far Enough?', in Humphries, Beth and Truman, Carole (eds), *Re-thinking Social Research: Anti-discriminatory approaches in research methodology* (Aldershot: Avebury, 1994), pp.21–36.

Tucker, Ivan and Powell, Con, *The Hearing Impaired Child and School* (London: Souvenir Press, 1991).

Tutu, D.M., 'Black Theology/African Theology – Soul Mates or Antagonists?', in Cone, J.H. and Williams, G.S. (eds), *Black Theology: A Documentary History Volume One: 1966–1979* (New York: Orbis Books, 1993), pp.385–92.

UPIAS, *Fundamental Principles of Disability* (London: Union of Physically Impaired Against Segregation, 1976).

University of Birmingham, *Presenting Your Thesis: Notes on the arrangement of thesis and their preparation for binding* (Birmingham: University of Birmingham, 2003).

University of Birmingham, *Student Guide to the Submission and Examination of Research Degree Theses* (Birmingham: University of Birmingham, 2003).

Uzukwu, Elochukwu E., *Worship as Body Language: Introduction to Christian Worship: An African Orientation* (Minnesota: The Liturgical Press, 1997).

Vanier, Jean, *The Heart of L'Arche: A Spirituality for Every Day* (London: Geoffrey Chapman, 1995).

Vanier, Jean, *The Scandal of Service: Jesus Washes Our Feet* (London: Darton, Longman & Todd, 1997).

Vanier, Jean, *Made for Happiness: Discovering the Meaning of Life with Aristotle* (London: Darton, Longman & Todd, 2001).

Vanier, J., *Befriending the Stranger* (London: DLT, 2005).

Visible Communications, *The Invisible Church* (Northampton: Visible Communications, 1996), [Video].

Visible Communications, *The Birth of Jesus Christ. The Gospel of Luke in Sign Language* (Northampton: Visible Communications, 1997), [Video].

Visible Communications, *Jesus Begins His Ministry. The Gospel of Luke in Sign Language* (Northampton: Visible Communications, 1999), [Video].

Visible Communications, *Jesus and His Disciples. The Gospel of Luke in Sign Language* (Northampton: Visible Communications, 2000), [Video].

Wainwright, Geoffrey, 'The Language of Worship', in Jones, Cheslyn, Wainwright, Geoffrey, Yarnold, Edward and Bradshaw, Paul (eds), *The Study of Liturgy* (London: SPCK, 1992), pp.519–27.

Ward, Graham (ed.), *The Postmodern God: A Theological Reader* (Oxford: Blackwell, 1997).

Ward, Graham, 'Why is Derrida Important for Theology?', *Theology*, XCV(766) (1992): 263–70.

Ward, Graham, *Barth, Derrida and the Language of Theology* (Cambridge: Cambridge University Press, 1995).

Ware, Kallistos, 'The Spirituality of the Icon', in Jones, C., Wainwright G. and Yarnold, E. (eds), *The Study of Spirituality* (London: SPCK, 2000), pp.195–8.

Watson, L., 'Oralism – current policy and practice', in Gregory, S., Knight, P., McCracken, W., Powers, S. and Watson, L. (eds), *Issues in Deaf Education* (London: David Fulton Publishers, 1998), pp.69–76.

Watson, L. and Parsons, J., 'Supporting Deaf Pupils in Mainstream Settings', in Gregory, S., Knight, P., McCracken, W., Powers, S. and Watson, L. (eds), *Issues in Deaf Education* (London: David Fulton Publishers, 1998), pp.135–42.

Watson, L., Gregory, S. and Powers, S., *Deaf and Hearing Impaired Pupils in Mainstream Schools* (London: David Fulton Publishers, 1999).

Webster, Alec, *Deafness, Development and Literacy* (London: Methuen, 1986).

Weedon, Chris, *Feminist Practice & Poststructuralist Theory*, Second Edition (Oxford: Blackwell Publishers, 1997).

Weir, Mary Kathryn, 'Made Deaf in God's Image', in International Ecumenical Working Group, *The Place of Deaf People in the Church* (Northampton: Visible Communications, 1996), pp.1–10.

Weisel, Amatzia (ed.), *Issues Unresolved: New Perspectives on Language and Deaf Education* (Washington: Gallaudet University Press, 1998).

Whaling, F., 'Scripture and its Meanings: A Comparative Perspective', *Studies in World Christianity*, 6(1) (2000): 78–90.

White, James F., *Introduction to Christian Worship*, Revised Edition (Nashville: Abingdon Press, 2000).

White, Susan, 'The Theology of Sacred Space', in Brown, David and Loades, Ann (eds), *The Sense of the Sacramental: Movement and Measure in Art and Music, Place and Time* (London: SPCK, 1995), pp.31–43.

Woll, B., 'Development of Sign and Spoken Languages', in Gregory, S., Knight, P., McCracken, W., Powers, S. and Watson, L. (eds), *Issues in Deaf Education* (London: David Fulton Publishers, 1998), pp.58–68.

World Health Organisation, *Towards a Common Language for Functioning, Disability and Health* (Geneva: World Health Organization, 2002).

Young, F., 'Imago Dei', in *Ecumenical Disability Advocates Network* (Nairobi: EDAN, July/September, 2002), pp.3–4.

Young, F. (ed.), *Encounter with Mystery: Reflections on L'Arche and Living with Disability* (London: Darton, Longman & Todd Ltd., 1997).

Young, F., *Face to Face: A Narrative Essay in the Theology of Suffering* (Edinburgh: T&T Clark, 1990).

Young, Pamela Dickey, *Feminist Theology/Christian Theology: In Search of Method* (Minneapolis: Fortress Press, 1990).

Zimbabwe, Department of Culture and Languages, *Dictionary of Zimbabwean Sign Language* (Harare: Department of Culture and Languages, 1998).

Index